47 Days
THAT CHANGED AMERICA

ISBN: 1439276633
ISBN-13: 9781439276631

Preface

There's a scene in the movie, *Network*, where Peter Finch screams, "I'm mad as hell and I'm not gonna take it anymore." This phrase aptly summed up my feelings, as I boarded the train in Trenton for my daily commute to work in New York City on September eighteenth. I didn't pick this day to start writing this book; on the contrary, I think the day picked me. A few days prior to this date, Lehman Brothers collapsed and American International Group (AIG) was effectively taken over by the U.S. government. Thousands of good, hard-working people were affected by these events, and their lives were thrown into a state of disarray. It just so happens my employer is AIG; thus, an increased level of uncertainty entered my life.

The Lehman and AIG events are emblematic of a financial system that is showing signs of crumbling, and you don't have to be employed by one of these financial institutions to be affected by its reach. Against this backdrop, the presidential election campaign was in full swing, with both candidates having been sent off from their respective conventions a few weeks earlier with visions of a November fourth victory dancing in their heads. The adopted buzzword for this election was "change," and both campaigns had latched onto this theme since it had been identified as something we Americans were craving. Change can mean different things to individuals, ranging from a simple desire to see a new administration take office to a more urgent need of finding a stable job to help provide for their family. I can't provide a pure and concise definition that eloquently describes what it means to me, except to say that I wasn't happy with the current situation. Fear of an impending, nasty, and deep recession dominated my thoughts, made more urgent and complicated by my employers' recent new-found relationship with Uncle Sam. My nervousness and apprehension were reaching a fever pitch, and based upon observations and discussions with friends and business associates, I had a lot of company sharing this same level of unease. This common denominator bound us together, and the election offered us a ray of hope that the change we desperately wanted was on the horizon.

My wife and I have five children, and we want their futures to be as successful as possible, in the same way our parents wanted this for us years ago. We were both born and raised in middle class families in Philadelphia, growing up in what are referred to as row homes, and have never forgotten this upbringing. We have done fairly well, with the primary driver being the work ethic we learned during our younger years. We've achieved a higher standard of living than our parents, but only because of the support they provided and the foundation they built for us while we were growing up. Recent events have caused me to question whether the attainment of a higher standard of living is slipping away for my children and their fellow generation "Y" compatriots, with the root cause of this gloomy outlook a failure on my generation's watch to address the serious issues confronting us. We have many challenging issues, and while our political system provides us the means to deliver change, it repeatedly ignores the warning signals and defaults to the status quo. Most people are aware of the major problems presented to us, such as Medicare, Social Security, Healthcare, and Energy, to name but a few, yet our elected politicians choose to take the path of least resistance and defer the hard choices to their successors. We've reached the point where inaction isn't the viable alternative it once was, and we need our elected officials and prominent business leaders to find bipartisan solutions to the pressing issues that need to be addressed. The government takeover of my company and the financial system springing a major leak are what led to my frustration level boiling over, and were the major drivers influencing me to write this book.

When I began writing this book, there were forty-seven days until we elected a new president, and hopefully ushered in a new beginning that not only promised change but delivered it, as well. I invite you to join me as I chronicle these next forty-seven days, and spill out my emotions and observations as I describe the financial meltdown and discuss how it affects me and middle class America, how it feels to be an unwelcome employee of the public sector, and also come to terms over reconciling which candidate is more likely to drive the change we want, starting on their inauguration day. I viewed this as the most important election in my life, and treated it with the urgency it deserved. My hope was that my fellow citizens were doing the same.

Acknowledgements

This book wasn't easy to write. Besides the fact that it represents my first formal entry into the literary arena, it also required me to jot down notes and observations during the day, recognizing that it couldn't infringe upon my AIG responsibilities. Train rides between Trenton and New York City were spent trying to translate my notes and observations into a cogent diary that captured not only facts from each day's observations, but my accompanying emotions and feelings as well. I spent many late nights at home further refining and editing the words I had put to paper to ensure I was delivering a story that conveyed my real-time impressions as to what was happening during those forty-seven days. I didn't realize when I started writing this book that the next forty-seven days would witness the onset of the worst financial collapse since the Great Depression, and usher in the dawning of a fundamental shift in the level of government intervention into our economy. This made it even more imperative that I ensure my words captured the historical significance of the events unfolding around me.

My writing methods were old school, as I relied on handwriting the story. The real workaholics on this story were my wife and children, who encouraged me to keep going and graciously accepted the task of translating my hieroglyphics into typewritten pages. I'm sure they made some selective edits themselves throughout the process, and I remember many discussions that ensued concerning what I had written. They didn't always agree with my choice of words and would politely acknowledge areas of disagreement. It would've been easy to throw in the towel and abandon this time-consuming project, but my wife and children encouraged me to keep going and to finish the story. I have a fantastic family, and I want them to know how deeply appreciative I am for their encouragement and assistance in completing this book. I never could have finished it without them.

Introduction

American politics have always fascinated me, and the 2008 election provided a perfect example of what makes our process so unique. It contained a variety of interesting and historical subplots, each one worthy of a separate discussion. Political commentators will point to key moments that defined the contest and offer their analysis of how these events influenced the election. Most of these experts will tell us why we voted as we did, often times missing the mark in capturing the emotions and pulse of the single most important voting bloc in our country, the middle class. This group is defined in Webster's dictionary as "the members of society occupying a socioeconomic position intermediate between the laboring classes and the wealthy." Most Americans know if they fall into this class, and no academician will be able to convince them otherwise. I consider myself to be a proud member of this portion of the electorate and thought it would be interesting to provide a perspective on this historic election through my eyes and those of my fellow middle-class voters.

At mid September, I was undecided on how to vote in this election. This was a surprising situation to be in, since I have been a reliable right-leaning voter for most of my adult life. I was conflicted by this uncertainty and wanted to know what moved me into the undecided bloc that would decide the election.

I was usually a given for the red team, the type that would proudly pull the same lever each trip to the voting booth. This year was different, and a higher sense of personal responsibility and urgency emerged to make the candidates fight for my vote. Each election is heralded as the most important in our lifetime, yet given the current state of our economy and world affairs, the 2008 contest was shaping up to be more worthy of this designation than any of its recent predecessors.

By overwhelming margins, people felt the country was headed in the wrong direction. Voter wrath was directed toward a President with an approval rating in the 25 percent range, and a congress that wished its approval ratings were as high as their chief executive's. This dissatisfaction and yearning for change had many incumbents feeling uneasy, and fortunately, for President Bush, he was in a lame-duck status. Voters had the final say on whether they wanted the four hundred, thirty-five members of the house and the thirty-five senators whose seats were being contested to stay in their jobs. And there was also the matter of electing someone to the most powerful position on the planet.

Each of this year's presidential candidates had based his campaign on a theme of change, recognizing this was what the electorate craved. Each considered himself capable of delivering the change we so desperately wanted, although there was a distinct difference in why they believed they could deliver on this promise. One candidate professed to be new to Washington and not beholden to any group. This storyline sounded familiar to our current president's pitch in 2000, which was ironic, given the difference in their ideologies. The other candidate wanted to convince us that he was the true agent of change, reminding us of his record as a maverick in bucking his party when he felt the need to do so. His basic pitch was that he knew what was wrong with the system and how to fix it.

The story begins on September eighteenth, forty-seven days before the election. The significance of this starting point is that on this day my frustration with where the country was headed hit a tipping point. Just a few days earlier, Lehman Brothers collapsed, and the government rescued AIG, which happens to be my employer. As I glanced around at my fellow commuters on our daily train ride into New York City I sensed similar feelings of unease and thought of our shared hopes that the presidential candidates would address the many issues confronting our country. I decided at that time to write a middle-class voter's account of this election, focusing on what we wanted from this election and how events that unfolded influenced our decision.

I consider myself to be a middle-class American voter, someone akin to being defined as an interested member of the electorate, as opposed to being labeled a political activist. I'm married with five children, with a son in the military and college tuitions to worry about. I live in Pennsylvania, which happened to be a crucial battleground state this election, and I commuted to work in lower Manhattan each day. Like most investors, I watched in shock as the value of my investments seemed to be in a free fall and worried about whether my best laid financial plans needed a major overhaul. I saw the effects of the crisis all around me and observed how middle-class America was being affected by the deteriorating economy. Each day brought visual confirmation of the gloomy economic conditions, and unease over job security and providing for my family crept into my thinking. I surprisingly discovered that my spending habits had multiple areas of untapped opportunities, and I transformed into a more thrifty and educated consumer. I found I was not alone with this metamorphosis, and recognized the monumental effect this subtle pullback could have on the economy, especially if this shift proved to be more than temporary.

A week into the journey, the United States experienced a financial crisis that many experts proclaimed the worst since the Great Depression. Government intervention to combat the deteriorating conditions occurred at an unprecedented level as the markets experienced sudden and severe wealth destruction. Most Americans felt this pain, and baby boomer hopes of an early and stress-free retirement started to melt, along with their life savings.

The economy took front and center stage as the single most important issue on voters' minds, with Obama and the Democratic Party the beneficiaries of the deteriorating conditions. Foreign affairs became a non-issue, rendering McCain's perceived advantage useless in the dogfight to win the presidency. World powers came together to coordinate policies to combat the financial crisis, reinforcing the global reach of the meltdown.

Against this economic climate, the presidential campaign was in full swing, and the current lame duck administration searched for remedies to aid the quickly deteriorating economy. There was no silver -bullet solution to the crisis, and the experts worked at warp speed to find solutions to the crumbling financial system. The Republican administration worked with the Democratic congress to enact policies of government intervention last seen in the darkest pages of U.S. financial history some eighty years ago. These steps were justified with both an implied and sometimes vehemently spoken warning that they were necessary to prevent a catastrophic jolt to our economy, thereby asking us to look the other way as the public sector extended its reach into American capitalism.

Recessions are normal in business cycles; however, their length and severity are what differentiates them. Depressions are infrequent occurrences, with one per generation considered unusual. The "D" word was whispered by some as the current crisis unfolded, and, as conditions worsened, it became a discussion topic mouthed more frequently than people would have liked to hear.

As the administration worked with global leaders to stave off a repeat of the 1930s, the election continued to heat up, and people's anger and frustration became more pronounced. Visions of funding college educations, retiring early, and dreams of purchasing a second home dissipated before our eyes, in a sudden and severe stock-market collapse, accompanied by a housing crisis that forced millions of homeowners underwater. Trillions of dollars of wealth was lost around the globe, and the reputation of capitalism took a beating.

The candidates maintained frenetic campaign schedules and criss-crossed the battleground states to convince voters why they should be entrusted to be the forty-fourth president of the United States. One vice presidential and three presidential debates occurred, providing voters with additional insight to help in their selection process. All remained quiet on the international scene, leaving the economy front and center as the single most important issue on voter's minds. The campaign had its defining moments, and the electorate grew increasingly angry and frustrated with the failing economy and its effects on their daily lives. The combination of an economic meltdown and campaign contributions that shattered fundraising records fueled Obama to a seemingly insurmountable advantage as November approached. McCain was on the defensive until Joe the plumber had his infamous encounter with Obama. "Spread the wealth" became synonymous with Obama, and voters were left to ponder if this phrase was a precursor to what his governing philosophy would be. McCain believed this ideology warranted our full attention, and sharpened his closing arguments around this theme. The Democrat stuck to his game plan of linking McCain to Bush and continued to squeeze all the mileage he could from this perceived political marriage. Lost in the intrigue and suspense of the election was a more fundamental issue as to what would be the longer-term effects of the growing government intervention in our economy. Voters seemed oblivious to this, since they were focused singularly on the downward-spiraling economy, and were more concerned with surviving the present than worrying about what seeds were being planted to enable an even greater government intrusion into the private sector. This lack of attention to the longer-term horizon was understandable, but it shouldn't have been completely overlooked, because the current interventionist steps would either be accelerated or unravel depending on who was victorious on November fourth.

In desperate times, leaders typically step forth to calm the masses and issue comforting words and a vision to help weather the storm. George Washington was there in the 1780s, Lincoln was there in the 1860s, and Roosevelt was there in the 1930s. Each of these leaders made his mark approximately four score years apart from the other, and it was ironic that we were at this same stage today. The difference was that no one was stepping up to continue this great tradition of leadership. The current president was a lame duck, and with his current approval rating, he did not have the support or the will to lead the way. Congress was too busy jockeying for political position in the upcoming election, which left our presidential candidates in the spotlight to showcase their true leadership abilities under these trying circumstances.

Commentators focused on the problems the new president would inherit, losing sight of the fact that this pivotal moment presented a unique opportunity for either candidate to set himself apart, take control of the situation, and comfort the electorate that a steady hand would be on the wheel, starting with his inauguration on January twentieth. The media, politicians, and maybe even the candidates themselves would say this was an unfair expectation, given the circumstances and nuances of our political system; however, I beg to differ and would say that the American voters were shortchanged in the candidates' response and decision to sit this out and take the safe route to limit their own collateral damage.

Both candidates stressed change in their campaigns; however, when offered an opportunity to set a clear vision of change that would lead us out of the crisis they declined. There would certainly have been risks associated with this strategy, but with risk comes reward. The candidates could have given us a sneak preview of their leadership attributes, but they deferred on this and chose to allow business and politics as usual to rule the day. I cannot help but think that a campaign that started with such historic implications withered when unprecedented circumstances arose. History was still made during this election, and years from now, its significance will be cited by historians as they discuss American politics. The forty-fourth president of the United States may yet turn out to be an exceptional leader, someone who rose to the occasion like his famous predecessors before him. I certainly hope so.

I understand the importance of attempting to speak for my fellow electorate, and take this task seriously. I hope to convey my feelings about the campaign and how events and perceptions surrounding it influenced my decision. To my fellow middle class comrades, I hope this story connects with your feelings about the 2008 election; to my fellow hard-working AIG employees and others affected by business failings, we should be cognizant that sometimes the actions of a few impact many; to the media and numerous commentators who claim to understand what makes us tick, I want you to know your supposed hidden bias is apparent and demeaning to middle-class America; to the candidates who reached out to us with promises of change, we want you to know that our vote carries with it an expectation that you will deliver on the promise of change you so eloquently spoke of during your campaign.

September 18, 2008

Today is Thursday September 18th, 2008. You couldn't ask for better weather. It's a crisp, sunny day with the temperature in the low seventies. Generally, on a day like this, I feel upbeat, but for some reason, today feels different, like something is missing. I find myself questioning a lot of things, wondering why I am not in my usual positive frame of mind. Could it be the realization setting in that my employer has been effectively taken over by the government, with the accompanying mocking and embarrassment sure to follow, as well as the threat of job insecurity? Is it the state of the economy, with fears reverberating up and down both Wall Street and Main Street? The Dow dropped another four hundred points yesterday, continuing the downward flight path it's been on for the last year or so. Is the state of world affairs causing me a feeling of unease? Every part of the globe seems to be experiencing some friction, with socialist versus democratic tugs of war in South America, famine and genocide in Africa, continuing conflicts in the Middle East, Russia trying to flex its muscles and recapture its once powerful status, North Korea continuing to thumb its nose at the UN over its nuclear program, and the threat of terrorism that continues to haunt people around the world. These are but a few of many troubling issues around the globe, and if I took the time, I could list many other hotspots where turbulence and unrest seems to rule the day. One particular topic closer to home is the interest in the U.S. presidential election, which, according to the pollsters, is a close contest. Both candidates are stressing change, which represents the adopted theme of this election. As I reflect on the state of our country, my individual employment situation, and world conditions, I too wish for change. Both candidates are confident they will win the election and receive a mandate to be the agent of change we voters desperately want. Each continues to hammer at the appeal of this popular slogan, and I start to question which candidate is more likely to convert campaign promises into actions of change.

We live in a country and a world where it is sometimes difficult to make the hard decisions, not because we're blinded as to what the problems are, but rather because most leaders lack the conviction and integrity to make the unpopular decisions that usually accompany change. Promises of change are accompanied by words and nebulous ideas, with boastful promises of generalities but no specifics on how to actually effect change. Both candidates and parties follow this formula every election cycle; however, this time we are in dire need of real change to right the ship. It doesn't take a rocket scientist to see the issues that need addressing, but I have yet to hear either candidate offer a plausible fix to solidify Social Security and Medicare, lay out a clear and reasonable energy policy, or chart a course for affordable health care in this country. I understand that specific proposals on how to address each would be hazardous to a candidate's health, since special interests would summon their armies to battle to protect their holy turf. Is it naive of me to assume that we can solve these problems using a commonsense approach, or should we resign ourselves to accept the same patchwork fixes that generally win the day? It's easy to give in and say that, individually, we cannot change the world, but we should never fail to recognize that, collectively, we can influence decision making in Washington. Are we guilty of accepting poor performance from our "elected" leaders, allowing them to deviate from their promises and succumb to the realities of governing? I want to believe this election will be different, that one or both of the candidates will offer specific proposals that will be converted into actions, once they are elected. I can give some slack to an elected leader whose goals and ideas are altered by events beyond his or her control. At the same time, however, I do not want (or expect) these uncontrollable events to be the leader's sole focus, thereby abandoning and dismissing other pressing issues. This is not meant to be a direct indictment of our current president, who exercised his best judgment, with congressional approval, to go into Iraq. I admire his conviction about how to protect our country, and what's missing in his detractors' scathing critiques is recognition that other attacks on our soil have been prevented. I am interested in results, and to me, the one that counts is zero, that being the number of attacks on our homeland since 9/11/01. The decision to go into Iraq is a very sensitive and divisive topic, and American blood has been spilled in a country thousands of miles from our shore. Why do we refuse to admit the possibility that history may judge this as a successful defining moment in world affairs? The naysayers are quick to call it a major mistake that severely damaged our international prestige. This completely dismisses the notion that preventive actions can have positive ramifications, although to their delight, such results can usually never be proven. Whatever your current leanings, let us at least agree that this decision has ramifications that will be felt for years to come. Let history, and not opinionated pundits with their own political agenda and leanings, be the judge as to the success or failure of the current administration's foreign policies. On the other hand, there is no disputing the fact that the current administration and congress have been a disaster on the domestic front. I find fault in that the president allowed spending to increase at rates far incompatible with what we can afford. This lack of spending constraint is unforgivable, and has been a major contributor to the unhealthy economic environment we find ourselves in today.

The more I think about this election, and the great promise that the orderly transition of power should bring, the more realistic I become that most elections are contests that crown a winner, not based upon true ideals and ideas, but rather a race to see which candidate's marketing machine will persuade people to pull their lever on election day. This does not mean the process disillusions me; rather, it makes it more incumbent upon each of us to sift through the rhetoric and promises and make a decision as to who we believe will make a better president. This is a tremendous responsibility that rests upon our shoulders, and we should treat it with the significance it deserves. Each of us counts the same with one vote. The teacher in Philadelphia, the fireman in New York City, the baker in St. Louis, and the single parent in Dallas, to the unemployed throughout this country trying to put food on the table for their families, all count the same. This is our opportunity to stand up and be counted and feel that we are participants in electing someone to the most powerful position on earth. I do not know how many voters focus on the importance of this privilege and recognize the true power that our founding fathers bestowed upon us. As I think about this more, I start to feel a sense of empowerment and responsibility, and a more serious focus to ensure my decision is based upon a clear and fair analysis of who will make this country and the world a better place, not only during the next four years, but will position America at the head of the class for years to come.

I am fifty-one years old, married for almost twenty-seven years to my wife Helene, and have five children, ranging in age from fifteen to twenty-four. We have lived in the same home in Pennsylvania since 1981. Two of our children have graduated college, one of whom was in the NROTC and is now a naval officer, currently stationed in Japan. The other received her degree this past June and will soon be starting her career with one of the Big Four accounting firms. Our middle child is a sophomore at Boston University, with our remaining two currently in high school. My wife and I are extremely proud of each of them, and we feel fortunate to have such a wonderful family. I work in New York City, so I have quite a distance to navigate each day. I get up early each morning (around 5 a.m.), have a light breakfast, and drive to the train station in Trenton where I board New Jersey Transit (NJT) for what I hope will be a one-hour, ten-minute train ride to Penn Station in Midtown Manhattan. I then take the metro to South Ferry, which leaves me about a block from my lower Manhattan office. This two-hour, door-to-door commute can be tiring, but I enjoy my work and feel I make a valuable contribution to my company. I wonder if the recent government takeover of my company will change my attitude, but for now, my intention is to work as hard as ever to maintain my focus and keep bringing my "A" game. On the way to work, I am always struck by the many different people I see. The NJT ride is generally relaxed, with the passenger mix skewed to the white-collar side. Most read a paper, some bring a cup of coffee, others bring a laptop to work on, and the remainder of the people get cozy in their seats and catch up on some needed sleep. Most days, the train is full, and if you have ever ridden NJT you know what it is like to get stuck in the middle of a three-person bench. The newer trains are much more comfortable, providing more generous seating space. Unfortunately for me, as luck would have it, I don't seem to get the newer trains that much. Fortunately for me, however, I get on at the beginning of the line and get a seat of my choosing every day. The train travels north through New Jersey, and the areas we pass embody a microcosm of what this great country is all about. I see people on the train who bring different faces each day, sometimes smiling, other days with a look of angst that indicates a world of worry in their lives. I wonder if the people on the train have given the same level of thought to this election as I have, and if they are as skeptical as I am about the ability of the winner to follow through on his promises once elected. Is it possible they share my level of concern, in some cases even surpassing my level of interest? I wonder how many are fixated on a single issue, which will sway their voting preference. Could it be that the woman sitting next to me is singularly focused on the abortion issue, and that a candidates' position on this issue alone will dictate her selection? Is the man sitting in front of me worried about his job and waiting intently to hear more about each candidate's economic proposals? I cannot help but think, however, that a decision should be based upon a multitude of issues, with the candidates' positions on each collectively weighed to determine who offers the best solutions to the many issues confronting us today. We have Iraq, the economy, immigration, and energy, to name but a few. It is our duty to weigh each of these and make an educated decision as to who has the best solutions to get us moving in the right direction.

Today, the government floated a plan to set up an entity similar to the Resolution Trust Corporation (RTC) to house troubled assets of financial institutions. This government-owned asset-management company was charged with liquidating assets that had been assets of savings and loan associations declared insolvent by the Office of Thrift Supervision as a consequence of the savings and loan crisis of the 1980s. The thought is to take these current troubled assets off distressed companies' books, thereby solidifying balance sheets to help them navigate today's economic malaise. The market responded positively, with the Dow jumping 4 percent today on the hope this would help resolve our current economic problems. I think back to the 1990s, when some developing countries were faced with dire economic conditions and were thinking of government intervention to cure the problem. The U.S. made it clear to them that this would not be the correct prescription, that they needed to take their pains to right their economies structurally to enable a lasting growth in the future. There seems to be some contradiction here. This conjures up the old phrase, "do as I say not as I do." Maybe I am not giving the current decision makers enough credit; after all, the credentials of Hank Paulson and Ben Bernanke are certainly impressive. It dawns on me that either of two things is at play here:

1) Is our current financial state much worse than we thought, with this unusual step needed to help fix the systemic problems?

2) Is it coincidental that we have forty-seven days to the election, and that the current members of congress want to improve upon their record low-approval ratings?

The answer is probably a combination of both; however, my skepticism pushes my leaning to the latter. The positive market movement pleases me and improves my investment portfolio, but maybe my age and maturity are looking beyond this short-term gain and thinking about the repercussions as to what is unfolding today. In the last couple of weeks the government has effectively taken over Fannie Mae and Freddie Mac, bailed AIG out of bankruptcy, and is now considering bailing out distressed institutions, by taking troubled assets off their balance sheets. We could be witnessing the early stages of the most dramatic government intervention since the Great Depression, and if so, should one assume that, without this intervention, we would revisit the 1930s some eighty years later? Have we made a successful preemptive strike, or are we just prolonging the day of reckoning? I can't help but think that, years from now, some might look back and conclude that it might have been best to allow "too big to fail" companies to go under. I now work for what some commentators refer to as the poster child of government bailouts, and although jobs may have been saved by this intervention, I wonder at what long-term cost to the economy. I facetiously start thinking that I should now consider working government-employee hours, since my stereotyped perception is that they live in an eight-to-four world, which is far from what we experience in the private sector. They may take umbrage with how I'm painting their work experience; however, I believe my depiction is probably closer to reality than they would like us to believe. I quickly realize, however, that I could never fulfill my role by working those cushy hours. I also begin to think that additional companies might soon be coming to the government for assistance, since, once we embark on this path, it will probably become blurred as to who should be deserving of this treatment. Mix in a presidential election, and thoughts of political motivations can't be dismissed. The Government, in effect, could help decide which companies are winners and which are losers. This sounds like a slippery slope, and I dismiss this possibility because of its obvious ethical and moral shortcomings. We wouldn't dare go down this path, or would we?

Watching the news tonight I saw that Paulson held a news conference where he announced the Treasury's plan. Flanked behind him were Harry Reid and Nancy Pelosi. The message was to imply bipartisan support, which has been on hiatus in Washington over the last few years. Could it also be to pump up their approval ratings before they leave town to focus on the upcoming election?

I believe this RTC-like proposal has some merit, although similar to the AIG bailout, there are those in both the public and private sectors who believe the federal government could actually make money in this over the longer term. I also believe the timing was politically motivated for a couple of reasons, one to lift congress into better stead with the electorate and the other to avoid a third-quarter earnings release panic in the market. Paulson has a successful track record from his days in the private sector, and he knew the deteriorating conditions were going to pummel earnings and balance sheets when third-quarter results are released in a few weeks, further compounding the problem. This preemptive strike may improve third-quarter pricing marks under fair value accounting, thus avoiding a somber October in the run-up to the election.

September 19, 2008

Everyone seemed to be in a good mood on the train ride into New York City today. Domestic markets had a huge run-up yesterday, and foreign markets are following suit today. Maybe this will be a catalyst for what will hopefully be another positive day in the U.S. markets. Today is also a Friday, with the official start of the weekend within sight.

The market was way up at the open, and the momentum continued throughout the day. As I think back on recent days, I am again struck by the magnitude of decision-making that has taken place at the government level. These actions could be viewed as a turning point in government "intervention."

On the ride home tonight, I sense an uplifting feeling on the train. Since most of the riders are white collar, I surmise they are aware of what is happening in the markets. Absent those who had to cover short positions over these last few days, everyone is worth more today than a few days ago. This paper advance makes everyone feel better, and merchants and retail establishments are probably expecting to be the beneficiaries of this uptick with an increase in consumer spending this coming weekend.

Most people are fascinated by polls, and we will certainly get our fill during this election season. If one were taken this weekend about people's feelings on the economy, it would be significantly better than last weekend. It is amusing how a few days and an eight-hundred-point movement upward in the Dow can uplift your spirits. As the train stops at Jersey Avenue, I gaze out the window and wonder how many people in the surrounding towns feel richer because of today's events. I wonder how many could care less about the stock market, since they are more worried about the food market, and how to feed their families tonight. A poll of their feelings would certainly provide a much different result than those of us on the train. This diversity of people in our country, whether differentiated by race, sex, or creed, is what makes our country what it is today. Each individual has the same voting rights, and each vote only counts as one. My twenty-four-year-old son, twenty-two-year-old daughter, and nineteen-year-old daughter count the same as Warren Buffet, Bill Gates, and Donald Trump, although the latter certainly have more influence on the electorate with their public visibility and access to the media.

At one time in my career, I worked for a credit card company and was indirectly involved in marketing campaign strategies. I see similarities to the election process in that, if a political campaign can successfully identify a specific group and understand its needs, they can tailor proposals to lift a candidate's vote tally within the targeted group. This is similar to direct marketing, where you target to specific demographics, only the stakes are significantly higher than getting someone to accept a credit card solicitation. It seems to me that each presidential election starts out 45 percent to 45 percent, with the remaining 10 percent of the "in play" population deciding who our next president will be. I'm usually in one of the forty-five percent groups, but not this time. My indecision could mean that this election's "in play" population is fifteen percent, maybe even twenty percent. With forty-five days to go until Election Day, single events will have a much greater effect on deciding the election, resulting in significant shifts in momentum on an almost daily basis. Each candidate will be attacking and counter-attacking, as events unfold, and seeking to gain an advantage on every conceivable front. We should expect this daily barrage to challenge our thinking; however, the real question for each of us is whether we will allow it to tilt our leaning toward a certain candidate. A single event can be magnified and have the potential to influence our thinking in selecting our next leader. Could the current government bailout be that issue, or will some other event capture the headlines and tilt our thinking in another direction, the closer we get to election day?

I consider myself fortunate to live in a great country like the U.S. Similar to the pride an Olympian must feel when he or she puts on that USA uniform, I feel a similar pride when recognized as an American when traveling abroad. I would be remiss to not recognize some resentment from foreigners; however, I'd be equally naive to not mention the jealousy I sense as to my nationality. I am more focused on this election than I have ever been, and I want to make the right choice as to who should be our next president. I do not take this mission lightly, and I hope my fellow citizens feel the same way. I have always thought of myself as being intelligent enough to edit out the bias and to form my own opinion, based upon my own interpretation of the facts. I have often wondered if my thinking on this subject is consistent with most voters, or if the level of seriousness and care I take in this process is more the exception than the norm. I desperately want to believe the former.

September 20th and 21st, 2008

I love fall weekends, with bookends of college football on Saturdays and the NFL on Sundays. My favorite teams are the Penn State Nittany Lions and the Philadelphia Eagles, with the early prognosis for each looking positive. My Phillies are also in a pennant race, and the next ten days will determine if they're playoff bound. The weekend is generally a time to recharge the batteries, spend time with the family, close out some open work items, and escape to sports viewing to help take my mind off the other serious issues in our daily lives. I think my ritual is fairly common among middle-class voters, and I believe most would nod in agreement that it mirrors their weekend routine, as well. I remember when my weekends would be spent attending my kids' sporting events, and with five children, my wife and I would split the cheerleading duties. It is much calmer now, although a part of me misses the excitement of seeing my kids compete in athletics. When I was running around to get to as many games as possible, I sometimes grew frustrated and impatient, although when it came to an end, I look back, reminisce, and wish I could relive those moments again. As I drive around and do some normal Saturday morning chores, I notice the signs in my township touting registration information for the various in-season sports. I served on the local Basketball Board for a number of years, and remember some heated discussions over how much to charge for sign up fees. Given the current economic climate, I would expect these fees still generate some heated discussion.

News surrounding the government-proposed $700 billion dollar bailout dominates the headlines, with Paulson and members of congress making the obligatory rounds on the Sunday morning news programs to tout the positive aspects of this initiative. The presidential candidates and their representatives weigh in, as well, with attacks and counterattacks continuing to be the norm. I watch some of it, but quickly succumb to a preference to retreat to my football-viewing ritual. This "time out" is a necessary escape for me before having to face the real world. It's now 1 p.m., and I flip on the TV to begin my escape.

I wonder what our forefathers did to escape, or did they maintain their serious demeanor 24/7. Were they much more serious than we are with the way we go about our lives, or did they have their diversions like us? Somehow, I believe the latter, although it would be foolhardy to not acknowledge the real-time information age we live in today that gives us updates as they actually unfold. If an earthquake hits at 1:30 p.m. in China we know about it by 1:31 p.m. Back in the 1790s, it might have taken them months to learn of such an occurrence. I remember when I started my career back in the late '70s, how information was not nearly as accessible as it is today. Select employees had personal computers then, as opposed to now, when it would be considered unusual to be without one. My children are certainly growing up in a different world than me. It is not uncommon to see young kids accessing the Internet for a variety of reasons, whether playing games, researching information for a school project, or updating their Facebook pages. Of course, with this accessibility comes parental responsibility to make sure our children are protected from the dark side of the Internet, although it's virtually impossible to eliminate all of these from our loved ones' surfing exploits. The Internet has spawned various innovative sites, such as YouTube. Candidates today need to be careful about what they say and to whom, because they never know when their own words can be selectively edited against them and posted on the Internet for everyone to see. A state of paranoia enters my mind as I now recognize that, as an AIG employee, someone may attempt to use my words against me and my company, regardless of the acquaintances I'm with or the context in which my words are spoken. There are over one hundred thousand of us throughout the world, and I wonder how many share my heightened need to limit the spread of AIG disinformation at our innocent expense. How's that for a side-effect of AIG's situation?

In one respect, it's a shame that innovation has almost effectively eliminated privacy as a right, with no differential as to whether you fall into the celebrity bucket or not. These innovative sites do not discriminate, and I would expect that many common folk will be getting their thirty seconds of fame at some point in the future, whether deliberate or not.

When I was young (My God, am I implying that I'm "old" at fifty-one?) I used to think that if Walter Cronkite said something on the news, you could bank on it being accurate. Unfortunately, I don't see another Cronkite from the vast array of newsmen and commentators who would like us to believe they are his equals. Back then, we had three main channels to get the news: ABC, CBS, and NBC. These same channels exist today, although most cable services provide access to a lot more news outlets. In addition, these three main news telecasts were on at fixed times only; whereas today, you can get news on TV twenty-four hours a day, seven days a week.

The same holds true for Internet news. Today, we know that certain channels are biased, such as NBC and MSNBC leaning left and Fox tilting right. Most of us have our allegiances, but I wonder how many use the news as a source of information to form their own interpretation, as opposed to treating the reporters' words as gospel. Maybe with age comes reason, but I feel confident I can weigh the news presented and make my own analysis and opinion as to how it should be interpreted. It never ceases to amaze me that a Democrat and Republican can have completely opposite interpretations of the same event. It has become a game to see who can win the minds of the listeners, and in effect, influence their thinking about a particular issue. This battle always heats up during the election season, most notably in a presidential campaign. The next time I hear Keith Olberman say something that even hints at a Republican compliment, it will be a first, likewise, for Rush Limbaugh with his democratic critiques. Fortunately, one is free to dismiss or zero out these commentators' opinions, which allows one to filter the information and come to his or her own conclusion on a specific topic. The frightening part of this is that there are voters out there who pledge allegiance to these left- or right-leaning fanatics, and blindly follow their pied pipers. I commend the commentators for this spell-like domination over their followers; however, I find it necessary to indict their cult followers for being so easily manipulated. These commentators are always searching for anything they can rail on about to critique their opponents, regardless of the minutia level they choose for the topic. I intend to focus on this as the election heats up and will provide specific examples to make my point. With forty-five days to go, I feel confident that I will have hundreds, maybe thousands, of examples to choose from. By the way, there was a major terrorist bombing in Pakistan today. A Marriot hotel was badly damaged, with over sixty people murdered. It concerned me that some Pakistani commentators blamed this on the U.S.' fight against terrorism. Wasn't this an attack on the civilized world? If the first words out of Pakistan were to spew venom at the United States over this tragedy, I wonder if the general population feels the same way, or is it just a guise by their elected leaders to deflect the blame away from their own shortcomings in protecting their populace.

Sometimes, it seems obvious to me, but why can't civilized nations band together to eradicate terrorist activities? We will always have our outliers, but I cannot help but believe a concerted effort would be successful. People in vastly different cultures have to share the common belief that life is sacred, and any attempt to forge a union to combat the evil of terrorism certainly seems worthwhile to me. I am sure that both the far left and the far right will find fault with this logic, but I believe the political center would support exploring such an initiative.

Markets will open Monday morning, and I fear the turbulence and volatility of last week will continue. I cannot help but feel we have entered a new phase in American capitalism, and that the backers of the massive bailout are still making educated guesses as to what the effects will be. I am semi confident in Paulson and Bernanke and want to believe they have this figured out. Once we walk down this path, there is no turning back, but I am willing to give them the benefit of the doubt, because I'm worried the status quo won't work. I am interested to hear more from the candidates on this bailout and get a feel for what their stewardship of the economy would look like. Both are espousing more government oversight, but I want them to say more and convince me of their leadership style in these trying times. I do not like them usurping or upstaging the President, but I need to know that, in forty-five days, I will be making the right choice. Will one of the candidates please step up to the plate and preview for me real leadership traits.

September 22, 2008

Mondays are always better after an Eagle's victory.

While eating breakfast, I flipped on the TV and wasn't surprised that the futures market was pointing toward an open to the downside. I thought that the euphoria of Thursday's and Friday's gains would succumb to the reality that the bailout bill still presented questions as to its specifics. In addition, the pessimists seemed to rule the media this past weekend and win the war of words versus the optimists. People can say what they want about different professions, but why are economists usually split evenly on different sides of an issue? It is never clear to a majority of economists as to whether an event is a plus or a minus, and I still cannot comprehend why supposedly intelligent people have such different views on ultimate outcomes. I heard differing points of view that the bailout is the "right medicine to fix the root cause of the problem" to the bailout causing "financial Armageddon." I can see why McCain and Obama have different views of what should happen with taxes. It is interesting that both camps acknowledge the bailout cost, yet neither has discussed how this unforeseen pressure on the deficit has caused them to rethink their spending priorities. They still profess that their policies are the right remedies. I may not be a mathematician, but I can see something has to give. Wouldn't it be refreshing to hear one of the candidates say that this turn of events had forced him to rethink his position on certain issues, and that his wish list has changed accordingly? Common wisdom whispered in the candidate's ear is to not flip flop on his or her initiatives, that to do so would be political suicide without a corresponding change of position from their opponent. This logic assumes that voters do not want to hear the truth, that we do not understand basic math, and therefore will not bother to question the logic of sticking to a position that reality dictates should change. Please do not insult me or my fellow voters. To borrow a phrase used earlier in this campaign—"you can put lipstick on a pig, but it is still a pig." Will someone please show leadership and modify his or her original promises? If so that candidate might have a better chance of securing my vote.

The Dow dropped almost 400 points today, reversing Friday's gains. It doesn't feel right that each day we are witnessing such wild swings. Congress is trying to alter the Treasury's bailout proposal by adding a provision giving the government an equity stake in companies participating in this troubled asset program. Similar to the AIG bailout, the government would in effect become a shareholder, with the potential for profit participation. Even though this has a semi socialistic feel to it, I am starting to believe that companies cannot be given a bailout without the government getting some upside opportunity, although the rates AIG will be paying the government can be likened to giving them your first born. I guess the price of survival is steep, however if AIG or another institution thinks they can get a better deal somewhere else, then by all means they could look elsewhere. I do worry, however, that a government ownership position may be more than passive in managing a company's daily operations, and if so, will they be able to dictate terms in areas such as which business lines to exit, which geographic locations to keep open, and employee compensation practices? It sometimes makes good politics to beat the populist drum, and in the process make innocent employees feel the brunt of this criticism. My company is now under government supervision, and I'll be watching closely to monitor the accompanying effect on me and my fellow employees. I need to mention here that since this book is a "personal" view of this important election, that any references to AIG are purely my own independent thinking, and any attempt to interpret them otherwise would be misguided. I could opt to shy away from such inferences, but that would be unfair to my goal of baring my conscience and describing this 47 day period in real time feelings. If I was investing time reading this book I would expect the author to have no preconditions or selective edits that would water down the emotions that were being felt during this period. I can assure you I will stay true to this objective.

This massive bailout has caused the dollar to weaken and the price of oil to spike to $120 per barrel. Goldman Sachs and Morgan Stanley have received approval to convert into conventional depositary institutions. Six months ago, we had five prominent investment banks; after this conversion, we will have none. An article I read today said that Wall Street will lose 40,000 jobs during this economic cycle. I hope that's all the jobs that go away; however, I sense the figure is too optimistic. I wonder how many jobs at my company will be lost over the coming months, or has the government bailout helped secure most people's positions? Wouldn't that be an unusual twist of fate if, by being bailed out, jobs were saved at AIG? Logic would dictate that this should be the proper course if the government wants to protect its new investment; however, that assumes politics doesn't interfere with business.

September 23, 2008

I was reading the newspaper on the train into work this morning, and two pieces of information caused me some pause. The first was an article with the headline, "Poll shows more Americans attuned to Presidential race." The article said that 43 percent of those polled said they were "very closely" following the presidential race, versus 36 percent who said so in September 2004. I am aware that this is a healthy increase, but I am equally aware that this represents less than a majority. I have always considered us to be the bastion of democracy, but should I rethink this given the polling result? We trumpet the virtues of democracy throughout the world, yet we cannot seem to get our own populace to embrace this sacred privilege. Just what is the cause of this voter apathy? Is it a feeling of frustration that nothing gets done in Washington and that it doesn't matter who gets elected? Have our elected leaders betrayed us by failing to deliver on campaign promises? Even if these have some semblance of truth, it is no excuse to surrender our voting privileges. I will make the counter argument that this makes it even more imperative to exercise our privileges, that we need to keep sending the message to our politicians that they work for us, and they need to act in our best interests. Candidates can speak all they want of being change agents, but we voters are the real drivers of change, and we send our message on Election Day.

Another article I read today was about the bailout program, and one quote in particular stood out to me. Harry Reid, the senate majority leader, said, "We're now seeing eight years of reckless Bush economic policies come crashing down with unimaginable speed and severity." Thank you, Harry, for exercising leadership and making us feel better about the situation. Thank you for your thoughtful analysis and your intelligent solution to the problem. We Americans should feel confident that we have someone like you in a position of authority. First of all, Harry, isn't congress an accomplice in economic policies, and aren't your approval ratings lower than the President's? People in the real business world would like to be able to pass the buck like you just did. Fortunately, or unfortunately, depending upon how you look at it, we accept our collective blame for mistakes. We don't want to hear partisanship from you; rather, we want reassurances of bipartisan support that would show unity in addressing the problems confronting us. I understand Mr. Reid is getting in his democratic election message, but there are times to step above the personal attacks, especially when the accuser is complicit in helping us get to where we are today.

The candidates continue to agree on more oversight and provisions on executive compensation for the bailout bill, but their silence continues to be deafening regarding how the increased deficit would affect their spending and tax proposals.

President Bush is scheduled to speak at the United Nations today. Ahmadinejad will also be speaking. It speaks volumes to our country's freedoms that we would allow the leader of a country who has publicly stated that Israel must be destroyed to step on U.S. soil and be given a platform to speak to the civilized world. Somehow, I doubt President Bush would be given a reciprocal courtesy by the Iranian leadership, although I believe the majority of Iranians are sane and would welcome the leader of the free world on their soil. It truly is a shame that so few can dictate a ruthless agenda to so many. Similar to the Shah being overthrown some thirty years earlier, I believe the same fate awaits the current regime. I don't know when this will happen, but I surmise the young majority will at some point move Iran into the free world.

Sarah Palin is meeting with various world leaders at the United Nations, as well. This is her coming-out party to the world, and this campaigning with the world leaders and diplomats is intended to help her standing with voters. I am going to go out on a limb here and say that she will reference some of these meetings during her vice presidential debate next week.

Paulson and Bernanke are pitching their bailout proposal to congress today. There is still some concern about giving the treasury a $700 billion blank check without the level of accountability and oversight congress feels its entitled to. I agree with this logic but don't want to see our congressional leaders do their typical grandstanding, so they can go back to their constituents and mention how they are looking out for them. If you're truly looking out for them, explain how our $10 trillion Federal debt is in their best interest. Tell them how much it translates to per citizen. The timing is perfect, however, in that it will provide incumbents free media time to trumpet their importance in Washington. Bernanke said that, without this "assistance," there is a strong chance of a recession. At least he didn't use the "D" word, which is being bandied about by some economists and commentators. When the debate is over, and some compromises have been reached, I think our elected officials will support the bill, unless of course their constituents convince them otherwise.

Most of my discussion has been on the economy, which is certainly warranted, given recent events. I continue to feel very uneasy about the future and would like to see some positive momentum in the economy. I read some analyst comments that said this holiday season is shaping up to be one of the worst in memory, which is not exactly going out on a limb, given the downward trajectory of our economy. I also noted that an economist used the term "capitulation," which to him was a good thing, because it implies we are near a bottom. Webster's defines it as "to surrender under conditional terms," but I don't believe any of us wants to give up yet.

The market dropped another one hundred, sixty points today. It appears there is a lot of anxiety over the tone of politicians' concerns about the proposal. A part of me is starting to think that the democrats are going to overload the proposal with amendments that Paulson and Bush will not feel comfortable with. If they oppose the bill, we will almost certainly have our recession, which may be what Reid and Pelosi want, because it would probably help Obama in the general election. Even though the Democrats control both houses of congress and are complicit in the economy's performance, the buck stops at the President's doorstep.

Most people I speak with share my concerns on the economy. It is the number one issue on voters' minds these days. Obama is leading in the polls, but he is far from having a safe margin.

September 24, 2008

Paulson and Bernanke continue to make their pitch for the treasury bailout program. Members of both parties are expressing concerns, although I am optimistic it will get done. I certainly hope it does, for I fear the market will continue in a downward spiral without its passage.

President Bush will address the nation tonight in a prime time speech on the state of the economy and make his case for passage of the Treasury plan. There must be some concern over its prospects for passage if he feels the need to make his case to the American voters. Neither Obama nor McCain has said whether they will vote for it. I guess they are waiting to see which way public opinion and the polls will tilt, thus providing them more time to have their decision made by the voters. I want decisive leadership, and neither of them is supplying it in this instance. Sure we need more oversight and limits on executive compensation, but I think most people agree with that. It's the level of oversight that I'm more concerned with. I wish one of them would step up and take a bold and decisive position; however, neither wants to take this chance. They are exercising safe politics and realize that a misstep forty-two days before Election Day could be suicidal.

The consensus of pollsters seems to be that the race will be won or lost in the battleground states of Ohio, Pennsylvania, Michigan, Florida, Virginia, Missouri, Colorado, and Iowa.

This is our Electoral College system at work, and it lends itself (as we found out in the 2000 election) to the possibility of the presidential victor losing the popular vote. Might we see a repeat of this on November fourth? If you believe the pollsters as to which states are "in play," I should feel a stronger sense of responsibility since Pennsylvania is on the list. This makes my vote take on added significance, and as such, I would expect a barrage of TV ads, media inserts, and even phone calls as the big day approaches. Speaking of phone calls, I wonder how many other voters share my disdain in receiving pre-recorded phone messages from a specific candidate. Please don't insult me or other voters' intelligence and insinuate you're reaching out to us on a personal basis. This annoying interruption has an opposite affect of what you intended, because it actually highlights an impersonal relationship you have with us. I equate these to the dreaded telemarketing calls, and I follow a similar routine of either hanging up or, if I happen to see an "800" or "888" number on caller ID, I let it ring. My home state does have a whopping twenty-one electoral votes up for grabs, which could very well give the election to the Keystone State victor. Obama lost the democratic primary in my state, which means he has some work to do. We have a popular democratic governor, which should help Obama. I wonder, however, if Obama's previous comments about "angry gun toting" Pennsylvanians will come back to haunt him. I would think we Pennsylvanians will be reminded of this comment in the latter days of the campaign.

I saw another article today that said 18 percent of likely voters in the country are undecided. This wasn't far off my prior assertion that perhaps 20 percent were in play. This is one of those statistics that can be very misleading. Even if the

18 percent is accurate, the more pertinent question is what this percentage is in the battleground states. The article cites as an example a married father of two children from New York and a mother of two on disability from Alabama. These states are going democratic and republican, respectively, so these undecideds will have no swing power in determining our next president. This is not to diminish their voting privilege; rather, it lasers in on where the election will be won. I doubt the 18 percent is consistent in every state. I guess in its simplest form, the election will come down to about five million voters combined, who comprise about 15 percent of the likely voters in the battleground states. Each member of this five-million-voter universe will have the fate of the election in their hands. This represents but a small fraction of eligible voters, and highlights the importance of each campaign's success in targeting proposals to this group's liking.

McCain offered to postpone the first debate scheduled for this Friday. His rationale was to focus his attention on helping to solve the standstill on the Treasury proposal. Obama still wants to have the debate; his reasoning is that this crisis makes it even more imperative that the voters get to see the two of them and judge for themselves who would be a better leader for the next four years. This week's debate topic is foreign policy, which most pundits would admit seems to favor McCain. Maybe he's thinking that if he could somehow postpone the foreign policy debate until closer to the election, possibly until the last debate, he could surge down the homestretch and leave voters with a comfort level, as they walk into the booth on November fourth.

A disconcerting thought that the economy must be in dire shape continues to haunt me. Are we really heading for a catastrophe, or is there some other motive behind the political posturing? I continue to get an uncomfortable feeling about this, and it certainly highlights why the economy is the number one issue on voters' minds. We all want to put food on the table and provide for our families. Any hint that this could be in jeopardy concerns each of us and makes us hope that whatever course our elected officials decide on will be the correct one. At this point, I think it is safe to say that most voters are aware of this issue, and since it remains the number one story, each politician will attempt to put his stamp on it.

Sarah Palin used the "D" word today. She said we could be heading toward a depression if congress does not act on the Treasury proposal. I certainly was not comforted by this and do not think it was a particularly smart thing to say. I am not a fan of scare tactics.

September 25, 2008

On the train into work this morning, my thoughts are consumed with fear of an impending economic abyss. If the President, Treasury Secretary Paulson, and Fed Chairman Bernanke were trying to get my attention they certainly did. The weather forecast is for rain today, which seems appropriate given the dreary economic climate.

Bush is having an economic summit today, with both Obama and McCain expected to attend. I can't remember another instance of this type of situation developing so close to a presidential election. I think it is proper that both candidates attend and have their say, because one of them is going to inherit this predicament when he takes office. Wouldn't it be refreshing if C-SPAN were allowed to film this summit? That would allow us to view each of the combatant's leadership skills under stressful circumstances. We may wind up seeing an obligatory thirty-second clip showing a fake bipartisanship moment, but I doubt we'll be allowed to see the candidates engaging in real issues.

It was encouraging to hear Obama acknowledge that the current crisis might affect his year-one economic goals; although he was quick to point out he would still provide middle-class tax cuts. McCain keeps pointing out that Obama will raise taxes, which the senator from Illinois acknowledges he will do for those couples earning over $250,000. In addition, he has talked of raising the capital gains and dividends rate above the current 15 percent level, although it's unclear how high he would like to increase these rates. I recognize that taxes will have to be raised at some point, unless we somehow get our spending under control. Taxpayers on average are okay with paying their fair share, but they don't want higher taxes to pay for frivolous items, such as a "bridge to nowhere."

Forty days until Election Day, and various polls indicate a close contest. We Americans like some suspense, and many of us want the election to be close. History will be made this year with the election of our first minority president or female vice president. This has excited people and given some of them a reason to vote. It is unforgiveable that only about half of eligible voters usually vote. Countries that get a taste of democracy, such as Iraq, have people come out in droves to vote when given the chance. Maybe it's the thrill of actually having this privilege that excites these people, and the freshness of the process that drives their participation. Maybe it is their belief that their single vote will make a difference and that this empowerment is something they take seriously. Isn't it ironic that people new to the process usually participate in much greater percentages than we Americans, who have been doing this for over two hundred years? We can learn something from the new kids on the block, who turn out in large numbers in the face of terroristic threats. Is our voter apathy due to a resignation that it doesn't matter who gets elected, that we will get the same old politics as usual in Washington? Obama and McCain are both appealing to this apathy with their promise of change, with one's credentials being that he is new to Washington and is not bound to business as usual, while the other trumpets his independence and maverick voting record. Both candidates have seized on the theme of change, and are working hard to be christened as the new sheriff more likely to shake things up in Washington. It is ironic that the vice presidential candidates have the opposite experience levels to the top of their ticket, which balances out their partner's experience or lack thereof. Most voters have misgivings about some part of each ticket. If it is experience you want, the Republican presidential candidate has it, as does the Democratic vice presidential candidate. If being new to the stage equates to change, then the Democratic top of the ticket and the Republican vice presidential candidate have it.

Most voters say they want change, and the candidates and their parties continue to hammer away as to why they are the best choice for making this happen. Whichever candidate is able to convince voters they are more likely to impose change in Washington will most assuredly win. There are moments when I think Obama is more likely to effect change, and similar instances when I think McCain is the one. I still have time to make up my mind, although something has to give for me to lean toward one of the candidates. I realize that change, in and of itself, is not necessarily a good thing and that there needs to be a reason and a will to change things for the better. Although we love to sign on to a change philosophy, I'm not sure voters have articulated just what it is they want changed. We certainly want the economy to change for the better, but do we really want fundamental and ideological change that will alter our way of life? Would we be open to game changing disturbances to our current routines? I'm not sure we do, and therein lies the danger this election presents to us. Our lust for this nebulous idea of change was born out of an emotional outcry, and it may embolden the victor to infer they have received a mandate to move the country in a direction of change we voters did not intend. One common change recipe both candidates espouse is to achieve bipartisanship in Washington. I say amen to that because we voters share that goal and despise the partisan bickering that has become the norm. I sincerely hope this change happens regardless of who wins, although our political system is tilting away from cooperation and more toward a philosophy of "to the victors belong the spoils." Our last two presidents were outside the beltway governors, and the current president pitched his change slogan in the 2000 campaign. Clinton did not have to work as hard in focusing on change, because he happened to have run in 1992 when the economy was experiencing a difficult time. People wanted the economy to change, and Clinton was in the right place at the right time. It is interesting how fortunes can change so quickly. I remember the first Bush having extremely high approval ratings about a year before the 1992 election. He was riding the popularity of a winning campaign in the international coalition he put together to remove Saddam Hussein from Kuwait, and seemed a sure bet for reelection. But in 1992, the economy took a fall and so did Bush, proving that voter moods are dependent on the present and not the past. Unfortunately, our attention span is rather short sighted, limiting the definition of present to no more than a few months at best.

September 26, 2008

The $700 billion bailout program is not yet a done deal, and the futures markets are responding in a negative fashion. In addition, there is still some uncertainty over McCain participating in tonight's debate. His surrogates are insisting this is consistent with his "country first" position, with the severity of the financial crisis warranting his full attention. He has not been overly supportive of the current proposal, and I think he is trying to take a position different than Bush's to highlight his independence. He is also attempting to show support for the middle class by taking a Main Street versus Wall Street attitude, with his hope being to sway some of these undecided voters to his side. There are other "conservative" Republicans trying to craft their own bill, with less of a dependency on a $700 billion giveaway. I personally want something done, and my preference at this point is for the current Bush/Paulson proposal. I understand that compromise is a vital part of our political system, but let's get something done before the market drops another five hundred points.

Word leaked out after 1 p.m. that McCain will be attending the debate tonight. I think this was the correct decision and agreed with Obama's position that the debate was more important than ever because, in less than forty days, one of them will be elected President. I am actually looking forward to seeing the two of them face off tonight. This event will likely sway some voters, although barring a major gaffe by either, my guess is it will not change people's minds. I think back to some of the prior presidential debates, and the mistakes or performances that truly impacted people's decisions. In 1960, Richard Nixon was sweating profusely in contrast to the young, vibrant-looking John Kennedy, who understood the importance of appearance and impression in the first televised debates. (I must put a disclaimer in here that I was too young to vote in that election.) In 1984, Ronald Reagan asserted that Mondale's age should not be held against him, effectively removing his own age as a negative in the campaign. In 1980, Ronald Reagan used the dismissive but effective rebuttals to Carter with the phrase, "there you go again," and continuing on about the current president's mischaracterizations of his positions. Michael Dukakis made weak responses to a moderator's question about if he would be for the death penalty if someone raped and killed his wife. Who can forget George Bush's apparent irritation and unease in 1992, as he constantly glanced at his watch in his debate with Bill Clinton? How about Al Gore's repeated exasperated sighs at George W. Bush's comments in 2000, and his invasion of Bush's space in the same debate. Are we in for a similarly defining moment in 2008? Since I'm on the topic of debate performances, I would love to know how the discussions over whether or not to bail out my employer went down. Was it a take it or leave it offer, with the government's position so strong that no hint of negotiations permeated into the discussions? I guess we'll never know, but some might view this transaction as one Paulson would be patting himself on the back over if he was still in the private sector working for Goldman Sachs.

I took a vacation day to go on my annual trek to Penn State for a football weekend. I have been doing this for over twenty-five years, and I always look forward to it. It's an annual ritual that started years ago, with some close friends and I, initially treating it as a guys' getaway for golf, tennis, and late night partying. As each of our families grew, the trip changed to one of bringing our kids along for the weekend, which necessitated a change in the trip's itinerary. I'm not complaining about the change; if anything, it has been a fantastic bonding experience for each of us and our kids. Each of my five children have participated, although because of space limitations, my friends and I had to invoke an age eligibility requirement of ten to get on the invite list. I remember trips totaling as many as twenty people, and I must admit those were some of the best trips we had. As our kids have aged and moved on with their lives, the number of participants has dwindled, although the one constant is that the core group of friends has remained the same. I think I can speak for each of them when I say we look forward to this trip with the same level of enthusiasm that we first experienced over twenty years ago. It won't be long until the circle of life is complete and the travel list returns to the same it was when we first started this annual occurrence. A football weekend at Penn State is one of the great spectacles in sports, spending time with 110,000 other fans on a fall Saturday afternoon (sometimes evening). I did not realize that this year's football weekend would coincide with the timing of the first debate, but it might be interesting to see the level of interest among the students and alumni.

The market finished up over one hundred, twenty points today, which is surprising, given the bailout proposal still being in a state of limbo. It is almost like hope is now driving the upward trends that occur all too infrequently, a hope built from a belief that the bailout will be a cure all. I think we will see upward movement for a period of time after its passage, but I do believe there are other structural issues that need addressing before we embark on a sustainable bull run.

The debate will be starting any moment, and the preparations can be likened to a football team game-planning for their next foe. Similar to a scout team, each candidate's camp brings in someone to play the role of his opponent in mock debates, trying to toughen them up and hone their one-on-one skills. They obviously understand the significance of these prime-time battles and leave no stone unturned in their preparations. Nine O'clock arrives and the debate begins. The moderator is Jim Lehrner, and although the topic of the debate is foreign policy, there are opening questions on the economy and the proposed bailout. One particular exchange, which I thought was very appropriate, was how the current fiscal crisis would affect their campaign promises and policy initiatives in their first year. Each candidate evaded answering the question and used it as a bridge to address some of their other pre-determined sound bites. Fortunately for the audience, Lehrer did not accept their evasive approach and pressed them to answer the question. Neither relented, and eventually, Lehrer had to move on to another topic. We have all seen this routine of evading the question asked and candidates delivering their own advertising; however, I would like to see the candidates answer questions directly. Most voters would prefer this, and although it may seem to the candidates to be a risky maneuver, some voters would actually reward them for their honest refreshing response.

I watched the debate in the lobby of the hotel with a group of people, and the level of interest was higher than I expected. This was encouraging, and I hope it is a precursor to a high participation rate among voters in the upcoming election. It never ceases to amaze me when the spin-doctors work their magic in providing their analysis as to who won the debate. Immediately after the debate, the magicians started working their magic. Each side spouted its reasons why their candidate won, and said they could not be happier with their man's performance. Can this media spin really influence voter's opinions? Unfortunately, I think it can in certain instances, which is an indictment of the independent thought process of some voters. Fortunately, however, most of the voters who are influenced simply reinforce their candidate preference. For example, most who watch NBC already lean Democratic, while Fox viewers tilt Republican. Barring an epic collapse by their man, these voters are a lock to stick to their original choice. We undecided voters, however, are truly torn in our decision process. We are undecided for a reason and are searching for something to help us make up our minds. Did the debate sway me? It did not. I thought the debate was fairly even, in effect a split decision. This was, however, supposed to be McCain's area of expertise, but I am not sure he outshined Obama. There were no major gaffes, thus this debate did not have a game changing exchange. I can draw another debate parallel to the private sector for when a company has its quarterly earnings release and subsequent analyst discussions. Some companies are much better than others at this, and the cat and mouse game between management and analysts is always interesting to hear. There are sometimes a few gotchas that occur, but major gaffes are usually few and far between. I would expect AIG's earnings release this quarter to be interesting to say the least.

A few friends and I went out on the town after the debate. State College is certainly a party town, and its reputation is well deserved. The problem we encountered was that all the bars and clubs were full, with waiting lines extending a block or so for the Rathskeller and other popular destinations. We did not want to wait in any line, and decided to walk along College Avenue to take in the atmosphere, which was its usual electric self. I wonder how many of the thousands of people enjoying the nightlife watched the debate. Should I infer that decisions to have a cold one versus watching the debate means a lack of interest? This would be too harsh of a verdict on my part, although I do believe the youngest eligible voters are more inclined to vote for Obama because of his persona and the fact that he visually defines change more than his opponent. This is my opinion, and it was reinforced from random polling I was conducting. This young vote will be crucial to Obama's chances of winning, and I am not convinced they will come out in the droves he is expecting. Polling may indicate their excitement to come out and vote this year, but let's see how many exercise their privilege if November 4th brings cold blustery weather in places like State College, PA.

September 27th and 28th, 2008

Penn State was a great escape weekend, made even better by the fact that they beat a ranked team and moved into the top ten. It was great spending time with my son and some of my friends who I see all too infrequently. The game did not end until around 11:30 p.m., and by the time we got back to our hotel it was about 12:30 a.m. Somehow the walk is much easier after a victory. The crowd in the stadium for the game was approximately 109,000, which qualified State College as the third largest city in Pennsylvania for that day. I was fortunate to have gotten tickets for the game from a friend of mine, while most of my friends were forced to go the scalper route. I have been in their position in some of my prior trips, and I know how expensive it can sometimes be to procure tickets through this negotiation process. The key is to wait as close to game time as possible before trying to get tickets, hoping you find sellers who either overestimated the value or are content that they've made enough with prior sales to call it a day. Interestingly enough, each of my friends was able to get tickets for approximately face value, which is very unusual for a game of this stature. I did not think about it much at the time, but in retrospect, one can assume that even scalpers recognize the tough times we're facing, and had to back off on their typical usury demands.

As I sat in the stadium gazing around at the 109,000 fans in attendance, I wondered how many would actually vote in

November. I also realized that this was only thirty thousand or so less than the margin Bush lost the state by in the 2004 election. From my view, there were two distinct groups in the stadium, the student and non-student populations. The former represent the group more likely to lean toward Obama, which only counts if they actually pull the lever on November 4th. For most of these students, this will be their first presidential election (although for some on the five and six year college plan, it may be their second), and I wonder if they will demonstrate the same enthusiasm on November 4th as they displayed at the game tonight. Most of the students are shielded or protected from the real world in their college lives and are focused on other things besides the issues being discussed in the campaign. Some of the students will take offense at this, but at this stage of their lives, I am not sure how many weigh the actual issues, versus looking for some obvious change in our political system. I think the student population views Obama as someone who defines change more than McCain, who for most is similar in age to their grandfathers. I think they understand that McCain has more experience, but if they are more interested in change, then Obama would seem to be their logical choice. Young voters are less inclined to exhibit reservations about a minority candidate being qualified for president, and, in an odd twist, I think this only adds to their feelings about him representing change. It's possible this election may witness a changing of the guard in race and ethnic prejudices, and that our younger generation is the first to be truly colorblind when it comes to their opinions on what is best for this country. Are we in the midst of a transformation that has taken years to achieve, where the crowning of an African American as our president will be the consummation of this metamorphoses? Is this election an indictment of our past and a preview of our future? I think this hypothesis has merit, and the exit polling on November fourth may provide a glimpse as to whether it is in fact a trend. Is it possible that our younger generation is teaching the rest of us something here, and if so, should we listen? Isn't it ironic that the party of Lincoln may be defeated in this year's election by the very principles and beliefs he espoused in his Emancipation Proclamation some 145 years ago? Somehow I cannot help but think that old Abe is looking down and smiling upon us today. If he had a crystal ball, might he have changed his opening remarks in the Gettysburg address from "four score and seven years ago" to "seven score and six years from now?"

When we got back to our hotel after the game, we congregated in the lobby to have some late night conversation, reminisce of times passed, and try to squeeze out some last moments of friendship that would not be rekindled until possibly next fall. The wisecracks of how it feels to be working at AIG came up, with the joke being that I had better be putting in long hours since I was indirectly working for them, because they're all taxpayers. There's not much of a response I can have to this, but it dawned on me that I had better think of a canned response, since I should expect to hear this quite a bit in the future. During our conversation, I threw out the election as a topic and found that most shared my passion about it, and some were leaning in a direction I would not have guessed. They were zeroed in on change as the desired outcome of the election; their definition of change was not based on color, but rather on who was more likely to bring real change to Washington. We discussed the major issues surrounding the campaign, and I was encouraged to find that each of my friends viewed this election with the sense of urgency necessary to get us on the right track. We may have had differing viewpoints on some issues, but we were all unanimous in our belief that something had to change. We all worried, not only about our futures, but equally or more so about what the future held for our children and their children. It was almost as if we felt a sense of urgency that, if we did not act soon to confront the major issues facing this great country, we would not leave it in better shape than we had inherited. None of us wanted to be part of the generation that took a step back.

On Sunday morning, as I headed east through the mountains on the way home from State College, I thought back to the discussions of the prior night. I wondered how many of us would be severely affected by the economic downturn and how many might join the growing line of the unemployed. My friends and I are a diverse group, some of whom share my professional field, quite a few in sales, with others in businesses ranging from contracting to manufacturing. I actually grew up in the same middle-class Philadelphia neighborhood with most of them, and I feel fortunate we've been able to stay good friends all this time. We have all attained what I will refer to as an upper middle class status, achieved through a combination of hard work and a hunger to succeed. Common characteristics of people at this level are that they never forget where they came from, and always maintain a drive for continual improvement. We all struggled financially at the start of our careers; however we knew that a strong foundation would serve us well as we progressed in life. I remember my first annual salary after college as being in the $12,000 range, a number that even after adjusting for inflation would still fall short of what today's college graduates receive. My friends and I have worked hard to achieve our current status; however we have no intention of ever relinquishing our middle-class state of mind. I would like to think we've passed the torch off to our children, who will attempt to chart their own success stories in life. I made a mental note to stay in touch more frequently, and keep abreast of their changing situations. I'm not sure what I could do to help, but I at least would want them to know I cared.

I almost forgot to mention the bailout package appears headed for adoption. There have been compromises on both sides, which is what generally needs to happen to get controversial legislation passed. I do not know all the specifics, yet, so I am interested to see what the final version will look like. History will judge if the right decision was made. I am sensitive to the fact that our country is being pointed to as the initiator of this crisis. Another level of sensitivity exists for me with my AIG label. Thoughts enter my mind about what this would mean if I ever opted to leave the company, and whether a resume showing time spent at AIG represents a major blemish that would move me to the bottom of a prospective employer's candidate pile. Not a day goes by that we're not mentioned somehow in the news. In addition, my wife receives the occasional call from a friend or family member asking if things are okay with me at AIG. I'm sure some of them aren't happy that the government bailed us out and wish we were left to fail.

September 29, 2008

The bailout proposal, which I will hereby refer to as TARP (Treasury Assistance Restructuring Program), did not muster enough votes to pass in the House. The vote was close at 228-207, and, as a result, the stock market dropped seven hundred, seventy-seven points, the biggest point drop in history. Isn't it ironic that some slot machines pay out big money with this combination? This drop could have been predicted by most people, since TARP's proponents were warning of dire consequences to our fragile financial system if it did not pass. The immediate reaction of the market seemed to vindicate this assessment. I am going to propose a thesis here that it did not pass because of Main Street's perception that it in fact was a "bailout," not a stimulus to help the overall economy. The congressmen voting "nay" on the proposal did so based upon their constituents' strong negative reaction to the proposal, especially given the timing of their own upcoming election on November fourth. I cannot fault their rationale in listening to the people who elected them; on the contrary, I applaud them. Voters have a lot of pent up anger and frustration with Washington, which is magnified when the economy is in such a poor state. In effect, Main Street blames Wall Street for the current state of the economy. I understand the thrust of this anger, but I am worried that this rush to judgment ignores the fact that what happens on Wall Street directly affects Main

Street. If credit markets continue to tighten, then business, consumer, and mortgage lending will be limited, putting a strain on all areas of the economy. The middle class will feel the trickle-down effect, and jobs will be lost in spite of their well-intentioned message to their congressmen. Obama and McCain both expressed reluctant approval of TARP, effectively trying to position themselves on both sides of the issue. Their cat and mouse game is tiring on me, and I would like to see one of them take a strong position on TARP. One of them should exert leadership and resuscitate the proposal, and help secure the needed votes for its passage. Something has to give, and I hope that something occurs before the Dow dips another 10 percent or so. Main Street will be opening third-quarter 401K statements in the coming weeks, and most will get sticker shock when they see the melting away of their nest eggs.

A few polls came out indicating that Obama was widening his narrow edge over McCain. Two reasons seem to be emerging, one is that people view him as being better able to steer the economy through difficult times, and the other relates to questions about whether McCain's running mate is fit for the VP role. Things can turn quickly, as evidenced by the fact that only four weeks ago, the pundits were impressed with Palin's convention acceptance speech, and the ticket was energized and riding a crest of momentum. Her limited accessibility to the press, and apparent protection by the McCain campaign, seem to be creating negative perceptions of her. Sarah Palin will have her chance to answer the critics in three days at the vice-presidential debate. Absent a riveting performance, the negative attitudes about her as a heartbeat away from the presidency will intensify. Most people admire her story, but as days pass, the focus on her has shifted toward the substance of her leadership qualities, and less on her hockey mom lifestyle. I feel it slipping away for her, although momentum can shift suddenly if she acquits herself competently in the debate. I believe she is a good person, and I admire her story, but that alone does not warrant my vote to be our vice president. Thursday night will provide us an initial glimpse as to whether she has what it takes to be a heartbeat away from the presidency.

Every day that the economy slips further is another good day for Obama and the Democratic Party. Today's seven-hundred, seventy point debacle will shift more of the undecided into his camp. I am frustrated with the economy, but not ready to commit to either candidate yet. I see a Republican president and democratically controlled congress. Each is to blame for this mess, although each would like the voters to believe the other is the guilty party. It is hard to discern political jockeying from people's honest opinions, and, unfortunately, some will be swayed by the former. I sense the McCain/Palin ticket is in trouble; however, I am quick to remember that the race will be decided in the battleground states. Voter moods can change in a hurry, and a major slipup by a candidate will create an opening to be exploited by his opponent. The Republican ticket is behind, but it's only the fourth inning. There is talk that the TARP will be reworked and another vote may be coming later this week.

One last point worth noting is the timing of the proposal. Most institutions and public companies' third quarters end on September 30th, which is tomorrow. Mark to market accounting for third-quarter results will be based on September 30th marks. Given the market's backlash to TARP failing to pass, marks worsened today, versus last week. If this downward pressure continues tomorrow, we will see third-quarter results feel the sting of this, further exasperating the situation.

September 30, 2008

I turned on the TV this morning to CNN and viewed a clip on "Rest in Peace the American Dream." The heading was self explanatory, with the main thesis questioning whether our next generation will be able to attain the middle-class American dream of home ownership. I feel a sense of anxiety over the current housing slump and the state of the economy, but to insinuate that this down cycle is a precursor to a long-lasting economic downshift is a little too much to take. We are a shortsighted culture, with most people wanting an immediate or near-term satisfaction of their wants. Whether it be Wall Street and the fixation on current quarter earnings or Main Street and its focus on the current price of a gallon of gasoline, as a culture we collectively crave short-term gains without worrying about the long-term ramifications. As a case in point, there were proposals to suspend the federal tax on gasoline to help consumers cope with the high pump prices, yet this seems to be counter intuitive if the real goal is to promote energy conservation. Lowering the price would allow commuters to continue their current driving habits, diminishing the outcry of getting a real energy policy in place. I understand there are people who live day-to-day; however, our lawmakers need to balance immediate assistance with longer-term planning. We had an energy crisis back in the 1970s, with an accompanying uproar of weaning ourselves off of gasoline consumption. Prices came down, the urgency for action dissipated, and thirty years later we are witnessing a reincarnation of this crisis. The one big difference is that we are now much more dependent on foreign oil, with domestic production falling from 60 percent of our usage to approximately 30 percent today. Petro dollars are going overseas, some to destinations I would not call pro-American (Venezuela). My overriding point here is that we need to develop goals and plans that incorporate longer-term thinking. Private sector companies develop strategic plans, which serve as a roadmap for where they want to go. Granted, the current crisis has altered these strategies, but most understand that economic cycles are normal, and that, at some point, stability and a return to normalcy will occur. I question whether the public sector has any idea of what a long-term strategic plan is and how to put one together. The political process may actually lend itself to this gap in planning, since politicians are more worried about getting reelected, which is contingent on satisfying their constituent's current needs, as opposed to focusing on longer-term solutions that may require short-term sacrifices. Here is a solution to the problem that makes too much common sense and would be considered a pipe dream in terms of it ever happening. Why not have term limits on politicians, which would allow them to be more forward thinking, since their jobs would not be contingent on giving in to short-term needs? I find it hypocritical that the current election has a theme of change at the presidential level, while at the congressional level, the incumbents will speak of their needed experience in working through the Washington political system to help their constituents. I think most people are opposed to career politicians, yet on Election Day they vote in the affirmative to keep their own lawmakers in place. We have the power to change the system; however, our votes reinforce the status quo. If we really want change, let's have a significant turnover in our elected officials. One of the things that motivate us to succeed in the private sector is the threat of failure, which helps drive us to perform at our best each and every day. Absent the threat of being fired would lead to complacency, which stifles innovation and efficiency. Any private sector CEO who has a 20% shareholder approval rate would be quaking in their shoes. It's a shame I don't sense this same level of panic in our politicians, since fear of losing their jobs might force them to tackle some pressing issues. The onus on instilling this fear with them rests solely on our shoulders; however I think we have been remiss in our responsibility.

TARP is back on the front burner, with talk of compromises being discussed and a possible vote on the revised proposal later in the week. The stock market liked hearing this and jumped almost five hundred points today. Another catalyst in this upward movement was the SEC issuing guidance on fair-value accounting, stating that companies are free to use internal modeling assumptions to value "hard to value" assets, in essence negating them from having to value at distressed or fire sale prices. The Financial Accounting Statements Board (FASB) is to issue additional "interpretative guidance" later this week. For the casual observer, this may not mean much, but for the business community, this is a potential game changer. Depending on FASB guidance later this week, it could mean that a good portion of write downs,

- which lead to forced asset sales to raise capital,
- which leads to shareholder dilution,
- which leads to lower share prices,
- which leads to rating agency downgrades,

- which leads to higher borrowing costs,
- which leads to bankruptcy or liquidations,

could be halted. This domino effect is breathtaking, and the Street is littered with the Bear Stearns, Lehman Brothers, and AIGs as proof of the dark side of this sequence of events. I know that Paulson and other knowledgeable people have been speaking of the dangers of "fair value," but what precipitated this change in tone today? For one thing, today is September thirtieth, the last day of the third quarter for most companies. Third-quarter results are forecast to be a disaster, and when the land minds start going off in a week or so, downward momentum will almost certainly intensify. This eleventh-hour reprieve can be likened to a death row inmate who has been granted a stay of execution. If FASB issues guidance in a favorable way, most financial companies could be the recipients of hitting the lottery. Pessimists will point to the fact that earnings will be lifted by accounting entries, but fail to point out that prior earnings were savaged by these same accounting entries. If FASB guidance is viewed favorably, then this occurrence alone has the potential to strengthen balance sheets, which would allow banks to have more lending capacity to help unfreeze credit markets and bring some sanity back to the lending world. If you couple a TARP passage later this week with this "fair value" guidance, you could see markets spring to life over the next few weeks. This could lift the gloom and doom over the economy, and improve voter psyche as the election nears. This lift could help McCain, who needs the electorate to focus less on economic issues and more on the leadership credentials of the two candidates. He has a chance in this type of debate, but as recent polls show, Obama is viewed much more favorably on issues that affect our wallets and pocketbooks. Conspiracy theories spring to mind, and I begin to wonder if the Republican administration, in conjunction with the SEC-appointed leadership, is attempting a full court press to get McCain back in the game. The mere fact that I suspect this indicates a level of skepticism about this series of events and the true reasoning behind it.

Oliver Stone's new film, *W,* comes out in a few weeks, and it is the first time a film will be released about a sitting president. Stone is a self-proclaimed liberal in the same vein as Michael Moore, and his interpretation of Bush will probably be unflattering and, in some cases, mocking of our forty-third president. The entertainment industry still doesn't get it. They feel their celebrity status gives them a platform and recognition of some belief that their holy words will influence voters and help sway the election to Obama (or any other Democrat for that matter). What they fail to realize through their jaded view of themselves is that middle-class America may like to be entertained, but it does not want or need some rich, pampered, out-of-touch entertainer to tell them how to vote. Ironically, I believe this celebrity endorsement works the opposite of its intended purpose and helps the Republican ticket. The McCain camp should pray for the Stones and Moores of the world to publicly show their endorsement of Obama. The celebrity factor could actually be worth a point or two for the Republican Party.

October 1, 2008

As the calendar turns to the month of October, Election Day is in sight. Only thirty-five days until we elect a new president. The polls continue to lean Obama's way, with the recent economic issues helping his cause. The electorate seems to think he will be a better steward for the economy. Is this because he is a Democrat? Is it because voters want a return to the economic climate of when the last Democrat was in office? Is it because Obama and the Democrats have been able to successfully link McCain to Bush, which would be a cancerous relationship for any candidate to overcome? Or is it because voters see the gridlock and partisanship in Washington and are willing to give the Democrats control of the House, Senate, and Presidency to push their agenda through? Although I am a fan of split branches to act as a form of checks and balances I think I have caught the frustration bug, and find it hard to believe I'm actually considering giving the Democrats this consolidation of power, but only if Obama can convince me he deserves my vote. We still don't know much about him, and this causes me some discomfort. This cloak of secrecy would be a negative in most presidential elections, but in this year's contest, it paradoxically could be a positive for him since the economy is dominating people's thoughts and the news headlines. This is allowing Obama to be judged on form over substance, which financial professionals learn early on is an inverted relationship of how real judgments should be rendered.

The Senate is set to vote tonight on its own version of TARP, and they have included some tax break provisions in their bill, including an alternative minimum tax provision to help twenty million middle-class taxpayers, and an increase in the amount the FDIC will insure from $100,000 to $250,000. Senate leadership is expressing confidence they have the votes for it to pass. A surprising defeat like the house episode would be a disaster.

It feels like the financial mess we are in is getting worse. I have yet to hear anyone speak in a comforting tone. The President, members of congress, the Treasury Secretary, and the Chairman of the Federal Reserve Bank all seem to be warning (even threatening) of a systemic implosion if the proposal isn't passed. Even the presidential candidates have shied away from delivering some kind of reassuring comments, which is a shame, because what voters are looking for is someone to take command and instill in each of us a sense of sorely needed optimism. Are they deferring to the President and his team, because they want the problem to stick to him, or are they working behind the scenes to get the proposal the support it needs to pass? I would be impressed if it was the latter, but in this day and age of negative campaigning, I am afraid it is the former. I keep asking myself why neither wants to step to the head of the class. McCain has always prided himself in putting country first, and Obama speaks of changing the way Washington works; both of them have been handed an opportunity to put into practice their campaign themes.

Another issue contributing to the uncertainty of this bill's prospect for passage is its billing as a "bailout." This term implies *giveaway*, which is the worst conceivable marketing this proposal could have. Every commentator is using the term "bailout" as well, with all of the major media outlets accepting this as its proper definition. I'm guilty of this as well, since I used the same phrase a few days ago. TARP means "Treasury Asset Restructuring Program," and I cannot understand why the focus is not on "restructuring" versus "bailout." No wonder taxpayers are expressing outrage. I will chalk up this government faux pas to two things:

1. It was a hastily cobbled together proposal that did not allow for the typical pre-announcement planning to provide the necessary positioning in people's minds;
2. The media was able to define this since the government did not. "Bailout" sells much better than "restructuring," and the former evokes voter anger and interest, which translates into higher viewership and ratings.

The first strikes me as reinforcing the belief that this is indeed a serious crisis, while the second supports my theory that the media will position an issue or situation in the way they feel will attract viewers and sell papers. Most learned economists and business people who have spoken on the various news outlets about this have stated that the government may actually make money on this or at worst lose much less than $700 billion. This is not a typical bailout, but more in line with a "restructuring." It does not matter at this point. The media won control of the issue, and influenced the electorate's vision of how we should think about it.

Another poll came out today and said that Obama is now leading in the three largest battleground states of Florida, Ohio, and Pennsylvania. The Quinnipiac poll has Obama ahead by more than the margin of error, and it's a certainty he will win the white house if he carries these states. Bush won all of these except Pennsylvania in both 2000 and 2004, and the electoral map shows that McCain will run out of real estate if he loses these states. It should be obvious why these states have turned to Obama—"it's the economy, stupid." The current economic crisis has marginalized McCain's perceived strengths on the war in Iraq, national security, and foreign policy issues, and elevated Obama into a front-runner status. The longer the financial crisis stays at the top of the news, the more positive it is for Obama. Is it hypocritical for me to think the Democrats might want to drag this out a little longer, shortening the amount of time McCain has to recover before November 4th? Are they so annoyed with eight years of a Republican in the white house that they would deliberately inflict a little more pain on Main Street to win this prize? How convenient to be able to do this and have a Republican president on the receiving end of Main Street's blame. This sounds similar to what happens when a new CEO takes the reins at a troubled company; they try to pin blame on their predecessor for any and all negative results. This is common practice, and I wonder at whose feet the AIG blowup will land. I'm not going to venture a guess; rather, I'll wait to see this play out in the future.

I mentioned on a previous day that, given the state of the economy, Obama should be running better than he currently is. He is picking up momentum as the economy deteriorates, but McCain is still within striking distance. It certainly seems a daunting task for McCain with thirty-five days to go, but stranger things have happened. Truman went to bed in 1948 thinking the election was lost, but woke up to a different verdict. Will there be another surprise in 2008, and if so, might that surprise be the race card? A recent poll said 33 percent of Democrats would be uncomfortable voting for an African American to the highest position in America. These same polls, however, indicate that Obama has a substantial lead among Democrats. Los Angeles Mayor Tom Bradley, an African American, was projected by the polls as the winner in the 1982 California governor's race. He wound up losing the contest, and it was concluded that white voters did not want to acknowledge to pollsters their racial attitudes. If this underground movement were to repeat this year, McCain would be the obvious beneficiary; however, the question is how big this group of voters might be. Do they come out and vote for McCain, or do they opt to stay home on November 4th and sit out the election? McCain benefits in both instances, versus the polling projections, but he doubles the pickup if this group actually comes out and pulls his lever on Election Day.

Lost in today's news is the fact that Russia says it is removing its troops from areas of Georgia, outside the two separatist regions. In addition, a general in Afghanistan said more troops are needed, and the U.S. is opening a new round of negotiations with North Korea on its nuclear program. Somehow these stories all pale in relation to the domestic economy.

October 2, 2008

The Senate passed the $700 billion proposal by an overwhelming 75-24 vote last night. The senate did add some provisions to the house version that failed earlier this week, and there have been encouraging comments from house dissenters regarding their current thinking on the bill. A House vote is scheduled for later this week.

I noticed on the Internet this morning that a Chicago woman had a winning bid of $1.75 for an abandoned home in Saginaw, Michigan. This story kind of sums up the state of the housing market, which is mired in a severe slump. This woman was able to buy a house for less than what it would cost her to buy a Big Mac.

Besides the economy, the big news of the day is the vice presidential debate scheduled for 9 p.m. Eastern Time. Both candidates have been preparing this week, and Sarah Palin needs a virtuoso performance to halt the leaking in the McCain ship. Her combatants in the Alaskan governor debates were impressed with her performances, and are warning Biden not to take her for granted. Polls indicate that Biden has a wide lead over her on who is more qualified to be vice president, which makes sense, given his name recognition, experience, and tenure in the Senate. I am interested to watch because of all the candidates, she is the one who, in my mind, signifies change the most, yet she is the one who causes the least amount of confidence to be a commander in chief. This is setting up like a David vs. Goliath story, and we Americans always root for an underdog. 56.7 million Viewers watched the 1984 debate between Geraldine Ferraro and George H.W. Bush, making it the most widely watched vice presidential debate of all time. I think tonight's audience will set a new record, which will further support the interest people have in this campaign and the urgency the electorate has to see this country moving in the right direction. An interesting sidebar to tonight's debate is that the moderator, Gwen Ifill, is writing a book, titled *The Breakthrough: Politics and Race in the Age of Obama*, which is scheduled to be released on January twentieth, the day of the forty-fourth president's inauguration. So much for impartiality as a prerequisite for a moderator. It smells of home field advantage for Biden; however, given the sensitivity of the moderator's leaning, I think she will go out of her way to ensure such bias will be absent from tonight's debate.

The time is 11:00 a.m,, and I am preparing for a noon business meeting. I am spoiled in that I have a nice view of the Statue of Liberty and Ellis Island from my office. There are a lot of white caps on the river today, but very few boats. The current economic downturn is affecting the number of visitor trips to the Statue of Liberty and the sightseeing tours that used to frequent the river. I wonder if the guides on the tour boats make any snide comments as they pass lower Manhattan, or if the visitors themselves make some mocking references to the street of dreams. Many people have indicted that Wall Street is the root cause of the financial crisis, which has spread across the ocean to most foreign economies as well. Many learned economists have said that globalization was causing the rest of the world to decouple from the United States. This crisis would seem to indicate the reverse is still true, that when the United States sneezes the rest of the world still catches a cold. AIG is the butt of many jokes and anger these days, and although most employees are aware of this venom, they continue to perform admirably under trying circumstances. An air of uncertainty hangs over all of us, yet we maintain a level of professionalism that I am proud to witness. I would expect additional wrath directed our way when we release third quarter results in a few weeks, although the numbers will be overshadowed by a focus on our new majority owner. My sensitivity about being identified as an AIG employee has reached the stage where I keep my badge hidden completely when not in the office. I continue to hear stories of AIG employees being verbally abused, but I haven't witnessed such, myself. I keep thinking that, at some point, there will be physical confrontations making the news. I have an AIG golf shirt I used to wear on weekends, but to minimize the whispers, it's no longer in the dress rotation. That's a pity because I do like that shirt.

New filings for unemployment claims were at their highest level since right after 9/11/01. A lot of middle-class families are being affected by the deteriorating economy. Optimism is one of my virtues, but I can't shake the feeling that this downturn still has a ways to go. I am confident we will come out of it, but the question is when. Another question is how much wealth will be destroyed when we finally hit bottom, and how many families' routines will have been turned upside down as a result? It's easy to see why people are hungry for change and why they view this election as their chance to speak up and be heard. Someone has to take the fall for this, and like a quarterback in football, our signal caller is the President, and he is the one pointed to as the problem. This is naivety and reality at work at the same time—reality in that the buck stops at the top, naivety in that the team of elected politicians is just as guilty and worthy of dismissal. Bush is a lame duck and has to leave; many of the others should leave voluntarily. We all want change, yet incumbents will probably win reelection at a 90 percent rate. Why should these incumbents push for change when we reelect them to another term in November? They need to be sent a real message, and the only way to do that is to put them in the unemployment line.

I hate the food they serve at luncheon meetings and usually run for a sandwich prior to a noon business meeting. This financial crisis must be getting to me because today I opted to take the free lunch. I must say, however, that the lunch selection was rather dull, so I don't want any taxpayers thinking we're abusing the system.

Psychology plays an important role in our lives, and given the constant drumbeats of disaster emanating from people's mouths if TARP doesn't pass, it's almost like we have talked ourselves into this being a "must do." I often wonder about certain people's motivations for being vocal supporters of proposals such as TARP. Quite a few noteworthy businessmen, such as Warren Buffet, Bill Gross, and Wilbur Ross, are pushing for passage and making their cases on the various media outlets. Each of these individuals has investors they are responsible for, which causes one to wonder if their intentions are pure or a guise to improve their own performance. Each is successful in what they do, but might their ulterior motives be to influence us to sign onto their positions to help in lobbying efforts to win their argument? If someone has a platform to speak from, they immediately have power within their grasp. Warren Buffet said today, "the nation has been hit with an economic pearl harbor, and the government must respond quickly." These are not reassuring words from the oracle of Omaha, and I am sure his choice of words was carefully chosen to achieve a desired result. The question is whether members of the House will heed his warning when it is their turn to vote on the proposal tomorrow.

There was a report today that McCain's campaign is pulling out of Michigan, effectively conceding the state to Obama. Chalk up one battleground state for the blue team, providing McCain with less available real estate to win the electoral battle. I guess throwing in the towel early makes sense to eliminate the wasteful use of time and valuable resources, but I wonder how the voters in Michigan feel. Do the state Republicans feel betrayed or disenfranchised, or is it a realization that the economy has taken its toll and anointed Obama as the more likely candidate to fix the current crisis? A fear is that a psychological blow has been dealt to McCain, and it appears he is running out of time and winnable states. He needs something to rejuvenate his campaign, which just two weeks ago had momentum on his side. Could Palin resuscitate his campaign tonight, or is he in a free fall from which there is no escape? Thirty-three days provide a lot of opportunities for something to happen, but as long as the economy dominates the headlines, McCain will probably continue to lose ground.

The market took another hit today, down over three hundred points. Every day brings volatility, with three-hundred-point-plus movement days being the norm as opposed to the exception. The market is hoping for TARP to pass, and it almost appears that investors are pushing the markets to sway those congressmen who voted against it previously to switch their vote for Friday's tally. Their constituents have had time to absorb the effects of the market drops, and they come to the realization that this affects them directly. Their 401Ks and IRAs will have suffered accordingly, and their anger is now being replaced by reality. They made their point, and now it's time to move on. This mood shift should provide the cover for their elected officials to vote in favor of the proposal.

I watched the debate, and thought both candidates acquitted themselves nicely. Biden reinforced his credentials and attacked McCain at every opportunity. His approach of saying John was a nice and good man but is out of touch is a recurring theme of his. He also continued to hit home that a McCain administration would be an extension of Bush policies. Palin, on the other hand, reiterated McCain's maverick image, criticized Obama on his policy of increasing taxes, and spoke of looking forward as opposed to the backward -looking critique espoused by the Democrats. I scored the debate a draw.

October 3, 2008

There is hope the House will pass the rescue plan today, with a vote expected this morning.

The last monthly unemployment report before the election came out this morning, and it showed the economy shedding 159,000 jobs. This was the worst showing since March 2003. The unemployment rate remained at 6.1 percent. This report is reinforcing the market's perception that the House will pass the plan, as the market opened in positive territory. McCain's hope is that its passage will stabilize the markets, which will hopefully stabilize his campaign. He cannot win on the economy issue, and he needs it to slip to page five of the news. I would expect Obama and his team to maintain their focus on the economy to solidify their position, and keep McCain back on his heels. McCain/Palin needs something, anything, to reignite their campaign. Her performance last night might bring some Republicans who had reservations about her back into their camp, which would be a good starting point.

Today is a Friday, which is most employees' favorite day of the workweek. Each day seems to bring with it more gloomy economic news, and today's jobs report kept this trend intact. I went out to grab a sandwich at lunchtime at a local restaurant (I will splurge occasionally), and the service was great, since I was pretty much the only customer my server had. My oldest daughter is a part-time waitress at an upscale restaurant, close to where we live. She is staying busy and keeping herself in money while she waits to start her professional career right after the New Year. She says that most days the restaurant has trouble keeping the few waitresses busy. She gets the occasional business-meeting dinner, which is where the big tips come into play. My wife and I go out less frequently, as well, and during the occasional trip to an Applebee's or Outback Steakhouse, we generally find no wait for a table. There are plusses to getting seated immediately, but it is depressing to not hear the laughter and loud conversations we had become accustomed to. This is part of the psychological affect of the current economic times, and it just reinforces the fact that things do not feel normal. I find myself looking closer at my own expenditures and will sometimes defer to a tuna fish sandwich at home for a late dinner as opposed to a drive through at Chic-fil-a or Burger King. These late dinners are the norm because of my commute, and it would be foolish to ask my wife and kids to hold off for a 9 p.m. dinner at home. The savings from this thrifty eating habit are minimal, but it represents one of my sacrifices to feel I am doing my part to rein in our monthly expenses. The savings will not pay for our kid's high school and college tuitions, but it mentally shows a level of discipline I didn't know I had. I won't insult your intelligence by saying that I need to exercise this frugality to put bread on my family's table, but I do hope to impress upon you this stealth type of dollar savings that affects the health of the economy. I could point to major expenditures such as car purchases, which are well off their historical norm; as a matter of fact, September was the first sub-million new car sales month since 1993. These items are quantifiable each month; however, the less obvious smaller expenditures are equally important in gauging the health of the economy.

Some of my coworkers feel uneasy about the status of their jobs. They look around and see what is happening to other New York Financial Service companies, and have that look of "not if, but when" we may experience the infamous RIF (reduction in force). I have tried to be upbeat and extremely positive to them about our contribution to the organization, and that we have to maintain our level of focus and keep our "A" game with us at all times. I feel a personal responsibility for their wellbeing, and I do understand their consternation. I think they know this, but at times like this, it is important for them to feel that someone is looking out for them. I keep my emotions in check, but deep down, I have the same fear they do.

The market closed down one hundred, fifty points today, which was a reversal from the positive territory it was in for the first half of the day. What makes this unusual is that the downward momentum kicked in "after" the rescue bill was passed by a 263-171 margin in the house, which was a fifty-eight-vote turnaround from Monday. Maybe it was the added sweeteners that swayed the previous "No's," or maybe it was a constituent reality check that Main Street will in fact be affected and that action was needed. The best quote I read on why some congressmen changed their minds came from Zach Wamp (R., Tenn.) who said, "Monday I cast a blue-collar vote. Today, I am going to cast a red, white, and blue vote for my country." Interestingly enough, although not surprising, the bill was loaded with the usual pork that seems to be a prerequisite for getting controversial legislation passed. The market slide serves as a reminder that economic fundamentals are weak, with each day's release of economic data pointing toward a seemingly inevitable recession. The rescue bill was touted as a needed injection into the patient, yet the market shrugged it off and continued the slide. It should take a while before its benefits will be felt, which is unfortunate in that McCain needs some positive economic developments in the near term.

When I get home from work, I usually check the mail to see what needs my attention. Today's mail had a couple of items that warrant further discussion. First was the weekly issue of *Time Magazine*, which had a picture of a soup kitchen line from the Great Depression era on the cover. During the 1929-1932 period, the stock market dropped a staggering 89 percent, reaching its nadir in July 1932. The index did not regain its 1929 peak until 1954. In fairness to the editors, the actual article goes on to say that a depression and/or a severe recession are avoidable, and that lessons learned from that era are being used by the Federal Reserve Bank today. This is comforting to know; however, the 1930s did not have the globalization, interconnectivity among economies, nor "derivatives" like we have today. The latter has become increasingly sophisticated, and I hope that the credit default swap market doesn't prove to be another negative surprise. Most people on Main Street never heard of this type of product, and don't realize that these types of financial instruments even exist. I am not an expert in them, but suffice it to say that they can compound a bad situation. In the never-ending search for earnings, I hope that greed did not usher in a set of products that will have colossal effects to our financial system. I sincerely hope the law of unintended consequences doesn't emanate from these sophisticated products. AIG's exposure to credit default swaps has been a major contributor in helping to bring the company to its current state.

I also received in the mail a few credit card solicitations, which continue to swarm my mailbox. The offers have diminished sweeteners, but they do indicate that money and credit are still available. My oldest children also continue to receive these credit card offers, which further validates that some financial institutions are willing to lend. I used to work for a credit card company, and I know what types of enticements were offered to reel in customers. I like to open these offers, curious to see the trend of where the particular offers are going. It does not seem that long ago that balance transfer offers of 0 percent for twelve months with either a zero or $25 maximum fee were prevalent. These offers have been replaced with shorter balance transfer periods, higher fees, and higher rates. The credit card trend mirrors other lending trends, but offers are still coming. Another trend is credit card rates going up on existing customers, even if you have been pristine in adhering to the issuer's terms and conditions. This is the infamous "universal default" gotcha, and helps lenders offset increasing delinquencies and charge offs. Most people do not read the literature they receive from their credit card companies, but amendment changes referred to as a "change in terms" are usually buried in these communications. These stealth change in terms were popular with one of my prior employers, and they were usually followed by a lift in earnings since they would result in higher rates, increased fees, or maybe even shortening the grace period. I would expect these to intensify as the economy weakens, and companies are challenged to grow their bottom line. When I ask friends of mine what their current rate is, most shrug their shoulders, while others will immediately go into a defense mode and say that they always pay in full each month, therefore it doesn't matter what their rate is. Point well taken, but these same individuals don't realize that if they're just a day late one time they will trigger two months worth of interest charges due to the two cycle billing trap. This flip to a revolver status could be expensive, especially if you're like my wife and I who pay just about everything with credit cards. We started this years ago to maximize the rewards offered, and also because we like the idea of using someone else's money for free for thirty days or so. The down side to this is that it becomes addictive and causes us to spend more than we should. This economic environment is making me rethink this strategy, and forcing me to weigh the benefits of those extra candy bars at the checkout counter. Check your interest rate the next time your statement comes in the mail. You might be surprised.

Seventy million viewers watched the Biden-Palin debate last night, surpassing the number who watched last week's first presidential debate (which was on a Friday). This easily exceeded the viewing audience that watched the 1984 Bush-Ferraro debate, setting a new VP debate record. Was it the mystique surrounding Palin, or was it an increased sense of urgency that drove the high viewing audience? Probably a combination of both, and I hope this interest continues into Tuesday's presidential debate.

I have continued to watch and read the commentators and pundits' reviews on the VP debate. Most of these experts judge the debate on what the candidates say, not how they say it. I think this is an Ivy League view, and dismisses the power of the how in the equation. Biden won the "what," while Palin won the "how." Do not underestimate the power of the latter. Joe Six-pack relates to this.

October 4th-5th, 2008

The weekend arrives, but somehow it is hard to escape the realities of what is going on around me. My retreat to watching sports and spending more time with my family is always welcome, but the Monday to Friday news and headlines spill into the weekend, effectively extending the sour mood into my retreat time. This is a shame, since Saturday should be an avid sports fan's dream, with Penn State on TV at noon and the Phillies attempt to sweep their playoff series against the Brewers coming on at 6:30 p.m.

I arise at about eight on Saturday morning, which gives me an extra three hours of sleep versus my Monday to Friday routine. I read the paper as I am having breakfast, and plastered onto the *Wall Street Journal* weekend edition is the lead story of the "Bailout Bill" (still cannot shake that name). I scan through the paper and notice that California is having problems securing funding, and that they may have to seek $7 billion in emergency federal loans until liquidity is restored in credit markets. Does this sound a little like the AIG story, or should we differentiate the two because one is a request from a public entity versus a private entity? I start wondering if California is the tip of the iceberg, here, in that other state and local municipalities may begin to severely feel the pinch of the downward pressures on our economy. Most middle-class Americans believe that state and local governments opt for tax increases as their first line of defense against deficits, avoiding the more logical step of cutting spending. We all know they have bloated expense budgets, yet they always look to dip into our pockets to ask for more. Are they afraid of cutting necessary services because Joe Six-pack will notice? Should infrastructure and improvement projects be put on hold, maybe even permanently delayed? What of the contractors who were hoping to get the work, to keep their employees in jobs, so they could feed their families? What about the recipients of the sprinkle-down effect, such as the local delicatessen or the hair salon? Will people delay getting their hair done or buying an extra pound of their favorite meat? If these habits were to shift noticeably, we could see a dramatic mood change, one which could have severe consequences. We are all concerned about what happens at the federal level, but what happens closer to home lends a greater sense of urgency to it. I mentioned previously about the severe housing slump we're in and the fact that many homeowners owe more on their homes than the property is worth. Natural outgrowths of this will be increasing numbers of foreclosures, which will continue to put downward pressure on home values. Local municipalities rely on real estate taxes as their primary revenue source. I would expect this income source to take a hit, forcing local governments to make tough decisions. Even though home values will continue to drop, I doubt we'll see many downward property reassessments, which will anger homeowners. If taxes are increased to cover the shortfall, people will be extremely unhappy. The problem is that there are various pieces of infrastructure in local townships, such as school systems, that need to be funded. This infrastructure isn't going away, and children still need to be educated. The next straw may be an attack on government employee and teacher contracts, with the latter being the single largest expense in school budgets. There have been rumblings for quite some time that teachers and government workers have the richest benefit packages, and I would expect voter wrath to be directed at these entitlements to help cure the gap. I believe those who educate our children have one of the most important roles in our society. I have no problem compensating them accordingly, but why do teachers always get their back up when we ask them to consider a performance based compensation system. They almost always recite their textbook responses why it's unfair to put them on a merit system that parallels the private sector. This is not a difficult concept to grasp, yet they assume their occupation is immune from any ranking system that weeds out the deadwood from their profession. If all they do is find fault with any recommendation of moving to a merit based system because of our lack of understanding about the nuances of their job, I have a simple answer – Agree with us it makes sense, and we'll allow you to figure out the particulars as to how to administer it. Don't bury your head in the sand and think you're exempt from this. As private sector employees feel the pain of the weakening economy why should public sector employees be immune from feeling the repercussions of this downturn? I would expect this topic to heat up in the near future. Another area to think about is association fees for those who live in a co-op or some other housing development that requires a sharing of costs. As some of your neighbors lose their jobs, and pressure to make up the shortfall leads to increasing fees to existing homeowners, I would expect some to start talking about cutting back on expenses, as opposed to increasing their costs. This seems prudent, but what about the electricians and plumbers who rely on these jobs to make a living? Without this work, they will be hard pressed to maintain their own work forces or provide some items for their own families. There is a waterfall effect, but I don't have enough ink in my pen to adequately discuss the numerous levels down it actually goes.

I went to the dermatologist the other day, and usually when I go, the waiting area is filled with patients. That day, I was the only one in the office and was able to get in and out in about twenty minutes, as opposed to the usual hour or so. I asked the receptionist if it has been like this recently, and she replied that it has slowed down considerably since my last visit two months ago. I wonder how many assistants in this office have been laid off or had their hours cut. I wonder how many patients are having second thoughts about coming in for a visit and paying their deductible (in my case it is $30).

At noon on Saturday, my son and I settle in to watch the Penn State football game. I have made the decision to escape for a few hours, and this R&R is most welcome. It turns out I cannot even escape the campaign here, since some of the commercials are election advertisements, or worse, a movie trailer with a political message. A commercial came on for the movie, *W*, and the background commentary spoke of our $1 trillion mistake. How is that for impartiality, or trying to influence people's opinion on the upcoming election? I still cannot believe that a filmmaker would put out a movie on a sitting president, at a point so close to November 4th, unless they had a serious political motive. Is this Hollywood's full-court press to influence voters? I can bet you the movie will be unflattering toward our current president, with the implicit message being that we cannot have four more years of this. Movies like this usually distort the facts, yet there are some voters who will be gullible enough to treat it as gospel truth. I have no intention of ever seeing this movie. Penn State won the game, and continues on their way to a potentially magical season. Next up is a Saturday mass at 5 p.m., followed by my second escape of the day, to watch the Phillies in game three of their divisional playoff series, versus the Milwaukee Brewers. The priest's homily today was on the abortion issue, and although the word "politics" or "election" was not mentioned, one would have to be foolhardy to not understand the intended message. As the offering basket was passed around, I started thinking back to the state of the economy and whether members of the congregation would be altering their charitable donations. Most people use envelopes, thus you cannot tell when the basket comes to you if contribution habits have changed. I have to believe that contributions are down, not only at churches, but across the whole charitable universe spectrum. There are many worthy charitable organizations that deserve our support, but they won't escape the outreach of this deteriorating economy. It's ironic that some of these noble organizations will have an increase in the number of people needing their assistance during this downturn, yet there will probably be a noticeable drop in contributions. It's not that people don't want to give; rather, it's a decision to feed their families first. I would think this drop-off won't only relate to individuals, but businesses as well. Companies may decide to reel in these expenses, given their variable nature. While at church most of us say a prayer for someone or something special; I cannot help but think that some of my fellow parishioners are now praying to keep their jobs and to be able to support their families in a way they are accustomed to. Some people go to church infrequently, but I wonder how many in attendance are making more frequent visits to seek divine intervention to watch over them and their families in these troubling times. This isn't meant to be disrespectful, but as the dollar is a safe haven in troubling economic times, religion is a haven in unsettling times, as well.

After church, my son and I settled in to watch the Phillies game. My wife and my youngest daughter joined us, which shouldn't have been a surprise, since Phillies fever is catching on. Baseball is a much slower game than football, and thank God for the remote control. This lifesaver enables us to change channels during commercial breaks so that we are viewing constant action. Those that have picture in picture are further blessed, although I find this annoying and stick to the reliable routine of one channel at a time.. My son is rather superstitious, and for some reason, he thinks it is good luck for our team when he controls the remote. I obviously do not believe in this, but nonetheless leave nothing to chance and defer to him and give him the remote.

We scream a little during the game, which the Phillies lose. My son immediately blames his mother and sister as being bad luck, completely ignoring the fact that the Phillies were outplayed. I immediately start worrying about the prospects of a possible choke, and thoughts of the Phillies being the first National League team to blow a 2-0 series lead start dancing in my mind. In Philadelphia, we have not experienced a major professional sports championship since the 76ers in 1983, and I believe this twenty-five year drought is the longest of any major city. I have five children, and none of them has experienced a title in Philly yet. Ronald Reagan was in his first term when we last tasted a championship, and the Phillies are our last chance to experience one during the Bush administration. We have come close, but no cigar. Sports are an outlet for most voters, and I do believe that a hometown win propels people into the work week with a positive attitude. It cannot offset the realities of daily life and the economic distress we feel, but for some people it comes awfully close.

Sunday is setting up as a Philly Sports paradise, with both the Eagles and Phillies on at 1 p.m. The remotes will be put to good use on Sunday, so I hope everyone's batteries will not let them down.

I wake up around 8 a.m. Sunday, and need to spend about four hours on my real job. It's hard to escape my AIG responsibilities, even when I prefer to. I have my standard issue blackberry, which keeps me on call 24/7. There's nothing worse than the dreaded ring alerting me of a message coming my way, although most times it's really another request that needs my attention. I often ask myself if I should ignore it and claim the battery was dead if pressed as to why I did not respond. Unfortunately, I have always had the work ethic and dedication to respond on a timely basis. I can accept the occasional request in the line of duty, but at AIG, weekends aren't really considered off days but just an extension of the workweek. I expect this intrusion to only intensify given our current state. I wonder again if my status as a quasi-government employee exempts me from having to work on the weekend, but realize I cannot succumb to the temptation of that work style. I have to admit, however, that it annoys me when I receive a request at 1 p.m. on a Saturday that requires a few hours of work to provide the sender the "most urgent" reply they've requested. It might just be me, but it seems as if every request is a life or death request from the sender, or from the senders' sender (I think you know what I mean). Most people love their blackberries, but I have learned to loathe it on the weekends. I'll bet most of our spouses loathe it just as much, especially when it infringes on our well planned weekend itinerary and throws these plans into a state of disarray. The obligatory thank you from the requestor usually comes when you've completed the assignment, but all this does is reinforce the hollow commitment that they respect our work/ life balance and want us to enjoy our family time. Innovation is great, but it has certainly contributed to a blurring of the work/ life boundaries. I must admit I have enjoyed indulging myself in writing this book, but with the responsibilities of my full-time job, I have been keeping a rather hectic schedule. There are times I ask myself why I maintain this frenetic pace, and not throwing in the towel on writing this book. The answer is that I think it needs to be written, that too often we rely on the professionals in the media to gain an understanding of how particular issues should be viewed. We allow these individuals to feed our minds and too often influence our perception of reality. These professionals like to call themselves independent or non-biased, yet most allow their jaundiced personal opinions to infiltrate their words and themes. My goal is to present an everyday person's view of this election, to comment on what I see and how I see things, and by going deeper than I ever have, to lead me to a conclusion as to how I should vote in this very important presidential election. I am no longer a *gimme* for the Republican ticket. They need to earn my vote this time.

The Phillies won today while the Eagles lost. My remote got a heck of a workout. If both teams had lost today, I fear there would have been a long line of jumpers on the Ben Franklin Bridge. Philly fans will understand this analogy.

As I watched the post-game shows on both, which were live from the same Comcast studio, the moods of each mirrored the result of the respective team. The Eagles' mood was summed up brilliantly by governor Rendell, who said they sucked. I am not criticizing the governor for his choice of words; rather, I think he connected to the Eagles' faithful by using his own Joe Six-pack description of how the team played. I like the "Gov," which is how he is referred to on the program. He is a regular on the post-game show and makes me feel that he is one of us, who shares in the highs and lows of the home team's performance. I think he connects with the voters, and this style plays extremely well on Main Street. He is a two-term governor, reelected overwhelmingly by state voters, and his style and substance make him very appealing to Pennsylvania voters. I have to add that I voted for him both times, thereby ruining some of my friends' hypothesis that I never vote for a Democrat. I start wondering if his down-to-earth style is apparent in any of the presidential and vice presidential candidates, and I think the closest to the Gov is Sarah Palin. I think she connected to the populace in both her convention speech and her VP debate, and I am wondering if she can translate this into votes for the Republican ticket in November. She has held up her end of the bargain with helping McCain, but I feel he has been the drag on the ticket over the last couple of weeks. She gave the campaign the adrenaline shot it sorely needed in her debate performance, now he needs to return the favor in his debate with Obama this coming Tuesday. Obama is still riding the momentum of a poor economy, and continues to hammer away at McCain being out of touch and in bed with Bush's policies. McCain cannot seem to escape this stickiness to Bush and seems to be on the defensive at all times. Obama is attacking and pressing forward, and the polls continue to shift in his favor by larger margins. I am still not convinced this election is over, although the Vegas odds would certainly indicate an impending Obama victory. Elections are very fickle and can change on a moment's notice. It has been eerily quiet on the terrorist front, the Ahmanajeh front, the North Korean front, and even the Chavez front. I sense that these flash points may be quiet for a reason, hoping that a softer and possibly new direction in American foreign policy is in the offing. Why should they stir the pot now, when in thirty days, American voters may help usher in a new foreign policy more to their liking? A sudden deranged terrorist attack or provocative comments from the axis of evil might move the U.S. economy to the back pages and return the issue of terrorism and safety to the forefront of the campaign. I give them credit for biting their tongues and showing a level of patience to allow the election to play out in the way they want. Isn't it ironic that our own democratic way of life is providing them the means to exit the Republican ideology out of power? Non-democratic countries have coups, assassinations, and other means of forcefully transitioning power. Ours is a peaceful process, one whereby we truly have the power within our grasp to alter history. We may disagree on which candidate is best for us, but we universally agree in the process. I sincerely hope that each of us votes this time, and that when it is over we will unite behind the victor.

It is Sunday night, and, as I sit on my back porch and put my final words on paper for the weekend, I realize that tomorrow is October sixth, which will leave just twenty-nine days until the most important vote in our lives. I am sure this is a refrain we hear during most election seasons; although I do believe for this election the hyperbole is warranted. Both candidates have their pros and cons, and, according to the pollsters, approximately eighty to 85 percent of the electorate has made up their minds. The remaining undecideds have a great responsibility, and the candidates themselves have a duty and responsibility to discuss issues over these remaining days. This is an interesting campaign, and it will almost end when the World Series ends. My Phillies are still alive, and so is each of the candidates. Most importantly, my vote is still alive and in play.

October 6, 2008

As I drove to the train station this morning, I noticed that gas was down to $3.29/gallon for regular unleaded. I was happy to see it at this level, but I am not happy that it is still this high. This drop from the $4/gallon level is certainly a relief, but I remember not too long ago when it was under $2/gallon. We have become so reliant on gasoline as a part of our lives that we now feel relieved when the price comes down to (still) astronomical levels. Have we now been conditioned to accept this $3-$4 range as the new norm, and should we be grateful for this easing? This is part of the psychological game that is played out every day. Where is our pressure point, and at what level do we cry uncle? I do not like being reliant on foreign oil, and I hope this temporary easing in price does not divert our attention away from domestic oil exploration and alternative energy sources as pressing issues to be discussed in this campaign. The dark side of me is suspicious of the drop in price, although common sense would equate an economic recession with lower prices. Why do I feel used then, that the price might be employed as a weapon to influence our opinions, and to distract our attention from getting the candidates to talk about it more. By easing back on the throttle, energy producing countries can play games with us, making us feel indebted that we now have more to spend on non-energy items. Are we being manipulated or gamed right now? It seems like energy is being

silenced as a campaign issue, which is benefitting the Obama/
Biden ticket. I worry that some of this is deliberate, and that,
combined with the recent lack of foreign policy incidents,
represents a type of conspiracy to influence our election.

Penn Station seemed overly busy today. Maybe it is because
of Monday and the influx of transients who make NYC their
home for the workweek, but whatever the reason, I am glad to
see increased activity. More companies are announcing layoffs,
and coupled with a continuing credit market displacement, it
seemed we were in a downward spiral. The crowds sometimes
slow the rest of my commute into the office, but I am comforted
that it appears busier than it has in the last few weeks. I just
wish people would exercise more courtesy when wheeling their
luggage through Penn Station.

The stock market was plunging right from the opening
bell, and I got the feeling it would continue all day. Not only is
Monday generally most people's least favorite day, but now the
market was going to pile on to this down feeling. I also have
read somewhere that Mondays are becoming the unpopular RIF
day at more companies. How many unlucky people will be the
recipient of this news today? I'll bet for most people on the
receiving end of this that the hardest part is calling their spouse
to give them the unwelcome news.

It seemed that I heard a lot more sirens from my office
today, leading me to sarcastically think that people were
jumping out of their office windows. I don't know why, but I
have this indelible impression of some frustrated people taking
this suicidal leap during the Great Depression. I am on the
fifteenth floor, so if I wanted to jump there would be only one
result. Why am I so fixated on the market? Is it because my

investment portfolio is plummeting and my carefully-laid early-retirement plan is becoming a distant memory? Most of my friends and coworkers do not even look at their 401K or IRA these days, hoping that they will wake up and find it was all a dream, just like when Bobby Ewing woke up in a season opening *Dallas* episode, effectively voiding the prior season. I am a realist, and I understand that markets go up and down, although the long-term trajectory has been up. I am fortunate in that I have experienced some above-average years, but new entrants to the work force are probably second guessing their decisions to set up retirement accounts. In the same vein, I would not be the least bit surprised if a lot of workers are now considering to either reduce or eliminate their contributions altogether. Being older (I have to start using the word "seasoned") I know this is the exact wrong thing to do, especially now that you can buy in at a low price (or so I hope). I am also cognizant that they need to live in the present and that it is hard for a twenty-five-year-old to plan for when they are sixty-five.

I noticed on the CNBC ticker that AARP said one in five baby boomers had cut back on the amount they are putting into retirement savings. The need to live in the present is forging this change, and coupled with the market drop we've experienced, I would expect that quite a few boomers who rely on defined contribution plans will be adjusting the age at which they thought they'd be able to begin to enjoy their retirement. There may also be some longer-term employees at AIG who might now consider getting out of the rat race, with their defined benefits at a level at which they could survive, as opposed to laboring through the workout phase we are about to enter.

Our domestic problems have spilled over into foreign stock markets, with some of these markets experiencing much worse declines than the U.S. Some of these countries look at our capitalist way of life and figure that their move into this economic system will reap the rewards we have achieved. Individual investors had visions of grandeur, but now they are being exposed to the risk side of investing. I hope they can stomach the losses, especially if they intensify.

The market was down as much as eight hundred points today but finished "only" three hundred, seventy points on the downside. The Dow did finish under 10,000, which for some represented a psychological barrier they did not want to see fall. As I scanned the Internet for stories about the market's tough day, I found an article that said six in ten people think a depression is either somewhat or very likely. This result is not surprising to me, given the constant media fixation on the problems we are experiencing today. Is it any wonder that the economy is front and center the single-most important issue on voters' minds? We see it and live it every day, and everyone is concerned about what lies ahead.

I am still amazed at the lack of leadership shown by our elected officials and prominent businessmen. I want to hear some reassuring and comforting words, but instead, gloom and doom rules the day. I feel that our President has taken a leave of absence and is literally acting like his lame duck status implies. I feel once again that Obama and McCain have a golden opportunity to show true leadership here, but instead they continue on with their attack ads on each other. I would like to see one of them step above the fray and project some leadership qualities. Be bold; tell us why things will get better (even if your improvement horizon is two years), and how you intend to make them better for us. Do not be afraid to separate yourself from your opponent. The voters will respond positively to this; you will be rewarded.

As I waited in Penn Station for my train to start boarding, I heard a musician playing the Adam's Family theme song on his flute. My mind immediately raced to thinking of Gomez, Tish, Uncle Fester, and Lurch. I loved that show and still watch it occasionally in reruns, when I surf the cable channels at night. I remember scenes where Gomez would be reading the stock ticker tape, and he always seemed to be on the winning side of a trade. We could all use Gomez's luck now.

My train was called for boarding, and as is typical, a mass of humanity converged on the four-foot-wide entrance to descend to the platform below. This is truly an experience, and newcomers could easily be intimidated by the rush of commuters positioning themselves in what passes as a line. There are no rules here, just get in position and go with the crowd. "Women and children first" doesn't apply to this ritual. The train was crowded tonight, similar to this morning. It just dawned on me why it seems so crowded. New Jersey Transit has cut back on the number of cars, cramming us in so they can maximize usage per car. I am not an engineer, but I am sure a combination of fewer cars with more people per car means a better bottom line to NJT. Even NJT is cutting corners, at the expense of cramming us like sardines into the cars. At least I got a seat, which I guess is something positive from the trip. Since we were packed in tight, I could hear the music playing in the ear phones of the person next to me. The song was "Living on a Prayer," by Bon Jovi. How appropriate.

I got home around 9 p.m. and was undecided on whether to exercise. I decided to stick to my routine of running three miles every other day and retreated to the treadmill in my basement. This proved to be a welcome escape from the daily grind, made more so by the fact that both Monday Night football and game four of the Red Sox-Angels series was on. I flipped between the two games while running, and for about thirty minutes, I was able to lose myself in watching sports. My Phillies play game one of the national league championship series this Thursday, and I am hoping their success will continue and help carry me and other Phillies fans through the end of October.

October 7, 2008

Before leaving for work this morning, I glanced at yesterday's mail and three pieces grabbed my attention. The first was a bill from my daughter's high school for the winter term starting in mid January, which is still more than three full months away from today. This seems a little early to me for asking for a payment. I do not mind paying tuition, but during these difficult times, they should be more sensitive to current economic conditions. The second piece of mail I opened was from the Days Inn at Penn State (where I stay for football weekends) with a notice that I can now request room reservations for the spring Blue/White game. It is not unusual to receive this notice six months out, but what struck me was that they lifted the two-night minimum and advance payment requirement. This gesture was very much appreciated, and is in direct contrast to my daughter's school tuition billing request. I wonder if they will repeat this policy change when I receive my notice for reserving rooms to next fall's games. The last piece of mail was a bill from Comcast for my cable and Internet service. My bill was up over $50 from the prior month, and I decided that this would warrant a call during my lunch-hour today.

The weather was chilly this morning, dipping into the thirties for the first time this fall. I turned on the car heater for the first time since last spring. I decided to read the paper on the train today, and got up the courage to check mutual fund performances. The fifteen largest funds are listed in the *USA Today* money section, and each one was down over 20 percent in 2008, except for one bond fund that was up 1 percent. The more revealing statistic was the fund returns over the last four weeks, which accounted for over half of the dismal year-to-date performance. For example, the Vanguard 500 index was down 27 percent YTD, 17 percent or almost two-thirds of the deterioration coming in the last four weeks (about the time I started writing this book). This increasing pain is hard to swallow and serves as a stark reminder that the markets have a cruel side to them that can be unleashed, which reduce paper wealth in a short period of time. This acceleration of losses seems to be a parallel to Obama's acceleration in the polls. I glanced at foreign market performances YTD, and saw that all of the markets listed were down considerable amounts, as well. So much for diversifying into foreign markets to balance risk. Our three hundred, seventy point drop yesterday (3.6 percent) compared favorably to a 19 percent drop in Russia and 9 percent drop in France. It must be hard to stomach a one fifth drop in value in one day, as most Russian investors are finding out today. I hope you are enjoying a taste of capitalism, comrades.

I made my call during lunch to Comcast to inquire about my monthly bill and finally got a customer-service representative on the phone after waiting for close to ten minutes. Any taxpayer reading this needn't worry about my use of company phones, since I made the call on my personal cell phone. I can't help but wonder if the wait was due to heavy call volume or as part of a cost-cutting program by Comcast. The representative was very helpful and said that my prior six month promotion had ended, thus the return to the normal rate. I was not giving up that easily and politely threatened to switch to Verizon. The rep got a supervisor, who was more than obliging to extend the promotion another six months. I gladly accepted and felt that I had done a good job in saving $300 over the next six months. I'm not sure I would have taken this route if the economic climate had been better, but I am doing a better job uncovering these types of opportunities and saving dollars wherever I can. If you magnify this occurrence by thousands or millions of customers, the dollar effect could certainly be significant. Businesses like Comcast want to retain customers, yet they have shareholders to answer to. If you multiply my $50 monthly savings by just 100,000 customers, Comcast would have some five million dollars less in revenues each month, which will probably translate to some employees losing their jobs at this cable giant.

If I feel a strong desire to cut costs everywhere I can, I'm sure other voters are doing likewise. No one likes to curtail spending, but sometimes the situation dictates that you do just that. I used to read in various articles about how consumers could save a significant amount by closely watching their spending. I never thought I would put this to the test, but now I wonder why I did not start doing this sooner. Is it possible my spending habits are witnessing a permanent shift, or will this prove to be only a temporary hiatus until better economic times return? If I revert to prior habits, I will be following the path of what happens when energy prices drop, which is what I previously condemned. Are my habits therefore short-term in nature, devoid of any longer-term planning? Maybe I should reevaluate all of my spending habits and stay consistent in both good and bad times. The deeper this economic crisis gets, the more likely it will have lasting effects on spending behavior. Educated consumers will be born out of this economic malaise, and companies will have to adjust their strategies accordingly. This is not to imply that an overnight dramatic shift in habits will occur, but given the size of our economy, a small shift could have huge side effects. I expect we'll see some noticeable company shifts in marketing strategies and less obvious changes to counterbalance revenue shortfalls, such as longer customer service wait times or even smaller servings of food at some eating establishments.

Yesterday was the first Monday in October, which represents the start of the Supreme Court session. There has not been much discussion surrounding this by the campaigns recently, since the economy is dominating the news. The current president has appointed two justices during his terms, with one now serving as the current chief justice. The Court currently consists of four left-leaning justices and four right-leaning justices, with Kennedy balancing in the middle. The two justices considered the most liberal are Stevens and Ginsburg, who happen to be the two oldest at 88 and 75 years of age, respectively. It is probable that one or both of them may retire during the next president's term, so the stakes are extremely high as to who will get to fill the next vacancy. As a citizen, I would like to interject some personal opinions here and state that we should have a mandatory retirement age for Supreme Court justices. I do not buy into these lifetime appointments, especially for positions as important as these. The naysayers will disagree and say that lifetime appointments are necessary, but I believe this politicizes the process even more, since a justice can opt to stay on until a president is elected who will appoint someone with similar leanings to their judicial way of thinking. Some think this is actually the most powerful branch of government, since their rulings can be considered law. Roe v. Wade is always on people's minds, and the next president may be able to tip the court a certain way. This is an enormously important issue, and I would expect the campaigns to elevate this to the front page before November 4th to energize their base.

I cringe looking at my screen to see the expected drop in the market. Today was no different, with the Dow down over five hundred points or 5 percent. The Dow currently sits at 9,447, which is about fifteen points below where it was when Bush took office in 2000. How's that for a piece of the Bush legacy? During Clinton's eight years the Dow rose over seven thousand points. Is there any wonder why people perceive Democrats as being better for the economy than Republicans? This ignores the fact that the Republicans controlled both the senate and house starting in 1994, but as I've stated previously, the buck stops with the President.

The market drop and continued angst over the state of the economy are providing Obama with more ammunition for tonight's debate. A news item on the wire today said that retirement accounts have lost $2 trillion in the past fifteen months. This erosion of wealth has significant impacts on the economy. It reinforces the psychological strain consumers are feeling and naturally makes us rein in our spending plans. This mood was borne out by August consumer borrowing falling at an annual rate of 4.7 percent. This was the first time since January 1998 that this index experienced a drop. Even our Federal Reserve Chairman was stoking fear today by saying tough times should continue into the near future. I would like him to define near future, since I don't like these nebulous open-ended timeframes.

We are witnessing massive government intervention. We were led to believe that the $700 billion rescue plan would stop the hemorrhaging, but after its passage, it seems like we have kicked onto life support. The Fed continues to apply new doses of medicine, yet the patient shows no signs of improvement. I cannot help but wonder if this meltdown still has months or years to go. I certainly hope not; however, I am growing more pessimistic each passing day. October was a cruel month in 1929 and 1987, and 2008 is shaping up to make this a trio we would rather soon forget. Over the past seventy-five years, bear markets that lasted a year or more have seen broad indexes fall an average of 52 percent. We are now at a 35 percent decline, since the peak in October 2007. Think about that for a moment—more than one-third of paper wealth has evaporated in the space of one year. What started out as a subprime issue has spread to other parts of the economy and the world. Nobody is immune from this sickness, and people all over the world are feeling its effects.

I am sensitive that it started on our soil. If we think our relations with other countries were poor before, wait until these countries feel the full affects of this tidal wave. A lot of people, friends and family included, openly say in my presence that my company is responsible for a lot of the pain. How's that for being subtle? Better yet, how's that for making me feel better and showing sensitivity to my situation? I still haven't figured out my canned response to the antagonism. There's some naivety to these attacks, but if you turn on any news program, I'll bet AIG gets a few snide comments thrown its way. The media continue to reinforce people's perceptions that we are the major cause of the problem. This condemnation of AIG is a popular attack, but remember that the company employs over 100,000 people. Most of these are your neighbors. Their kids play soccer with your children and attend the same schools. Don't crucify the vast majority because of the business mistakes of a few.

If ever the cards were stacked against anyone, it would be John McCain and his campaign. The economy continues to dominate the news, and deservedly so. Obama is riding a wave of momentum, being driven by a surge of poor economic results. I doubt the economic story will brighten anytime soon, which means continued gloom for McCain. I cannot remember an election campaign where this level of economic distress was so painful this close to the day we go to the polls to vote. A part of me feels sorry for McCain to see him swimming upstream against this strong current. Given this situation, he has nothing to lose in tonight's debate. I would expect him to come out swinging from the opening bell and throw some haymakers when the opportunity presents itself. He might even consider something novel, like telling us exactly what he would do to remedy the current crisis. I have been saying for awhile now that neither candidate has projected leadership during the current turmoil, and that such an approach would be refreshing to me and the American people. Why are they afraid to grab this crisis by the throat and tell us how they would fix it? We want leaders who face challenges head on, and who can provide us a blueprint to return to prosperity. I do not want to see them get into a hissing contest tonight. We deserve better, and I hope they will deliver. There is no baseball playoff or football game tonight, so the stage is all theirs. I would hope that my fellow voters tune in to watch and carefully weigh the issues being discussed. I am excited to watch this debate, and it won't have competition from the Phillies, since they wrapped up their series in four games.

The two principals are scheduled to do battle, and we the people will decide who wins. Only listen to the commentators and pundits for the post-debate analysis if you have to, but please remember that most of the lines you hear are already rehearsed. Keep an open mind and form your own opinions. Please do not fall prey to the media biases, which will envelope the post-debate theatrics. We have serious problems, and we need someone to convince us they have the right plan and leadership qualities to change course and steady the ship. We all want someone to make us feel optimistic about the future, and get us through this crisis.

The debate proved to be non-eventful. McCain did not deliver the knockout performance he needed, and I thought Obama handled himself well. Obama continued his refrain of linking McCain to Bush and his "failed policies of the last eight years" that led us to where we are now, while McCain stressed his leadership credentials and his opponent's lack of such. Anyone could have predicted these scripts. The only item that seemed bold or new to me was McCain's proposal to spend $300 billion to purchase bad mortgages and negotiate new terms based on a home's current value. We will see over the next few days if this gains any traction. There were some negative attacks, but in the end I scored it a draw. Companies usually have to pay for TV advertisement time, but tonight, AIG received free press as both candidates mentioned us in an unflattering way during the debate. I cringed when I heard it, but I understand it plays well to the masses. I went right to bed afterwards, refusing to watch the post-debate commentator theatrics.

October 8, 2008

Less than four weeks to go until Election Day, and the economy remains the number one issue. As a matter of fact, it seems to be the only issue. World stock markets are down this morning, and U.S. futures are pointing toward a much lower open as well. The $700 billion rescue plan seems like a distant memory, now, with the euphoria around its medicinal value swamped by the realization that there are other fundamental issues that need to be addressed. Additional remedies are being applied at a fast and furious pace, both in the U.S. and overseas. When decisions are made this quickly, it either implies that well-thought-out solutions are being brought off-the-shelf or that a patchwork band aid approach is being applied. I assume that a combination of both is at play, with the one consistency being that a quick response is needed to try to stem the tide of this financial crisis. I am hopeful that policy makers will find a cure, but I'm pessimistic that quite a bit more damage will be left in its wake.

On the metro into work today, I noticed a young woman reading *The Audacity of Hope* by Barack Obama. She seemed to be very engaged in the book, almost as if in a trance. I must confess that I have not read the book, but at some point I probably will. This young woman stayed fixated on the book until we had to exit the train at South Ferry. Commuters generally rush to the doors to exit so they can beat the rush to the stairway that takes us up to ground level. The woman reading the book did not rush to get up; rather, she continued reading as if oblivious to the fact that she might miss her stop. As I glanced back, she eventually did get off, although she continued reading as she made her way up the steps. Something in this book seemed to have her under a spell. Have the economic events that have unfolded left her frustrated with her own situation and grasping for some level of hope? More importantly, has she found it in Obama's words? She seemed to be passionate in her reading, and if passion were a barometer of a wave of emotion, this would bode well for Obama. Should I dismiss this apparent interest as nothing more than curiosity, or should I view this as one of those stealthy leading indicators that foreshadows a wave of Obama enthusiasm that will overwhelm McCain? How many other people are feeling like she is and are willing to give this new entrant on the stage a chance? Not that it should matter, but this woman was white.

During my two hour commute to work, some significant financial activity happened. The Fed cut interest rates a half point, lowering the federal funds rate to 1.5 percent. This move was coordinated with other central banks, with the European Central Bank, the Bank of England, Swiss, Canadian, and Swedish Central banks announcing rate reductions. This sparked a reversal in the U.S. future's markets, with investors enthusiastically welcoming the moves.

Sometime during mid-morning, I noticed a cruise ship making its way down the river on its way to the Atlantic. It looked like a Celebrity ship, with the insignia familiar to me, since I have cruised this line before. As it passed between my office and Ellis Island, I got a good look at it, almost like a postcard setting. It was a clear day; I could see the ship as if it was right next to my office. Most passengers would be out on the deck during the bon voyage part of the cruise; however, that didn't seem to be the case today. Maybe they were all gathered on the starboard side facing Ellis Island, or maybe the tourist industry is experiencing a slowdown. I know this is offseason, but I was still surprised at the ghost-town-like appearance on the decks facing me. Tourism is a huge industry, with most people travelling and vacationing at some point throughout the year. Everyone needs to recharge their batteries and get some much-needed R&R. I am not currently thinking of any extravagant trips, and I doubt if many others are entertaining such thoughts now as well. My daughter at Boston University is a Hospitality major, and thank goodness, she is only a sophomore. Something tells me that employment prospects for the class of 2009 will be several notches below recent years. Jobs will be available, but the number of openings will be cut back significantly. I take solace in the fact that when she enters her senior year, the economy has to be in better shape than it is today (doesn't it?). She in essence will be able to ride out the downturn, and I hope benefit from the recovery. In the meantime her winter term tuition bill will be due sometime in December or early January, with the later the due date the better. I deliberately put some of my portfolio in cash about a year ago, although, in retrospect, I should have done more. I can cover her tuition with cash, but I think of others who might have to sell some assets into a distressed market to fund the winter term for their children. This scenario will play out all across America, and with student loans becoming more difficult or expensive to get, universities might see a drop in enrollment for next semester. Community colleges should be the beneficiaries of this trend. I would like to see Universities put some of their endowment funds to use helping students and parents meet their tuitions and fees in these difficult times. Is it too cynical to think that this should be a good reason for them to draw down on the tax-free endowment earnings they've accumulated over a number of years? Boston University is a great school, and my daughter loves being there. The tuition is steep using any barometer, and if she was graduating high school this year, I might have strongly recommended she consider another great school such as Penn State, which is half the cost and has a top-notch hospitality program like Boston U. I guess those PSU football weekends didn't achieve the advertising success I had hoped for a few years back when she decided on Boston U. I've been shut out so far in that my first three have chosen to attend schools other than PSU, although my oldest did get to attend for one semester when he was displaced from Tulane University because of hurricane Katrina. I was able to get to more games that year under the pretense of visiting him, and if I can successfully persuade one of my remaining two on the merits of being a Nittany lion the number of games I'll have the pleasure of being able to attend will go up significantly. If their reading this I don't want them to feel pressured, but I would want them to be cognizant that the tuition burden is more manageable at PSU than many other institutions of higher learning.

At noon today, the Dow is down about two hundred points and, at this pace will drop below 9,000 by Friday. This reversal from the early morning uptick of approximately two hundred points is alarming. I made a previous decision not to sell into a rout, which certainly seems to be at play, given the negative volatility we are experiencing.

It has been a painful twelve months, and an even more painful last month. The last week has been brutal. The Fed has been getting a lot more active, with the latest half point cut in the Fed Funds and discount rate, adding to yesterday's Fed promise to buy commercial paper. Each of the Fed steps has had less and less of an impact on the markets. This aggressive government intervention has had no effect, except to heighten concern and push the market lower. Are we nearing a bottom, which stock experts like to say happens when we have total capitulation? I would like to think so, although it is hard to sound the all clear when so much negative sentiment exists. This is deflating to a lot of people, and it will continue to force us into a more cost-conscious mindset.

Time for lunch. I went to get an anniversary card for my wife and found that the Hallmark store has already set up their Christmas card display section. The holidays are over two months away, yet the early blitz has started. I guess this is an attempt to get us thinking of better times ahead and to improve our morale. Sorry, I cannot quite get in the holiday spirit, yet. It may actually have the opposite effect, since people may realize that their holiday shopping will be severely limited due to the more pressing needs of providing the necessities to their families today. We all try to squeeze out extra-special gifts for our family during Christmas, but I fear this year's giving will be the lowest in quite some time. On my way back from Hallmark, I passed a Starbucks. This would usually be a busy time, but the wait in line appeared to be non-existent. Upscale establishments, whether in the food and beverage industry like Starbucks, or in the clothing store business like Nordstrom, have to be experiencing a major drop-off. If this trend continues I'm sure some of these companies will be laying some employees off. The moderately priced stores such as McDonalds and Wal-Mart are benefiting from this shift in spending habits, and in some cases, these customers will be lost forever to the upscale businesses they used to frequent. I draw a correlation to AIG, here, since we have many customers across the globe, and I wonder how many will be deserting us as we work through our problems. The company has many good people working to address this, and I hope these efforts prove fruitful. Our competitors must be salivating, not only because they're hoping to be the recipients of some of our customer departures, but also because they may benefit from AIG employees leaving for greener pastures. We have many good people that I've come in contact with during my time at AIG, and they have nothing to do with the root cause of the problems at the company. They and their quality businesses are collateral damage, and I couldn't blame them if they look for new opportunities. I hope they don't leave, because we're going to need them to weather the storm, but I think we should prepare for above-average turnover, especially when the economy and job markets improve. I don't know if I'm being foolish or naive, but I actually feel more motivated than ever to help AIG overcome our current adversity. I can't promise this feeling will last indefinitely, but I can guarantee I will do my part to help us survive this crisis.

I got my Subway fix for lunch. I am perfectly content to spend $6 for a sandwich, cookies, and a soda. By the way, Subway was extremely crowded, with its affordable menu, popular in these trying times.

The market had a roller-coaster day, ending down almost two hundred points. Overseas markets were a bloodbath, with European indexes down 5 percent and the Nikkei down 9 percent. All markets and economies are caught in this downdraft. I have never seen volatility like this. We are swimming in unchartered territory. Paulson came out and said there is much pain ahead, and although I appreciate his candor, I want to hear some positive news. I read an article in the *Wall Street Journal* that said 16 percent of homeowners are under water, meaning their mortgage debt exceeds the current value of their homes. I wonder how many of my neighbors are in this unenviable position, especially those who moved in recently. I worry this problem will only make the current downturn that much more severe.

There was one piece of good news today; home sales were up 7.4 percent from July to August. This was unexpected, and hopefully will foreshadow that we are near the bottom. We have been teased about being close to a bottom before, and I remember some experts saying we were at a stock market bottom fifteen hundred points ago.

As I ride the train home tonight, I look around and wonder how many of my fellow commuters have similar feelings about the current economic crisis as I do. It is hard to not be down about it, unless you have had an extended stay on another planet. The pain I am experiencing in wealth deterioration hurts, although most of it is paper loss. At some point in this cycle, I might have to bite the bullet, but I am fighting and strategizing on how to prevent from selling low. I am very optimistic that, a few years from now, my investments will be worth more than they are today, so I want to be able to reap the rewards after living through this carnage. Various experts give different guidelines on how much to sock away to protect you and your family in the event of a job loss. I felt real positive about my safety net up until about a month ago. I am still okay, but I figure I have lost about three months' worth of cushion in my rainy day fund. Job losses are picking up, and I have heard economists speak of unemployment as a lagging indicator. Some prognosticators are saying the unemployment rate might hit 8 percent, which would be 25 percent higher than where we currently are. This is a depressing thought; however, it is nowhere near the peak of 12 percent reached in the 1987-1988 recession period. I hope for all of our sakes we do not challenge that level.

All of my commute time is now in the dark. It does not matter if I am leaving for work or on the way home—it's dark. It mirrors the current economic climate for sure. As the train heads south toward Trenton, I am thinking again of the people who live in the communities we pass on the train. We pass through dark areas, but along the way, I witness quite a few pockets of light where people are resting in their homes with their families. I wonder if they are discussing the travails of the stock market, or talking about what necessities they may need to cut back on during this crisis. Most of these people are feeling some hurt in their daily lives, and I feel guilty that I am thinking my paper losses qualify me for pity. These people are living the real pain, and stretching to make ends meet, and I can understand why they want change. They do not like what is going on now and how it is affecting them. I can look at my relatives and see how the current situation is hurting them, too. My parents are ninety-one and eighty-seven years of age, and to people like them on fixed incomes, these are trying times. Higher food prices mean the difference between meat and tuna fish. It is not right that people in this situation are suffering because of the greed of people they do not even know. My brother-in-law is on disability and sometimes stretches his check to squeeze out a night for dinner and a movie. These types of diversions are needed escapes, but the economy is infringing on his routine. My younger kids like to go out with friends on the weekend; however, I do not feel the need to be as generous throwing them a twenty-dollar bill as I did a few months ago. I think of my oldest son whose ship is currently out at sea somewhere in the Pacific. His job is more secure than most; however, his life is always on the line defending our country. Although he is thousands of miles from home, he is feeling the affects of our financial distress. I sometimes peek in his investment portfolio mail delivered to our house and I see him taking some hits on his savings. He is young and has a lot of time to recoup his losses. I tell him to increase his savings in the emails I send him, but how do you convince a twenty-four-year-old to save more, as opposed to possibly taking a well deserved shore leave at a fantasy location in Thailand? I hope he is enjoying one of those shore leaves now. Those in the military have an extra keen interest in this election. Democrats are traditionally more dovish, and stressed military personnel may actually welcome a change in policies. I do worry about North Korea, since my son's naval base is too close to this member of the Axis of Evil for comfort.

October 9, 2008

Futures are indicating a positive opening today, but this has almost become meaningless, since we have experienced false starts throughout this current crisis. Four Asian country central banks cut rates, following on the heels of yesterday's coordinated effort between the U.S. and European Banks. The statistics of damage that this current bear market has inflicted are impressive (in a negative context).

1. $7.4 trillion in stock market value has been wiped out.
2. The Dow is down 37 percent since October ninth, 2007, making it the third worst bear market since the mid 1940s.
3. The S&P 500 has given up 20 percent since September 1, 2008 (thirty eight days).
4. 160 stocks of the S&P 500 have lost more than 25 percent in the first eight days of October.
5. 325 of the S&P 500 stocks are at fifty-two week lows.
6. 2,232 of 3,203 issues traded on the NYSE made new fifty-two week lows. That represents 67 percent of all the issues traded.

Although this bear is about a year old, its ferocity has intensified over the last four to five weeks, with excruciating body blows delivered in the last ten days or so. As I ride the elevator to my fifteenth floor office today, the infomercial monitor in the upper right corner of the car said, "komodo dragons leave 10 percent of their prey uneaten while a lion leaves 30 percent." I wonder how much this current bear will leave.

Polls indicate that Obama continues to widen his lead, and that McCain is entering the danger zone. I would like to know the makeup of these surveys, because my own polling of the race indicates its closer than the ten-point edge the polls give to Obama. The economy has assuredly helped Obama, but has a knee-jerk reaction of anger spouted venom at the Republicans because of Bush? With four weeks to go, will people cool off and look more closely at McCain, and will some of them realize that he is not the problem? Will they start thinking about the wisdom of an Obama/Biden/Reid/Pelosi team leading America for the next four years, and maybe take a second look at McCain? Or has the current economic crisis permanently wounded McCain, with Obama benefitting from this pent-up anger? With twenty-six days to go, it certainly appears bleak for the McCain/Palin ticket, but I sense it is not completely out of reach yet.

All has been quiet on the international front, and if this continues, the threat of terrorism will be a non-issue in voters' minds. The price of oil and gasoline continues to drop, so another Republican advantage has been marginalized. This leaves questions of judgment and leadership as chips to be played, and I would expect the McCain campaign to go all in with this card.

The markets were down again at noon, off about one hundred points. Morgan Stanley is showing signs of being in trouble and some are starting to think it might follow the fate of Lehman or Bear Stearns. Using recent history as a guide, I wouldn't be surprised if by this time next week they file for bankruptcy, receive a government bailout, or see a shotgun marriage. We are a co-tenant in my office building with Morgan Stanley, and the question is whether they will follow our path and receive a government bailout.

As the crisis intensifies, I think of all the paper gains that have been destroyed, and draw an analogy to playing monopoly. Stocks like GE could have been Boardwalk, but now would be adjusted to Indiana Avenue. The pecking order is changing, and companies like Wal-Mart are positioned to perform extremely well in this tough environment. They announced today that they would not be undersold and announced that ten well known toys, including some Barbie dolls, will be priced at $10. The retail pricing wars for our holiday shopping dollars has officially begun.

By the closing bell, the Dow had plunged six hundred, eighty points to its lowest level in five years. The Dow has now lost 5,585 points, or 39 percent, since closing at 14,164 on October 9, 2007. This represents the worst run for the Dow since the two-year bear market that ended in December 1974 when the Dow lost 45 percent. The S&P 500, meanwhile, is off 655 points, or 41.9 percent, since recording its high of 1,565. Today's one-day stock market paper losses were estimated at over eight hundred billion dollars (ironic in that it's more than the total of the rescue plan passed last week).

This constant battering is the norm. I actually feel violated. There comes a point where you can't rationalize it anymore. The stock-loss drop in the last year has now eclipsed the value of the housing drop. Each day brings more pain, and it is being felt all over. It is hard to get into a buying mode when you feel this deterioration of your personal assets. I wonder how many people are now prioritizing what expenses to cut back on. We all have our lists, although there might be some disagreement over the prioritization. Some bills will be automatically dropping off, such as the lawn service when the cold weather hits. Of course, higher heating bills will offset this, unless of course you opt to tough it out with the thermostat at sixty degrees. Do I need to keep the exterminator service, or the extra cable channels? Maybe we'll cut back on trips to the movies by using pay-per-view. Should I re-evaluate my insurance coverage deductibles? These are but some of the items that might be considered, and although a decision to drop one of these services will save me money, there will be a drop-off in revenue to the business affected, which might force more hard working people into the unemployment line. It is amazing to what extremes we take things when we feel we are under duress. I saw an article that said OPEC was going to hold an emergency meeting on November 18th to discuss falling oil prices. They want to halt crude's steep losses (down 40 percent from a high of $147 per barrel). What about when the price was going up? I did not see a rush to increase production to lower the price. Notice the date of the meeting—after our election. Oil is a national security issue, and I hope the candidates give it serious discussion between now and Election Day. Pardon the pun, but I do not like our country being held over a barrel. One of my pet peeves is the movement of gasoline prices at the pump. Why is it when the price of oil goes up, gasoline seems to follow in tandem? When oil comes down there is always a protracted delay before we see the benefit at the pump. Now is as clear an example of this as ever. I was paying about $4 per gallon when oil was at its peak, now I am paying $3.25. The math doesn't compute, since a 40-percent drop in oil prices should equate to more than an 18-percent price drop at the pump. I'm sure the oil companies can find a way to justify this with some of their industry jargon, but to this middle class citizen, it defies logic and common sense. End of debate.

I did get a few pieces of good news today. My son will be taking some leave and coming home in December for two weeks. His round trip flights from Japan are costing him $1,800, and I sensed from his e-mail he was hoping we would pick up the cost as we did last year. Given the current state of the economy, I did not feel compelled to duplicate last year's offer. We still cover his cell phone bill, since it's part of our plan, and allow him an occasional use on the joint credit card. I would've closed this joint account sooner if not for the fact that both of our credit scores would be hurt by doing so. Speaking of credit card bills, I had to read the riot act to my two oldest daughters about their usage. I am the primary cardholder, but I expect them to feel my pain in this climate by cutting back sharply. One of the hidden costs we parents bear is the expenses our children incur on the credit card during their college days. All I have to do for my recent graduate is show her the rewards points earned to highlight the amount she spent during her college career. I haven't thought of this before, but maybe I should redeem these reward points for my wife and me. This might make sense if I want to maximize their value, because I would expect credit card companies, airlines, and hotels to consider increasing redemption levels to ease the burden on them of people wanting to cash in for free rewards. These companies know there will be an uptick in redemption requests, and this increased activity will necessitate an adjustment to their expense projections, which will strain their bottom line. We should start perusing our mail closely because these changes will be buried in terms and conditions, and we might be shocked when we attempt to redeem and find out we are woefully short of the needed points to secure a reward.

I received a call from my dermatologist today, telling me that the biopsy results came back negative. With everything going on at work and in the economy, I forgot about this test. The news did provide me a sense of relief, because there's always a worry when you might hear bad news on this front. It does help put things in perspective, though. This medical issue brings to mind the cost of medical care. Double-digit increases occur all too frequently, and most companies will be sending out information to their employees for benefit selections and costs for the coming year. Employers will be asking employees to bear more of the cost, either through a higher payroll deduction or higher deductibles. I would expect the majority of companies to want to save on their medical expense contributions for next year, and although our politicians always talk about the problems we are confronted with in health care, they never seem to act in a bipartisan manner to address it, and they never seem to change their own medical benefits package, which are provided for the rest of their lives even if they're a one term congressman. Maybe a significant increase in each employee's share of their medical premiums and the accompanying cry for help from distressed workers will bring this issue into the forefront in the next president's first hundred days in office. I feel for the unemployed on many issues, with medical coverage during their unfortunate circumstances being maybe the most important. I understand that Cobra is available; however, the cost of this extended coverage can be prohibitive to an individual and his or her family when their earnings stream is at its lowest point. A country like ours should provide coverage during this transition period. The rolls of the unemployed are increasing, so this issue needs to be elevated in the campaign as well.

My Phillies will begin their series against the LA Dodgers tonight. We are starved for a title in Philly, and I hope the magical ride continues for another few weeks. Sports are a great diversion from our daily lives, and it can provide a tremendous psychological lift to people when their team accomplishes something special. It is unfortunate that the price of going to a sporting event has skyrocketed. I doubt if we will see prices come down to help the fans during this economic downturn, although I was encouraged to see the New Jersey Nets offer a season-ticket program with delayed billing. This pioneer idea may not catch on with other teams, since their guaranteed players' salaries and costs of building new stadiums continually put pressure on their bottom line. Taxpayers balked at the $700 billion rescue program, yet they gladly agree to support taxpayer funding for new stadiums. I read where certain seats in the new Giants stadium will require a $25,000 seat license. Given the population base, I would expect they would sell out, however I wonder how deep they will be dipping into their waiting list to find the necessary buyers. Obama seems to be a sport's fan, but his two Chicago baseball teams got eliminated last week. I am not sure who McCain supports, but I do know his vice presidential candidate will be dropping the ceremonial opening puck at the Philadelphia Flyers home opener this Saturday. I wonder how many swing votes this will be worth in this battleground state.

I caught the last three innings of the Phillies win over the Dodgers. The markets may certainly put us in a down mood, but I felt rejuvenated with the victory. We Philly fans have been disappointed many times before, so I am going to temper my enthusiasm for the moment. It does feel good though.

October 10, 2008

Today is my twenty-seventh wedding anniversary. I have been lucky to have a fantastic wife and partner all these years. She generally lets me handle the finances of the household, and I think she would admit I have done a pretty good job most of the time. When she calls me and asks if we are okay financially, I take notice. I received such a call at work today and tried to reassure her everything will be okay. I feel like Bill Murray in Groundhog Day, with each day seeming like the one before. The futures were way off early this morning, and foreign markets were taking another pounding. I do not know how anyone could be oblivious to the financial meltdown we are experiencing. My wife is certainly in tune with what is happening, and her concern and anxiety is probably being replicated in households across this country and across the globe as well. Consumers are the engine that drives our economy, and a hesitation to spend or a shift in their sentiment will dictate the future economic picture. It certainly is pointing negative, and there does not seem to be any relief in sight.

I dropped off a shirt at the cleaners this morning and asked the attendant owner if business had slowed recently. She smiled and said "absolutely." This business is located on the bottom floor of the building where I work, and there are other small business owners on this floor as well. I will occasionally grab a donut at the Dunkin Donuts across from the cleaners. It costs a dollar for a donut, which probably contains a nice profit margin. I do not ever remember the line being less than eight or ten deep at around 8 a.m., but today there was only one person in line. In prior times, I would have viewed this as an opportunity to get in and out quickly, but today I opted to forego a morning delight and headed back to my office.

Futures are still way down, and the opening bell in about an hour appears to be headed for a repeat of the last couple of weeks. Noted investor Wilbur Ross was quoted this morning as saying the equity markets will not improve until the credit markets do. Wasn't that the intended purpose of the rescue bill, the coordinated drop in rates, and all of the other actions taken over the last few weeks? It is almost like the markets are a disease that is immune to everything thrown its way. Rather than the pandemic flu, which took many lives, this disease is destroying wealth in its wake. At the current rate, we could see another 20 percent market drop in a week.

I have been negative about the leadership I have seen from President Bush and the two candidates throughout this crisis, and I am starting to believe that the private sector will have to take charge and lead us out of this crisis. Jamie Dimon, Warren Buffet, and Donald Trump—please step up and provide a guiding hand and instill some confidence in this market. Sometimes words can be a powerful tool, and when fortified with actions, can ignite people's optimism and start changing the mood of the situation.

The president is scheduled to speak to the nation at ten this morning. I think I will walk over to the sitting area to watch.

I watched Bush speak, and his words did not soothe me or my investment portfolio. The channel his speech was on had a split screen, with Bush on the left and the Dow Jones average on the right. When he began, the Dow was off under one hundred points, and when he finished it was off almost two hundred points. He reiterated the actions taken thus far and attempted to project calm among the financial storm swirling around us. I was hoping for some new initiative or action to give me a dose of hope, but none was forthcoming in his speech. I did not feel any better after his speech than I did before.

Polls continue to lean toward Obama. It's possible that over the last week or so as he has solidified his lead that a realization is setting into the market that Obama will win and, thus, we can expect an all-democratic branch of government to control the purse strings. Is Wall Street's verdict a resounding thumbs-down to the prospects of the next four years? There is excess being squeezed out of the system, but is an Obama victory on top of this too much to stomach? I must admit I am a little uneasy with this potential leadership in Washington, but can it get much worse than it is now?

I am still puzzled why neither candidate is taking the opportunity to project leadership in this crisis. Are they fearful that the economy will deteriorate further, and therefore do not want to step up until they and their teams feel a bottom has been reached? This borders on cowardice, yet they both are following the safe course. I get the feeling that Obama wants to nurse his lead, much like a football team running out the clock in the fourth quarter. This is not leadership; it is complacency. McCain is attempting to throw a few Hail Mary's, such as his proposal for the government to spend $300 billion on homes under water to get homeowners into a mortgage, based on today's market values. This does not seem to be gaining much traction, with Obama and his team trying to mercilessly pan it.

Obama's team must think this race is in the bag, because he is certainly not talking in specifics. He continues to speak about Mom and Apple Pie, a safe route until November 4th. McCain is playing from behind, but I do not sense urgency or a two-minute drill to cut into the lead. He has the perfect crisis at his disposal to show why he is best to get us through these trying times, but for whatever reason, he is afraid to seize this opportunity. Although there are twenty-five days remaining until the election, he needs to strike now and attack the perceived idea that Democrats are better stewards of the economy. Attack the senate and house leadership. They share in the blame, so why give them a free pass?

At the final bell, the Dow Jones Industrial Average was down one hundred, twenty points, making it the "best" day of the week. The net movement could lead you to believe that it was a calm day; however, a look inside the numbers reveals the exact opposite. The Dow actually traded in a range of 1,019 points. At one point, the Dow was down approximately seven hundred points, while at another point it was up approximately three hundred points. As was true of most days in this volatile week, the last hour of the trading day was a Jekyll and Hyde act. At 3 p.m., the index was at 8,200; at 3:30 p.m., it was around 8,900; at the close, it was 8,451. Fortunes were won and lost in this last hour. I do not know if anyone can state with certainty the prime reason for the last hour of volatility, and, in truth, there is probably a combination of various factors that contributed to the wild swings. Did individual investors finally cave in and surrender to the market? Did shrewd investment managers sense this panic and start putting money to work on blue chip stocks? Were investors opening or closing positions at the end of the day to position themselves for the G-7 meeting this weekend, betting on what the outcome and resultant effects to the market would be? Whatever their intent, I for one, am glad the weekend has finally arrived. Most markets around the globe had their worst week ever, and most people will be licking their wounds before the battle commences again on Monday. We survived, although thinner in the wallet, and can soothe our wounds with a cold one or a glass of wine. Today is my wedding anniversary, and my wife and I were planning to go out for dinner to celebrate. My daughter is working tonight at the Brick Hotel, so maybe we will have her as our waitress. I hope she is not expecting a big tip. Only kidding!

When I left work, the Phillies and Dodgers were tied at one in the second inning. The Phil's winning would be a nice anniversary gift. On the train home, I could not resist to get an update, so I called my son who told me they were winning 8-5, although he was quick to point out that their previous lead of 8-2 had shrunk. I could've checked the score on my blackberry, but for some reason, I wanted to hear from my son. We have had our hearts cut out by our sport's teams before, so I have learned to almost expect defeat being snatched from the jaws of victory. I should get home to catch the last couple of innings, and hopefully a win to go up 2-0 in the series. This would provide a much-needed jumpstart for the weekend.

October 11th-12th, 2008

October 11ᵗʰ-12ᵗʰ, 2008

The Phillies did manage to hold on and beat the Dodgers to go up 2-0 in the series. They are halfway to the World Series, but they have not closed the deal yet.

Obama spent time in Philadelphia Saturday, attending four events at different areas throughout the city. The news accounts said approximately 60,000 people attended these events. Philadelphia is the largest city in a remaining battleground state, thus its strategic importance. Pollsters say he needs to win Philadelphia big to offset the Republican strength in other parts of the state. Registered Democrats outnumber Republicans 4.4 million to 3.2 million in the state, which is a significant advantage. Since last November, Democrats have enrolled 500,000 new voters. The key is how many of these people will actually come out and vote on Election Day. It is an uphill battle for McCain in my home state, and if he loses Pennsylvania and its twenty-one electoral votes, his margin for error shrinks to a razor-thin margin.

There are meetings in Washington this weekend about the financial crisis. All major countries will be represented, and the good news is that everyone recognizes this is a global crisis and coordinated efforts are needed to stem the deteriorating conditions. The weekend offers a reprieve in that markets are closed.

As I think of the events of the past week, I realize that we witnessed a historic drop in the markets, one that will weigh heavily on people's minds as we ponder what the next week holds for us and what each of us should do. As it unfolded last week, we were all a bit stunned. We knew there were problems, but I do not think anyone envisioned the speed and severity of the meltdown. I felt completely helpless, and decided to stay the course with my investment mix. I was afraid to make rash decisions and did not want to rush into making changes that I would regret later. I have always believed in setting my investment mix based on a longer-term strategy, understanding that there would be ups and downs along the way. It is hard to time the markets, and my philosophy is to not deviate from this plan. I must admit however, that the prior week's events caused me to reconsider my strategy. If I believe that the current momentum will remain on the downside, should I pull the trigger and shift into cash, CD's, or other safe investments? Or should I hold tight, keeping to my long-term belief that, over time, markets will go up? On Saturday, I was not sure what route I would take, but on Sunday, I decided to stay the course. This was a tough decision, but I think my fear of missing an uptick won out over my fear of a continued decline. The market has dropped too much in too short a time, and I think a panic mentality ruled the day. I never want to ride with the herd, and I hope I do not regret this decision in the future. I am hopeful that saner minds will prevail and that markets will recoup some of the last week's lost ground. I came to the conclusion that the worst thing I could do is sell at this low level, and have some vulture investor benefit at my expense. My time horizon is not a day, week, or a month; it is much longer than that. I am holding my breath and closing my eyes to the market. I will not give in to this hysteria. As I draw comfort in my decision, I realize that others are going through the same analysis to determine what they should do. I am sure some will opt to get out and put everything into the safest investments available, while others will follow my thinking and still others may opt for a combination of both. This is a personal decision, and individual circumstances will weigh heavily in the process. Each of us does have a breakpoint, however, and a few more days of six-hundred-point drops may cause some to reconsider their stance.

Penn State won big at Wisconsin in their Saturday night prime-time battle, and the magical journey continues. They may move up into the top three, since some teams ranked ahead of them lost. I am enjoying their success immensely, and it is a soothing feeling that helps offset the sting of the economic climate. Their success does not influence my financial decisions directly, but it does provide a needed psychological lift at this time. Next up for the Nittany Lions is Michigan.

What makes my investment decisions difficult is that I need to consider my wife and children. They count on me to make the right decisions, and I do not want to let them down. I try not to show the anxiety I feel, and I think I am doing a good job of hiding any hint of unease. I shoulder this burden and do not want them to think about it. I want my high school and college children to focus on their task of doing well in school. I do not want them diverting their attention to the financial environment; I want them to maintain their grades, which are more important for them in the long term. They cannot help but see the market drops in the news, so it is not that they are oblivious to it. As a family, we are cutting back on some things, but I do not want them to get alarmed and have a drop off in studies. I cannot control what their friends and their families are doing and how this might influence their thinking. I can only control the Krouchick message, and I am trying to project an image of calm. My oldest daughter is aware of what is going on, and I cannot shield her from the real world. She is pretty perceptive, and since she has a business degree, she understands what is going on. She is even thinking of investing in the market now. Good for her. My oldest son is in the navy, and he continues to invest about a third of his income in the market. He has job security, which is important in this climate. I read an article that said military recruitment is up. I guess the current economy and accompanying tight job market are causing people to take another look at a military career. One plug for the military is in order; they learn good leadership and discipline skills, and past companies I've been with have had success in hiring ex military people. I would guess their discipline helps them survive this current economic environment better than most.

My wife has been great throughout this. She is smart and intuitive and tries to maintain a calm facade. She recently went back to college and received her nursing degree and is now back in the work force as a registered nurse. I am extremely proud of her, and I know it was difficult for her to balance home and school responsibilities. This added income is a huge plus in this environment, and the healthcare field she is employed in should always have job opportunities. Our population is aging, and the average life expectancy is increasing. Given these dynamics, is it any wonder that healthcare and social security are major issues? You do not hear much talk by the candidates on social security, although it deserves to be on the front page. I can honestly state that I do not know what their proposals are for this program, except that current social security recipients are off limits. This is a politically sensitive topic, and each of us knows it needs to be addressed. Are we smarter than the candidates on this? Of course not, but the obvious solution is to either increase taxes or reduce benefits. The candidates and their camps do not find either of these choices appealing, thus the silence around solving the problem. I do not like the steps that will need to be taken, but I am willing to incur some pain to make Social Security solvent for generations to come. My feelings are obviously biased, since I can now see off into the distance the day I'll be eligible for benefits. Why can't we have a bipartisan solution to this? Both parties know something needs to be done, but they choose to ignore it and delay more painful decisions until after their Washington stay is over. If you need to lower annual benefit increases, increase the eligibility ages, or raise taxes to solidify the program, then do it. Most people would be upset with these changes, but I think most would find a way to adapt, as long as they know its coming and can plan accordingly. The one thing I will not stand for is complacency, and a total dereliction of Congress' duty to strengthen this program. One other sore point; Congressmen, don't you dare increase my taxes with a promise to shore up this program and then divert those funds to enhance or set up new entitlement programs. Keep these funds in a bucket (or the infamous lock box Al Gore referred to during his debate with Bush in 2000) directly related for their intended purpose. Taxpayers know a bait and switch when they see it.

At some point, the dam has to burst, and I found it both amusing and alarming that our national debt clock ran out of zeros as it passed the $10 trillion mark. Yes, that's trillions with a "t." We simply cannot afford to continue to spend like drunken sailors. Every candidate likes to talk about controlling spending, yet his or her actions belie these words. Why should we expect citizens to balance their budgets when our government is the worst abuser of this fundamental rule? Some discipline at the government level might actually impress people to follow this lead in their own financial matters. This dilemma is not only at the federal level, but the state and local levels as well. I do not want the cascading effect, whereby all of my taxes go up. We are heading in that direction, unless we do something about it now. Failure to act will not only have domestic ramifications, but diplomatic and foreign affairs consequences as well. If we cannot pay our bills, we will have social unrest and a greater level of foreign dependency to fund our habits. It seems that throughout history the wealth of nations has caused their strengthening and weakening status. Lincoln said that our downfall would not be from invading powers, but from within our own borders. I do not want us indebted to foreign powers with their oil wealth. Foreign armies cannot destroy us, but our overdrawn bank account can.

As I watched the Eagles and Phillies games on Sunday it was clear that the candidates were targeting the viewing audience in my home state. Most commercial time consisted of advertisements from both candidates, although Obama seemed to have significantly more air time. He did opt to forego the matched funding due to his substantial war-chest, while McCain accepted the $85 million that goes with the program. I would expect this bombardment to continue until Election Day, unless of course McCain follows his Michigan strategy and concedes Pennsylvania to Obama. I guess I will be seeing less of those funny Miller Lite and Bud Light commercials, which I have to admit I do enjoy. I happened to see a clip on a news program Sunday about Obama meeting residents in an Ohio town, and one of the residents got into a conversation with

him about his tax plan and how it might affect this individual
personally. It was an interesting exchange, and what struck
me was Obama's comment that "when you spread the wealth
around that's good for everybody." It was said in such a casual
and innocent way, which is how people often times reveal their
true feelings. He didn't have time to check with his campaign
strategists about how to answer this question, and I was left
wondering how I should interpret this comment. It may die
on the vine, but I think it warrants further insight, and I'm
curious to see if it gets more publicity in the coming days. The
Eagles won a close one with a fourth quarter comeback. It was
especially satisfying since division rivals Dallas and Washington
lost. This psychological lift gave me the motivation to do my
running, and I chose to run outside instead of on the treadmill.
I ran my course two minutes faster than normal. It was crisp
outside, with a full moon and what seemed like thousands of
stars. The run felt great, and I was hoping it was an omen for
the Phillies and the world markets. The Phillies got hammered
early and lost, but they still have a 2-1 lead in the series. The
futures are looking strong, and Asian markets did open on the
positive side. We will soon find out if U.S. markets will follow.

October 13, 2008

Foreign markets are positive today, with the Hang Seng leading the pack up 10 percent. The Nikkei is closed today for a national holiday, so in Japan, investors will have to wait another day to recoup some of their recent losses. European markets are up 6 percent so far, and U.S. futures are up approximately 4 percent. Volatility has ruled the markets recently, and although it is looking positive early, there is no guarantee that the markets will be ahead at the closing bell. The coordinated attempts by central banks and foreign governments are providing a boost to the markets, with the intention to loosen up credit markets. If this massive intervention to provide unlimited dollars to financial institutions does not thaw credit markets and bolster banks, then I am not sure what the next step would be. Ben and Hank must have this figured out, haven't they?

As a result of recent moves, taxpayers will become shareholders in banks, most notably in Britain, where the government is making a major cash infusion into three of the nation's largest banks. The Bush administration is attempting to move quickly to get the $700 billion rescue plan up and running in the U.S., hoping to further prop up the financial system. Events are unfolding in a fast and furious fashion, and although I am comforted by the unprecedented coordination among the world's nations, I still have some lingering reservations about the haste in implementing these measures.

Will the law of unintended consequences apply to these rushed actions, in effect causing unintended pain in the future? Major policy changes generally take time to be developed and vetted, with implementation only after a thorough educated analysis of the repercussions. Granted, we are experiencing an unprecedented crisis, and time certainly seems to be of the essence. Thoughts of selling into this relief rally cross my mind, but I decide to stay the course. It is unrealistic to think that the markets will recoup their losses quickly, and I would be happy to accept a bottoming process with subsequent slow and steady gains.

The suddenness with which this crisis hit overwhelmed everyone, whether it was politicians, businessmen, or Main Street. We have paid a huge price for the excessive greed of prior years, and I hope we can soon talk of this episode in the past tense. Each of us has been affected, and will continue to be affected into the foreseeable future. Job losses will continue to increase as businesses retrench and rebuild. Each of us will continue to worry about how it will affect our families, and when we will be able to signal the "all clear." Against this backdrop, we have an election in full swing, and the new president will have a mess on his hands, although for his sake and ours, I hope that the foundation being laid in these trying times is the right course to get us back onto the road to prosperity. Government intervention is now the primary lever (maybe even the sole lever) helping us out of the current downturn. I continue to worry over the level of intervention and continue to think that voters aren't paying enough attention to how much Uncle Sam is getting involved, as long as the situation improves. I am starting to focus on this because this recession may be ushering in the dawning of a new philosophy of government intervention that we are currently ignoring. Are the seeds being planted that will be hard to reverse?

At noon, the U.S. markets are up 6 percent, which reduces this bear's decline to 36 percent. Overseas markets are up almost 10 percent. I wonder how the investors who panicked and exited the market last week feel today. They got their peace of mind, but at what cost? Will they stay on the sidelines or get back in, effectively buying high after selling low? This volatility is unnerving, with each day bringing more wild swings to the market. This environment is where the experts and savvy investors shine, feeding on the mom and pop kitchen-table investors who are usually on the wrong side of this trade. If the market has truly bottomed, then three months, six months, or a year from now, we will be reading about these funds and investors whose opportunistic buying yielded them sizable returns. When the dust settles, will we wake up and find that the financing system has been transformed into a quasi government funding backstop? Has risk been removed as a key element in decisions? One could infer that the government has set up a stop-loss program for investors, in effect limiting downside exposure (although some AIG shareholders may disagree with this sentiment). I don't want to lose anymore, but at the same time, are we changing the dynamics of how business and economies work? I will go so far as to say that this is an indictment of capitalism, that it is okay during prosperous times, but it is not the right formula during a time of crisis. Governments had to intervene or we would have had massive failings, not only in the financial system but also in the way we live. Without this intervention, we might have witnessed the tipping point to social unrest, causing political upheaval around the globe. It still may happen in certain countries, as their populations feel the wrath of a global recession. Will governments in these countries be able to bring stability and calm, or will rioting and civil disturbance rule the day? We may have been so close to a worldwide catastrophe that governments had no choice but to act quickly to limit the collateral damage. This was a coordinated global effort, and if we can see such coordination in this crisis, why can we not get the same cooperation in other types of crisis? Is it because money was involved, which strikes right at the core of our societal values?

Obama and McCain are still fairly quiet about the crisis, although McCain is planning a "comeback" strategy that will focus on tax cuts and appeal to those who like the underdog. Each day that passes is one less day for him to make up ground. Some polls show him behind in Virginia and North Carolina, usually safe and reliable red states. Compound this with a double-digit deficit in Pennsylvania and we have the potential beginning of the end. The Clintons campaigned for Obama in Pennsylvania yesterday, and former president Clinton will be on the stump in Virginia today. McCain seems outnumbered, and I do not see anyone on the horizon helping to prop him up. Is the Republican Party abandoning him, or biding their time for a full court press in the final weeks?

U.S. markets extended their gains throughout the day, with all major indexes up 11 percent. The Dow and S&P set new records for one-day point gains, with the Dow's nine hundred, thirty point increase almost doubling the prior record of four hundred, ninety nine. My wife called me around 5 p.m. to talk about the markets rise, and although everyone is happy about the increase, I cautioned her that these types of movements are not normal. I prefer surprises to the upside, but I wonder if this dramatic increase is another head fake or the beginning of a sustained rally. This increase is certainly welcome, but the reality is that we recouped less than half of the damage done over the preceding eight days. I will feel a lot better if the market can build off these gains over the next few days and weeks, thus providing some comfort that we are not in the throes of a bear rally.

This is earnings season, and over the course of the next few weeks, the market will be digesting third-quarter earnings reports. The prognosis for these results isn't exactly bullish, and it is possible that poor earnings may be a somber dose of reality and relapse the patient into the intensive care unit. Will today's euphoria be eclipsed by sour reports, and if so, am I missing an opportunity to get out on an uptick? I have rolled the dice so far, and will continue to do so for the foreseeable future.

Obama detailed his economic rescue plan today, which contained some items that sound appealing. He proposed new legislation that would give families the option of withdrawing up to 15 percent of their 401ks, up to a $10,000 max, without facing a tax penalty this year or next year. He also called for a temporary lifting of taxes on unemployment insurance benefits, and a ninety-day foreclosure moratorium for homeowners acting in good faith. One last item he called for was a temporary tax credit for firms that create new jobs over the next two years. These proposals are going for the jugular, and I must admit they might be closing the deal with some of the middle class. There was noise that McCain would be coming out with some new proposals of his own today, but if he does, they might be run over by the Obama train.

McCain and his campaign are really struggling. They appear to be on life support, with a miracle cure needed to revive his chances. There is a debate in two days, and this will be his last face-to-face encounter with his opponent. Obama has held his own in the prior debates, and I would expect him to play it safe and force McCain to swing for the fences. With twenty-two days to go, McCain is running out of days and issues. Fair or not, he has been the victim of the worst economic crisis in years and had been successfully painted as a Bush clone by the Democrats. He needs a miracle, and I am not sure where it is going to come from. Foreign affairs are now dwarfed by the economic crisis, which may actually be enhancing Obama's position. It does not appear that Iran, Venezuela, Syria, North Korea, or any other foreign adversary is going to help the Republican ticket. They are lying low, keeping the U.S. electorate focused on the economy. They only have three weeks to keep their powder dry, and usher in a new foreign policy era in U.S. history. This silent treatment scares me some, and if elected, I would expect Obama to be tested early by our foes. This election has been fixated on nothing but the economy, with Americans more concerned about putting bread on the table than worrying about a rogue nation obtaining nuclear weapons. Who can blame someone for thinking this way? American voters' priorities are to help ourselves first, and then worry about outside our borders later. The economy is dominating all domestic issues, including off-shore drilling, which was a top issue only a few weeks ago. Voters are shortsighted, and if we have banished energy issues to the backburner, we have no one to blame but ourselves. Prices at the pump are down, and so is our interest in a well-thought-out energy policy. Both candidates are mum on this, now, and I guess it is hard to get the electorate charged up about it when prices are falling. Our long-term strategic energy issues have not changed in the course of a few weeks, and I hope that the victor will prioritize this in their administration.

What about Medicare and Social Security? How about immigration? I cannot remember the latter being discussed at all in the last few weeks, and I have yet to hear concrete proposals to address the solvency of Medicare and Social Security. Why the silence? Speaking of immigration, I see Ellis island every day from my office. This was the point of entry for immigrants to our country, and is a visual reminder that we're a country of immigrants. This is an extremely sensitive political topic, and I'm not sure what the right answer is, but I would certainly like to hear more about each candidates position on this.

As I raced through Penn Station to catch my train home, the theme from *F Troop* was being played by a vagabond flutist. I would guess the percentage of transients who recognize this song to be about twenty percent. Wait a minute, that's the percentage of undecided voters in this election. Am I on to something here? Is there a direct correlation between undecides and those recognizing the F Troop theme song? This was another of those classic TV shows I loved; unfortunately, I cannot remember the last time I was able to see this one in late-night cable reruns. Unlike the *Adam's Family*, *F Troop* never made it to the big screen. I'm not ashamed to say one of my favorite TV shows was *Happy Days*, which contained a blend of family values and characters we could relate to. The Fonz and Richie never had to log on, and they had Arnolds to today's Starbucks. My kids are probably embarrassed as they read this.

The Phillies play again tonight, trying to rebound from last night's loss to the Dodgers. A win will give them a stranglehold on the series, whereas a loss will conjure up visions of past heartbreaks, and create some real anxiety for Phillies's fans. While I am on the topic of sports, I cannot remember a deflationary cycle in the history of major American sports. It will be interesting to see if this current financial crisis spills into the professional sports world. Player salaries continue to escalate, supported to a large extent by corporate sponsorships and television contracts. Common sense would dictate that, at some point, revenues will flatten, causing some upheaval in the contracts negotiated. Up till now, professional sports have been immune from down cycles, but this recent crisis may cause a shift in behavior. We all enjoy our sports release, but at some point, the cost of attending a game will drive more fans into their living room viewing chairs, at which point I would expect Direct TV or pay-per-view to be the main avenue for watching sporting events. I'm always surprised at the sticker shock I get when purchasing food at a concession stand during a professional sporting event. It doesn't seem right that to feed a family with four hot dogs, sodas, and popcorn should necessitate a bill with Grant's face as opposed to Jackson's . Let me do the math as to how a 1,000% percent markup happens. I can buy 8 hot dogs for $3 in a supermarket, which translates to thirty seven cents per hot dog. I'll generously add in a cost of the roll for twenty five cents, bringing the total cost of the hot dog to sixty two cents. They charge me $6 per hot dog, which contains a markup that even a loan shark would be envious of. Is there any other business in the world that has this type of markup? Anyone been to a movie theatre recently? I would expect people to be less generous with their hard earned dollars at concession stands during this economic climate. Sports are certainly one arena where advertisers look to promote their products or brand. The next time soccer powerhouse Manchester United highlights on Sports center, look at the front of their uniforms to see their corporate sponsorship proudly displayed. Yes, taxpayers, AIG is proudly embroidered on the front of their jerseys. I wonder how many Monday morning quarterbacks will beat the populist drum and question this business decision, even though this deal was consummated before our troubles surfaced. Man U is extremely popular around the world, and the belief was we would leverage their popularity in solidifying the AIG brand. Unfortunately, given our circumstances, it may reinforce our company's current situation.

October 14, 2008

I went to bed last night with the Phillies trailing and woke up to find they had won 7-5 for a three-to-one lead in the series. I wanted to stay up and watch, but I was just too tired.

Foreign markets are up this morning, and the Nikkei roared ahead 14 percent after reopening today. Futures are pointing toward a higher U.S. open, while European markets are up 5 percent, so far this trading day.

Paulson and the Treasury have decided on a $250 billion cash injection into various large banks, in return for equity stakes. The thought is that it will help shore up capital positions and help unfreeze the credit markets. Bush had a news conference to announce the program this morning, while Paulson and Bernanke will provide more details in a briefing later today.

I found it amusing this morning that, on the metro, I noticed one bench of about five people all attempting to get some last minute rest before starting their workday. They must have stayed up to watch the Giants lose on Monday night football to the lowly Cleveland Browns. Sorry, but I had to get that dig in at one of my Eagles division rivals.

Before going to my office, I went to the cleaners to pick up a shirt I had dropped off last week. The Dunkin Donuts across the walkway was still relatively empty, with only two people in line, and for some reason, I felt I needed a donut this morning. That marble frosted donut tasted great. It is amazing how a market uptick provides a shot of adrenaline and improves my mood, although I have no intention of extending this sudden splurge at the expense of my new-found thrifty nature. I remind myself that we are not out of the woods yet, and as I scan the business news this morning, I note that Pepsi is laying off 3,300 workers to reduce costs. My daughter at Boston U has a friend whose father works at Pepsi. I hope he isn't one of the employees losing their job at my favorite soft drink company. It seems every day there are more job cuts and more families' lives thrown into disarray. Those affected workers have more pressing needs than to get euphoric about the market uptick. They join the ranks of the other ten million workers in the unemployment lines hoping to find a job to limit the disruption to their lives. I saw a forecast that projects the ranks of the unemployed will hit 8 percent by year-end 2009, which would swell the number to thirteen million, about the size of the total population in my home state of Pennsylvania.

The *USA Today* newspaper had an analysis of Pennsylvania's electorate, and the theme of the article was that the state is very much up for grabs with its rich twenty-one electoral votes. Democrats have superior numbers of registered voters; however, we have a lot of conservative Democrats that are not sold on Obama yet. Tom Ridge, a former governor, plans to headline a "we're not bitter" tour to remind voters of Obama's controversial remarks that people in small Pennsylvania towns "cling to guns or religion," because they are bitter over the loss of manufacturing jobs. I thought this infamous quote would be given more ad time by the Republicans, who have decided to unleash it just three weeks before the election. I think this gentle reminder will have some legs to it, and I have to agree with the premise that Pennsylvania is still in play. If McCain could grab this rich prize, his chance of winning the White House would increase significantly. I would expect both he and Palin to be spending a lot of time in Pennsylvania over the next few weeks, and for our airwaves to continue to feel the bombardment of political ads. The Democrats have dispatched their vice presidential nominee to the state to shore up support for the Obama ticket, and they like to speak of his Scranton roots. Good ole Joe wants voters to feel he is one of them, and it may come down to a contest of him convincing them of this over their annoyance of "clinging to guns and religion." The Clintons were in the state the other day talking up Obama, who seems to focus his trips in the Keystone State to the large metropolitan areas, such as Philadelphia and its surrounding suburbs. Obama is hoping Biden and the Clintons will be able to smooth over the sharp words of his infamous quote. I would like to believe these people would vote based upon the real issues in this campaign and not on a selective quote made during the nominating process many months ago. Although issues will count in their decision process, they may opt to punish Obama for his stinging and condescending words.

I had lunch today with a friend who I had not seen in a while. I coached his two boys in basketball years ago, and our paths had not crossed in quite awhile, until we met on the train a number of months back. We exchanged business cards and finally got a chance to meet for lunch. He works at one of AIG's competitors, and during our luncheon conversation he seemed genuinely concerned about my situation. I appreciated his sincerity, and must say it was great to hear him have some encouraging words. It was great to reminisce and catch up on old times. I remembered his kids as very talented players and also as very respectful and coachable kids. I was glad to hear they are both doing extremely well, which would have been consistent with my expectations of them many years ago. As we exited the restaurant, I noticed that the market was almost flat, which was a surprise, given where the futures were earlier and the capital injections to banks announced earlier today. Most of the big banks were up almost 10 percent, so the drag was being applied by other sectors. Some investors were cashing out of gains achieved in yesterday's run-up, while others were betting that the rally would be short-lived and would mimic some of the other false upticks experienced over previous months.

European markets ended up about 3 percent, off of their highs for the day. They were at least able to hold onto gains and give their investors their first consecutive days' winning streak in what must have seemed like an eternity. The U.S. markets are less bullish, and I wonder if this is an indictment that the steps taken and the amount injected is short of what will ultimately be needed. This hesitation was unexpected, and the failure to join other world market's upward momentum is causing me some angst. I am not changing my stay-the-course strategy; however, I keep thinking that maybe the market was giving me one more chance to get out on a high note.

McCain unveiled a new $52 billion economic plan. The centerpieces of his proposed plan were an elimination of taxes on unemployment benefits, a 50-percent cut in the capital gains tax, and a 10 percent tax rate on retirement withdrawals up to $50,000. The proposal had similarities to Obama's plan and there was not much of a difference in price tags. McCain said a couple of things about Obama he hoped might get voters to thinking about his leadership and past voting record. His comments were: 1) "Never before have the American people been asked to risk so much based on so little," and 2) "Obama cannot turn a record of supporting higher taxes into a credible proponent of cutting taxes." Both plausible arguments delivered to us as soul-searching questions to think about. At the least, his proposals and comments show he has a pulse and that the remaining three weeks strategy will be to get voters thinking about Obama's leadership credentials. Senator Clinton tried this strategy against Obama in the primary and was unsuccessful. McCain needs to hammer away at this theme, because Obama is not going to self-destruct and beat himself.

The market ended down a modest seventy-five points, which represented the first time in nine sessions that the Dow did not close up or down in triple digits. It did swing in a seven-hundred-point range, however, so volatility is still in fashion. Everyone has an opinion as to where the market is headed, and my opinion is that it is headed up over the long term, although I think it will trend down in the near term. How's that for hedging my bets? While on the topic of hedging, I wonder how many investors are in hedge funds which have taken short positions in the stock market. These individuals are probably hoping the market continues to tank to further improve their returns. I doubt many middle class Americans are in these type of investments, which are usually for the wealthier investors, given these funds minimum investment levels and strict redemption criteria. I would think those wealthy investors in long position hedge funds are feeling miserable these days as they are trapped by redemption restrictions in a severe bear market.

The vagabond flutist was playing "When Johnny Comes Marching Home Again," as I raced through Penn Station to catch my train. This song conjures up memories of the classic movie *Stalag 17,* with the U.S. prisoners singing the lyrics as they paraded through the barracks. The escalator to the train platform was off again, which is turning into the norm each day. I always thought the idea of an escalator was to assist us in our foot travel, but I'm actually getting pretty good at walking up and down escalators. I wonder how much they save in power usage each day, and combined with the fewer number of cars, they are certainly displaying their austerity kick. The train was crowded tonight, and a woman sat down next to me. She dropped a button on the floor and my gentlemanly instincts made me reach down and pick it up for her. It was an Obama button, and when she thanked me for picking it up, she unashamedly said, "I cannot lose that; he is going to be our next president." She sounded so confident about this, I just nodded and went about my business. As I thought about her comment, the first thought that came into my mind was passion, similar to my thoughts when I witnessed a woman reading *The Audacity of Hope* a few weeks back. She seemed to be passionate about Obama, and that he would not only win but also lead us out of the abyss we are in. Was this fanaticism at work here, and if so would it represent a clear advantage to Obama and improve his chances of winning? A common wisdom has been that Republicans are better at bringing out the vote on Election Day. If this woman is a leading indicator of the movement, which the Republicans are facing come Election Day, they are in trouble. The passion seems to be missing on the Republican side so far this election season. The economy is driving the passion this time, and, according to a recent poll, 91 percent of Americans are unhappy with the direction in which the country is headed. This is a phenomenal percentage, and it mirrors the downward trend of the markets, the accompanying elimination of wealth, and the worsening unemployment picture.

The President has been more visible over the last week, trying to comfort us with his comments on steps being taken to turn the economy around. His visibility may actually be inflicting more damage to McCain, since the Democrats have been successful in linking the two together. McCain needs to rid himself of this ball and chain, but the Democrats are relentless in keeping the two joined at the hip. I do not know why McCain and his campaign do not use the same strategy by linking Obama to the Reid and Pelosi leadership team. The approval ratings for congress are actually lower than the President's, yet the dialogue around this seems to be almost non-existent. This opening has been there for McCain, yet he opts to ignore it. Maybe he is holding it in reserve, but time is running short.

The polls continue to indicate an Obama lead, with some showing a sizeable advantage. He seems to actually be getting brazen to an extent, venturing into sacred Republican states that may be teetering a little. He has a sizable money advantage, and can afford to dip his toes into enemy territory. McCain has no such luxury and needs to concentrate his resources in states where he has a chance. An article I read today said that the money spent during this campaign season, including the primary, will top $1 billion (about the same amount the Dallas Cowboys' new stadium will cost).

Senator Clinton said today that she will probably not run a campaign for the White House again. This makes sense, since an Obama victory would mean she would have to wait eight years to make her next run. At this time last year, she seemed a lock for the Democratic nomination, but it all came tumbling down with Obama's powerful message of change. I thought she would not only win her party's nomination, but the general election as well. I remembered some comments made by her husband during the primary season when he insinuated that Obama's lack of experience was being ignored, and that he was being given a free pass on this by the media. It's now déjà vu, since McCain is experiencing the same frustrations as Clinton in trying to find a strategy that will work against him. With three weeks to go, he is facing the same fate as Clinton.

October 15, 2008

U.S. futures are trading lower today, while European markets are down 3 percent this morning. The mood is darkening, with a realization that we are in a recession that might go much deeper than the normal downturns. We're told the government's moves yesterday were necessary to prevent a major catastrophe; however, they will not be a cure-all for what ails the economy. I have had this sinking feeling for the last few weeks, and each time we get a burst of good news, the subsequent reality of poor economic conditions wins the day. The Treasury and the Federal Reserve Bank have announced a number of initiatives, with each expected to have a positive effect on the financial system. They may be producing the desired result, but why do things continue to stagnate or get worse? If these steps have been so positive, then the only conclusion I can come to is that the economy and financial system were in much worse shape than the experts initially thought. We may have been on the cliff, and if so, I hope these steps have brought us back from the edge.

At noon today, the Dow is down 4 percent, a better showing than the 7 percent drop in Europe. Oil has dropped to $75 per barrel, which is half of its high reached earlier this year. The price of a regular gallon of gas is down to $3.15, which is a 20-percent drop from its previous high. This is a needed relief, but why is there such a mismatch with the 50 percent drop in the price of oil (I know I'm belaboring this point, but it does irritate me to no end)? Some economic news was released this morning, one showing that retail sales in September were down by 1.2 percent, almost double the drop analysts expected. I don't think I needed any analyst to tell me this, for any trip to a mall would reveal much less customer traffic. Wholesale prices fell for a second straight month, declining by 0.4 percent, thanks to a big drop in energy costs. Core wholesale prices, which exclude food and energy, rose by 0.4 percent, double what economists had been expecting. In addition to these negative results, we are in the midst of third-quarter earnings season. JP Morgan Chase results were on the low end of expectations, and this reality check is dampening investor expectations. We still have a few more weeks left in the earnings season, and a dark cloud is hanging over these impending results. Maybe the government steps were preemptive strikes to limit damage as results are being released, and that without these steps, the third quarter would have been a bloodbath. At least the steps taken provide a dose of hope, with the thought being that those actions will take time to seep into the economy before they start paying the needed dividends. "Dividends" is an interesting choice of words, since I have not talked much about the dividend cuts and eliminations announced by many companies over the last few quarters. I wonder if these cuts will be reversed when we pass into greener pastures, or if the current crisis will result in a more conservative dividend philosophy at many institutions. Dividend cuts will probably affect many retirees who are counting on a dividend stream to help fund their income levels. This strategy seemed prudent, but I wonder how many retirees are now at risk of losing a portion of their retirement income stream. I guess this current market is forcing investment advisors to rethink the wisdom of a dividend strategy as part of an overall retirement plan. Obama is proposing to raise the tax rate on dividends, and if company announcements of dividend reductions continue, the net effect to federal tax revenues if his programs ever would get enacted may actually be zero.

The federal deficit for the fiscal year just ended is $455 billion. Next year's deficit has estimates ranging up to $1 trillion, a lofty number by anyone's standards. Someone has to pay this back at some point, and without some long-term plan, I fear that our path is to keep spending more than we can afford. It's a refrain I've often mentioned, but we need a plan that should address programs like Medicare and Social Security. This campaign has avoided addressing these issues, with a focus on fixing the current situation. We will come out of this at some point, but at what cost to our future long-term health? I do not want, or expect, my children to pay for our fiscal mismanagement. We need to address it now. Most Americans do not want our politicians to come up with another stimulus program that spends another $200 billion. Why don't they ever consider cutting some of the current spending on frivolous programs? Everyone who works for a business knows that there is some unnecessary spending which occurs in his or her own organization and when cuts are necessary we get them done. I would like the government to follow this same philosophy with its spending habits. Here's a novel idea. Why not put a team together of private-sector individuals schooled in expense efficiencies and task them with finding $300 billion of Federal spending opportunities? I picked three hundred billion because this represents approximately 10 percent of total government expenditures. I'm confident they could find such; however, they are not allowed to be shackled with any preconditions. I think the savings they find could be real, and I would gladly volunteer to be part of this worthwhile effort. It probably wouldn't get much support, however, since the political establishment would be fearful of its findings, especially when pet projects of each and every politician are recommended for the chopping block. I know Washington politicians do form commissions on various projects, but why is it these commissions are always packed with political retreads and politician-friendly members? If they truly want to do it right and have the public embrace its usefulness, then why not actually assign people with actual business experience to the commission. Their business mentality would be a fresh approach and would diminish the watering-down effect that occurs when politician-friendly experts issue supposedly sound recommendations.

A residential building next to my office is being renovated, and each day I notice fewer laborers working on the interior of the building. These renovations were started some time ago, when the economy was doing better, and with the downturn, I wonder if it will remain empty for months and maybe years to come. It is a nice location, with a view of the river. Given the job losses that have occurred, and more that are in the offing, I would expect this buildings owner to hurt for a few years. As companies continue to downsize, space will become available, adding to the woes of my next-door neighbor. Restaurants, jewelry stores, clothing stores, and convenience stores counting on these residents to help make them profitable will fall short of their income projections, forcing them to cut back and, in some cases, close their doors. The manufacturers and wholesale distributors who survive on delivering goods to these stores will have fewer orders to satisfy, and they too will have to retrench. New York City will reap lower tax revenues, forcing cuts in services. At some point, we will bottom out and see a reemergence, with the cycle reversing itself. The question is, how long until we reach this stage?

I am sitting in the middle of this environment, watching it happen, and powerless to do anything about it. This financial crisis has many tentacles to it, and it is not pleasant to witness. I often wonder if I'm being too pessimistic in my outlook because of my AIG experience, but each time I think this another dose of bad economic news reinforces my gloomy forecast for the overall economy. I take the train home each night and escape to the tranquility of my wife and family. I return each morning, hoping for signs of an improving economy, but I only see signs of a worsening climate. Each day on my drive to and from Trenton, I can't help but notice the lettered sign on one of the bridges surrounding the city that proudly boasts, "Trenton makes, the world takes." I'm not sure exactly when this sign was first put up, but given our current economy and the shift in this country out of manufacturing and into a greater dependency on the service sector, I'm not sure it still applies. I wonder if the city will ever again be worthy of that slogan. It's now been about a month since the government bailed out my company, and I have not as yet noticed or felt any significant changes in our day-to-day operations. We continue to receive our paychecks every two weeks. One thing we shouldn't count on are bonuses this year, since my initial reaction is to assume they'd be non-existent, since we'd want to avoid an uproar from politicians and Main Street. One of my first mentors cautioned me years ago about bonuses, and said to never spend a bonus you hadn't yet received. I have never forgotten these wise words, and consider it my duty to pass them along to my staff. I hope they have heeded this advice as I have. I thought more about this later and started to worry about future-year compensation being at the whim of politicians who are always searching for populist messages. Even though they would help protect the government's investment in AIG, the reality is politicians are more concerned with form over substance, which helps get them reelected. I don't think this bodes well for the future compensation practices at AIG, or any other companies who have the government as a major shareholder. I do get it however, in that the outlandish compensation packages some CEO's receive while their company languishes in mediocrity warrants a closer look. These packages need to be aligned with performance, and I believe even the recipients of the current mismatch would have a hard time defending against a change in practice.

The last presidential debate is tonight at Hofstra University, not far from my office in lower Manhattan. If you believe the current polls, McCain needs a stellar performance to get some momentum back into his campaign. Most polls show Obama lengthening his lead, and barring a blunder on his part, he should be able to maintain this lead. There are hundreds of polls, with some showing wider margins than others. We are always fascinated by polls, and in some cases, they may actually influence our decisions. If your candidate has a substantial lead or is way behind, are you less inclined to feel an urgency to actually vote, since it will not alter the verdict? The reverse is true in a tightly contested race, where each individual feels his or her vote will make a difference. These polls can also influence a candidate's campaign supporters in that they may psychologically let their guard down or lessen their enthusiasm if they sense impending victory or defeat. Polls have become so scientific that they are almost always directionally correct. These polls take a lot of the suspense out of the process, providing us with a result before the voters actually cast their ballots. Whenever I receive a call from a pollster asking for my opinion on something, I always decline. Maybe I should reconsider this tactic and answer counter to my actual preference. If enough of us could band together to follow this strategy, we could put a dent in the reliability of these polls. One poll that recently came out was about the government bailing out my employer. Suffice it to say that, if Main Street had its way, we'd be in bankruptcy right now.

The Dow continued to drop throughout the afternoon, and finished down seven hundred, twenty-five points, representing its second largest point loss ever. The Dow has almost given back all its gains from Monday, leaving one to think Monday's uptick was only a mirage. There's a word that conjures up visions of Las Vegas, since I've visited the Mirage hotel and casino in the oasis in the desert. It would make sense for the gaming industry to experience severe revenue drops in this environment, but there probably are some who will still gamble away their earnings in this economic climate, hoping for a jackpot to help them through these troubling times. I know its counterintuitive thinking, but I would bet it's happening to thousands who are falling further into debt. I wouldn't be surprised if some are actually trying to get cash advances on their Visa or MasterCards to fund this excursion. Credit card companies aren't dummies, and I would expect their customer service departments and analytics groups to be working closely to install preventive and detective measures to limit their exposure and possibly save some customers from falling further into a hole they can't get out of.

I am not sure how many tools the Fed has left in the toolbox, but I do know they have less now than a month ago. It's like a battle where you try different strategies to repel your advancing enemy, with each failure adding to the anxiety that you may lose. From a national security perspective, I question what would be happening today if our country alone had this financial crisis. Would our enemies destroy us with their wealth, and not need a military advantage? This crisis is global in nature, but it should cause us to think of the consequences of financial mismanagement. Some of our worst enemies are rich in oil, which is a precious resource that we need to survive. Will a drop at the pump take our eye off developing a responsible energy policy?

It is ironic that the last debate is being held in the New York City area, which is considered the epicenter of the current financial crisis. It is also ironic that the market had a significant drop today, in effect welcoming the participants to New York. Any glimmer of hope McCain may have had that Monday's market uptick would stabilize things and get voters minds away from the economy was shattered with today's performance. It is a numbing reminder to each of us that this crisis is far from over, and that the occasional upswing is just a temporary interruption in a downward march. Paulson and Bernanke are stressing patience, trying to reinforce that the medicine they have applied will work in time. I am not sure what their time frame is for this healing process or how much pain is ahead of us before it starts to improve.

A soon to be completed U.S. intelligence report was leaked, and it has a dim assessment of Pakistan and its progress in confronting the Al-Qaida-backed insurgency. The report describes Pakistan as on "the edge," and is a grim reminder that danger lurks outside our borders. Anti-U.S. sentiment has grown in Pakistan, with our drone assaults into their territory worsening the situation. As I think about drone combat tactics, my initial thought is that these type of assaults minimize the need for foot soldiers, and therefore limits U.S. casualties. When I was younger, there were science fiction movies where a star wars battle strategy was being employed. Are we now on the cusp of this being reality, and ushering in a new phase of warfare? What will the next generation of weapons be like, and how much will it cost to lead the way in this "progress?" Back to Pakistan—how can a country of 160 million people, about half of our population, succumb to an insurgency that is greatly outnumbered? I still cannot understand why citizens of that country do not see the evil associated with the terrorists and adopt a campaign to expunge their foes. Foreign affair's experience does matter in elections. Our next president will have to deal with this as well. One thing I've always wandered about is how terrorists can make significant profits on their actions or threatened actions. For example, if they threatened to target a specific company, they could short the company's stock, benefitting from the expected drop in price. How's that for using capitalism to profit in a way we would never imagine?

The Phillies come on about a half hour before the debate tonight. I doubt if many people use their picture-in-picture feature for two such different events, and I decide to flip back and forth to view both. The Phillies led 1-0 when I switched to the beginning of the debate. I prefer this debate format, with the participants at a table facing each other and the moderator. I stayed focused on the debate for about a half hour, and switched to the Phillies to see that their lead had increased to 3-0. I switched back immediately to the debate and thought McCain was more than holding his own. Obama was his usual eloquent self, and in my view, fought back to make it a draw. McCain failed to land the knockout blow that my Phillies handed to the Dodgers, although he did have his best performance to date. Domestic issues, most notably the economy, were front and center. I did not remember one specific question on foreign affairs. McCain tried to distance himself from Bush, while Obama maintained his attacks, linking the two as one. McCain looked his age in the close-ups, while Obama maintained his cool, almost emotionless, demeanor. I still get the feeling we don't know enough about this first-time senator from Illinois. Luckily for him many people view this as a positive in this election. The real winner in this debate was Joe the Plumber, who received more that his thirty seconds of fame. He became the single most identifiable difference in the two candidate's positions. I did sense more passion in McCain's words, with Obama sticking to his same message in his typical oratorical style. McCain needed more out of this debate, and with twenty days to go, the economy continues to haunt his campaign. Barring a major event on the world stage, the economy will continue to grab the headlines, and Obama will continue to leverage bad news to his good fortune.

October 16, 2008

The Phillies are in the World Series, which means we could have our first major sport's title in twenty-five years, although I am cautious in that we have been down this road before. It will add another couple of weeks of excitement to my sporting interest. I almost feel spoiled with Penn State joining the Phillies in their quest for a title. Late October is fun again.

Foreign markets are down this morning, although Dow futures are pointing to an open on the up side. Japanese investors are feeling our pain after the Nikkei lost over 11 percent today. Earnings continue to pour in, with Citigroup reporting another dismal quarter. Oil is at its lowest level in thirteen months, with the threat of a global recession weighing on investors' minds. The question is no longer *if* we will have a recession, but how long and deep it might be. Expert views differ on the severity, with each of us hoping for the optimistic leanings to come true. They say that markets start improving halfway through a recession, on the expectation that better days are ahead. I would like the market to start feeling this way, since I am reluctant to get bullish until some signs of improvement emerge.

I wanted to enjoy my lunch, so I did not bother to peak at how the market was doing at midday. On my way to Subway, I passed a couple of police officers who had just taken someone into custody. I do not know what the particular disturbance was, but it made me think that, in trying financial times, we will see an increase in criminal activity. We have our career criminals, who do not differentiate nor care about how the economy is doing. This crisis will give birth to another set of criminals: those who have no other way to put food on the table. They have tried to make a decent living and have become frustrated as they go deeper into debt, or worse, have tried to get a job but found no takers for their services. They are willing and able to work, but the current state of the economy offers them little, if any, opportunities. I do not condone this behavior, but I understand what causes it. I am not talking about someone who becomes a perpetrator of heinous crimes; rather, I am focused on the petty thief who preys on small business vendors for his or her basic needs. I have not checked any police blotters recently, but I would bet they show an increase in this type of activity.

I got up the courage to check the market after lunch and felt relieved the Dow was only down fifty points. The Dow had been down almost four hundred points earlier, making this a down week, even after the huge run up on Monday. Volatility continues to reign in this market, and I think there is an equal chance the Dow could be up three hundred or down three hundred at today's closing bell. This uncertainty is driving investors crazy, although for stay-the-course investors like me, it's still paper losses only. I am committed to ride this out; however, psychologically, I would feel better if we had some stability return to the market. I don't need an eight-hundred-point upward movement, only to see it reversed in a couple days. I would settle for some twenty-five-point consistent movements, preferably to the upside. The Dow continued its volatility in the afternoon, closing up four hundred points on the day. The daily swing was eight hundred points, which used to be considered the exception, as opposed to the norm. The Dow changed direction seventy-five times in today's session. This market is anything but normal, trying to figure out where the economy is headed.

The Queen Mary cruise ship appeared out my office window tonight. I could actually see the Queen Mary name in white lights near the top of the ship. I remembered reading somewhere that a cruise on the Queen Mary is very pricey; however, I guess the people who can afford to vacation on this ship aren't feeling the pain as much as middle-class America. Cruise ships sometimes reposition to new locations as certain seasons end, and maybe the Queen Mary is in the midst of doing this now. Many investors may have thought of repositioning their assets during this downturn, but besides cash, there isn't any other asset class you could have successfully hidden in. "Preservation" has supplanted "growth" as today's investment strategy.

As I think back on last night's debate, it dawns on me that this may have been McCain's last stand. Polls continue to point toward an impending Obama victory. McCain is now being forced to defend reliable Republican states, such as Georgia and Kentucky, which is draining valuable resources from the battleground states that were to be the true deciding contests in this race. The media is portraying Obama's campaign as unstoppable and that McCain seems to be getting run over in its way. Obama has significantly more money than McCain and can afford to spend in some states he wants McCain to have to defend. The map is starting to look blue, and McCain's margin for error is shrinking each day. The Obama money machine is on a roll, and his campaign will not leave any stone unturned. Obama has even purchased a half-hour of airtime on CBS, NBC, and Fox in the 8-8:30 p.m. time slot for Wednesday, October twenty-ninth, less than a week before the election. Fox has even said they will push back the start time of a potential game six of the World Series to accommodate him. I have not seen the cost of this media buy, but it has to be a substantial sum. His campaign seems to be leaving nothing to chance, maintaining its relentless and full-speed-ahead strategy. McCain is in the way of this blitzkrieg, and he almost seems helpless to do anything about it. If Obama's momentum continues up to Election Day, he may well have long coattails, ushering in an era of Democratic Party dominance in Washington. They may win enough seats to be filibuster proof and dictate Washington business for a number of years. This scent of power must be heaven for the labor unions and trial lawyers, who are hoping to restore their prominence with a big Democratic win. The Democrats are not taking any chances, and they are unified in this quest for power. It is interesting in that, if typical economic cycles repeat, they could be in a sweet spot for a number of years. They could be the beneficiaries of an improving economy and get all the credit for this rebound. The stars are aligning for them, and if this scenario unfolds, I hope they have the sense to address the major issues that have not been discussed enough in this election. With power comes responsibility, and I hope their quest to reclaim this throne does not blind them to the need to implement positive strategies for our nation's problems.

I am talking as if McCain has been defeated, allowing the media to influence my perception of this election. People I speak to claim they are undecided, yet the polls are predicting a huge victory for Obama. How can my face-to-face polls be so different than the scientific polls taken by the experts? One of us is being conned, and I am not ready to surrender and say it is I. There are still nineteen days to go, and a lot can happen. McCain was riding high until this financial crisis shifted the momentum, and he has been on the defensive ever since. Anyone who has been through what he has does not have *quit* in his DNA, and I expect him to take the fight to Obama over the remaining days. We Americans like a close race and do not like suspense removed this early in a contest.

October 17, 2008

CNN had another poll that showed that, if the election were held today, Obama would have a firm two hundred, seventy-seven electoral votes, making him the forty-fourth president of the United States. McCain's sure-win electoral votes were much lower, with various states too close to call at this time. When you look at the map and the accompanying blue and red leanings, it is fascinating to see the red for McCain bunched in the south and in the middle of the country. The Blue surrounds him on the coasts and in the north. The map does not look much different than it did in the prior two elections, except that the current "too close to call" states were mostly red. Pennsylvania was listed as firmly in Obama's column, but I am not sure I agree with this assessment. Maybe I am dismissing the accuracy of these polls, but the reading I get from friends and relatives is that it may lean Obama, but only by a slim margin. I know that there are certain blocs that will vote heavily in his favor, but the pulse-reading I get is different. Besides, I want my home state to matter in this election, and I want to hear what they have to say to us. Do not toss me and my state into an "over" category when we are in play.

As I watched clips of Obama and McCain speak at the Alfred Smith dinner in New York City, I saw two different personalities, one appearing calm and almost lackadaisical, and the other more intense and hungrier. It dawned on me that these contrasting styles have become clearer as Election Day nears, with Obama being able to taste victory, while McCain is determined to not give up regardless of the odds. Obama talks of not getting complacent, yet his style contradicts his words. I do not sense an urgency to fight for votes on his part, while McCain is struggling to keep his head above water.

With eighteen days until the election, a radical thought crossed my mind, one I hope I can adequately articulate. The biggest plus for Obama has been the state of the economy, for which President Bush and his party are receiving the bulk of the blame. All sections of this country are feeling the effects of this meltdown, and people's reactions have been to direct their anger at someone to get it off their chests. McCain has felt this in the polls, resulting in his consistent drop over the last three weeks. When someone gets angry, he or she screams to clear his or her mind, yet most will calm down and rethink his or her actions later on. There is no denying that the economy is in bad shape and that people will continue to hurt for a period of time. As they think through the situation, will they come to the conclusion that they overreacted toward McCain, and take a closer look at his proposals and leadership credentials? In essence, have they blindly shifted to Obama out of anger and frustration, and not because of rational thinking around his positions? Is it possible that McCain will experience a rebound as voters calm down and reevaluate the candidates? Maybe it was fortunate for McCain that the worst of the crisis hit when it did, because if it were just starting now, the angry voters would not have time to calm down before pulling the lever on November fourth. This is just a thought, and I am interested to see if developments over the next few days and weeks support this hypothesis. Of course, if the economy deteriorates at a quickening pace, then all bets are off.

European markets were up modestly this morning, while U.S. futures are pointing toward a lower open. New home construction in the U.S. dropped to the lowest pace since 1991. This news was overshadowed by Warren Buffet, saying he is buying U.S. stocks now. Finally, a dose of optimism from a prominent and influential business person. He reiterated his stance to "be fearful when others are greedy, and be greedy when others are fearful." There is no doubt fear has a substantial advantage over greed in today's market, and Mr. Buffet is saying that is his signal to get in. This may help reverse the future's trend today, although Fridays have been extremely volatile trading days.

Bush is speaking to the U.S. chamber of commerce this morning. I am sure he will try to comfort investors, but I do not think his words will soothe their feelings. Buffet's words will carry more weight than Bush's.

Consumer confidence suffered its steepest monthly drop on record in October, as the financial crisis sent shock waves through the economy. This University of Michigan survey came in well below economist's expectations.

The market is holding up today, with no major change up or down so far. The president's speech had the recurring theme that he, Paulson, and Bernanke have been saying, that it is going to take awhile for the credit system to thaw. This plea for patience is understandable, but no one has a clear answer on how long this thawing process will take.

I ran out to a deli for lunch and saw a double-deck tour bus running along Water Street. These sightings are common; however, it is unusual to only see two tourists on the upper level. Today is a nice, sunny day, with a mild chill. October is not the heaviest vacation period, but the lack of tourists is still a surprise. Maybe foreigners have decided to stay home, due to their own country feeling the wrath of this crisis. Foreign exchange rates are contributing as well, with the dollar on a strengthening trend over the last three months. Say what you want about our deficits and financial markets, but the dollar continues to be a safe haven in uncertain times.

Joe the Plumber had his picture and a story in the *Wall Street Journal* today. If McCain goes on to win, he may want to invite Joe to a front-row seat at his inauguration. Joe was given a platform to speak with the media, and based on his opinions, I feel it is safe to say he leans toward the Republican side. Are his feelings representative of others in his state or in this country, or should he be dismissed as a person whose views are inconsistent with Main Street? He is an eligible voter in Ohio, one of the battleground states, which is considered extremely close. Bush won this state by 118,000 votes in 2004, and the margin is trending toward a photo finish in 2008. Could Joe influence the result in Ohio? Will his conversation with Obama in which the Democratic nominee said that "spreading the wealth around is not a bad thing," strike a nerve with voters who do not subscribe to this philosophy? We should note that Obama has not tried to disavow this comment. Should we infer then that, if elected, he will practice what he preaches? I continue to wonder if this philosophy isn't being given the level of attention it deserves by voters. Are we so frustrated with the current state of affairs that we're blind to something that might be staring us right in the face?

As I approached the south ferry terminal to hop on the metro, I was greeted by people soliciting me to sign a petition against changing the city charter to allow Mayor Bloomberg to run for a third term. They did not know I was from Pennsylvania, and probably didn't care. They were belligerent with the tired workers wanting to get home for the weekend. I believe strongly in term limits, but I just want to get home.

My Penn Station flutist was playing, "The Halls of Montezuma," this evening, and visions of Richard Widmark in the movie of the same name crossed my mind. I'll bet no one under forty knows who Richard Widmark is, let alone recognizes the movie's name. With the selections I've been hearing recently I think it's safe to say my musician is targeting the baby boomer audience. Even these individuals have their target markets. I occasionally drop a tip in the jar, however if a song I don't recognize is being played no donation would be forthcoming.

New Jersey Transit was experiencing delays, which would add another thirty minutes to my commute home. As a NJT customer, it gets frustrating when these delays occur, which seems to be at least once or twice a week. They share the line with Amtrak, although Amtrak gets the priority when dueling schedules collide (I shouldn't complain about this since Amtrak customers pay three times as much as I do for their monthly commute). As I stand and stew waiting out the delay, I think of the infrastructure supporting the rail system, and how poor the conditions must be to have consistent delays. I'm not sure how to fix this without major inconveniences, but it's obvious that infrastructure investment is sorely needed. Where would the investment dollars come from? Probably from Uncle Sam, in the form of higher taxes.

The Dow finished down one hundred, twenty-five points for the day, a reversal of the two hundred points it was up at mid-afternoon. At least we held on to some of yesterday's gains. The Dow had its best week since March 2003, advancing almost 5 percent. Speaking on behalf of fellow investors, we will take it, although this gain recoups but a small portion of the obliteration of the prior three weeks. Warren Buffet's comments today may have kept the market from imploding, and I agree with his views that there are some great companies at bargain prices waiting to be bought. A lot of people may share this thinking but are probably leery of committing liquid assets at this time.

As I scanned the Internet, a particular story caught my attention. It was titled, "Nation could face short election night." The article talked about how media executives were contemplating how to manage their newscasts in the event of an Obama blowout. Networks are planning to have election-night coverage until 2 a.m. east coast time, which would be a lot of airtime to fill if one believes some of the polls. Although I understand the reason for their preparation, it annoys me nonetheless. What about the voters out west, who have already seen a victor declared? Will they feel disenfranchised and opt to stay home? They might be motivated to vote if there are state and local contests, which interest them, but their vote for the top of the ticket will be insignificant.

This has been a tough week from a work perspective, but a memorable week in other ways. My Phillies are going to the World Series, and will open play in the American League Champions' city next Wednesday. Penn State attempts to stay undefeated against Michigan tomorrow, while the Eagles have their bye week.

The candidates will continue to press on, and the news will be dominated by their words and actions. Will something besides the economy grab some headlines, and change the direction of the campaign and voter's preferences? Obama wants quiet while McCain needs a game changer.

October 18th-19th, 2008

The weekend ushered in some cool weather, with temperatures in the thirties each morning. Polls continue to show Obama leading, although a Reuters/C-Span/Zogby poll released on Saturday had Obama's lead shrinking to four points, revealing some momentum tilting McCain's way. The poll revealed that McCain led in only one age group—those aged 35-49. I was surprised that Obama led with older Americans, although this group represents those nearing retirement, who have felt the impact of the deteriorating economy more than younger Americans. This explains why Obama would be leading in Florida, a state that has a significant number of retirees. If McCain loses Florida he loses the election.

ABC News with George Stephanopoulos showed a political map that has Obama with a firm two hundred, sixty-four electoral votes, leaving McCain no margin of error. The problem McCain faces is that he is trailing in most of the battleground states that Bush won in 2000 and 2004. He is being forced to not only defend red states, but go on the offensive in these states to recoup lost ground. Obama has a tremendous money advantage, and his campaign knows how to put it to use. He raised $150 million in September alone, which is almost double what McCain received in federal matching funds. He will have raised almost $700 million, more than Bush and Kerry combined in 2004. This election is painted green, the color of money, which Obama has been able to successfully raise. There is nothing illegal about his fundraising efforts. It does however call into question the role of money in the election process. We do not want our election to turn into a contest, whereby money-raising success declares the victor, detracting from the candidate's positions on key issues. Money allows a campaign to pay for their ground forces and infrastructure, and common sense dictates that the more they have the greater their chance of achieving victory. They need to spend it wisely, but with an overflowing war chest, they can afford some misfires.

The airwaves continue to be dominated by political messages this weekend, with their frequency only intensifying. National and local candidates keep popping up on TV, and most of their messages are negative. Nothing annoys me more than a candidate whose sole pitch is why you should not vote for his or her opponent. I see this frequently in local races, and I immediately am biased against this individual. I want to hear why a candidate is qualified and deserving of my vote. McCain has gone more negative than Obama, and it is a high-risk strategy that his campaign feels is necessary to make up lost ground. The sad part is that I believe there are fundamental differences that he should be trying to exploit, as opposed to going negative. This negativity weighs into my thinking, and others probably share this view. An influential Republican came out Sunday morning to endorse Obama, and I was struck by some of his reasoning. Colin Powell is the endorser, and he went on to talk about the negativity and divisiveness of Republican attacks against Obama. He called for unity, for us to rally behind Obama and visions of change and hope. Powell's endorsement could make a difference in some undecided voters, and I must admit I take notice when someone like him speaks up. I generally dismiss endorsements because of their political bias. Will the *New York Times'* endorsement of Obama or Limbaugh's endorsement of McCain sway my vote? Not a chance. The people who read and listen to these media sources already have their minds made up. They were successfully brainwashed years ago, and their views are so entwined with their pied piper that they cease to think independently on most issues. Powell is a different type of endorser, and I suspect this can only help Obama. The irony in this endorsement is that Powell was mentioned at one time as a potential McCain running mate. During the interview, when Powell explained his endorsement, a reporter asked what party he was aligned with, and he said he is Republican. It is interesting that he maintains his Republican leanings, but decided to support Obama. Some people will immediately say that his endorsement is race driven, but I do not believe this. I respect Powell enough to believe his motives are purely in the best interests of the country, and who he believes can lead us out of the dire situation we are in.

Bush is meeting with European leaders at Camp David this weekend to discuss the financial crisis, with talk of holding a world summit to discuss the crisis some time after the election. This summit will include leaders throughout the world, not just the large developed countries. Numerous actions have been taken by global leaders to attempt to fix the problems, and when this summit convenes after our election, they will have had time to digest the preliminary results of their efforts. This will be an interesting summit, and I would like to see our newly-elected leader join our lame-duck president representing the U.S. This would be a great experience, and I hope politics does not preclude it from happening.

My Nittany Lions ended years of futility by finally beating Michigan on Saturday. The stage is now set for their showdown with Ohio State next weekend in Columbus, and this game will decide if their journey toward a national championship continues. The Phillies' opponent in the World Series has yet to be determined, with the Red Sox forcing a game seven with the Rays on Sunday night. The Penn State game is at 8 p.m. next Saturday night and will run opposite game three of the World Series. My remote will get another workout.

On Stephanopoulos' Sunday morning show, there was a clear view that Obama will be elected president on November 4th. The panel discussed what little chance McCain has and focused more on the enormous problems Obama will face when he takes office. Even Newt Gingrich had a sort of resignation in his voice to this outcome, although he tried to maintain some semblance of hope by saying what McCain should focus on in the last two weeks of the campaign. Everyone is writing McCain off, believing that the polls are right. The pundits are going so far as to talk of a Democratic rout in the house and senate, with a mandate for change coming from the electorate. The wave of anger and discontent is strong among the voters, and McCain is unfortunately in the way. This view assumes nothing will happen in the next fifteen days to alter this momentum. I must be removed from reality to think the election is not over, or so listening to these commentators would imply.

Palin was on *Saturday Night Live* this weekend, and, coming on the heels of McCain's appearance on Letterman Thursday night, gives the Republicans some free ad time. I thought the Palin skit was funny, and although it may not sway people's political views, it was a risk worth taking.

McCain is now focusing his message on our wallets and how we better hold onto it with Obama's proposed tax increases. Obama is firing back by saying that anyone making less than $250,000 will see a tax cut, and that 95 percent of Americans will be the beneficiaries of this. I think back to Obama's recent exchange with Joe the Plumber, and his comment about spreading the wealth around being a good thing. On the surface, this may sound enticing to a lot of people, but the fundamental issue is where the tax increases go. I am okay with any hikes going to help lower-earning individuals, being applied to reduce the deficit, or used to shore up our Social Security system, but it strikes a nerve with me when it is suggested that a tax credit to people who pay no tax will be the recipients. I am all for sharing, but less enthusiastic about it when it is going to non-taxpayers. I know this may sound cold, but at some point individuals have to take responsibility and try to improve their lot in life. I am aware there is a percentage of people who truly warrant our assistance, and I am fully committed for us helping them in whatever way is necessary. The problem is that the number eligible for this assistance usually trends up as people game the system, regardless of which party is running Washington. We all can probably cite instances where we know of such occurrences, and in some of these cases the recipients actually boast of their circumstances. I wonder how many of these individuals on assistance are using their iphones to make calls, or their ipods to listen to music. I'm not pointing a menacing finger at Apple, so I don't need Mr Jobs scolding me as he reads this. I love their products, but I'm merely drawing an analogy that seems to contradict what certain people's priorities should be. In my opinion, "spreading the wealth" will only encourage people on assistance to remain on it indefinitely, and increase the entitlement burden for taxpayers to shoulder. It took an innocent guy like Joe the Plumber to raise this issue and give McCain something to build off of. I would expect the Republicans to push hard at this issue in the remaining days and force Obama and the Democrats to play some defense for a change.

It annoyed me the way the media attacked Joe the Plumber by delving into his personal life to see what they could uncover. This guy did not ask for the spotlight; rather, Obama gave it to him. This episode reinforces the media's bias toward Obama, which borders on protectionism. I cannot remember any election where this bias was so obvious. It should also strike fear in each of us because it shows that no one is immune from the public spotlight, and if someone has a bone to pick with you or disagrees with your views, they can delve into your personal life to try and dig up any speck of negativity they can find, and perform their own selective edit to form a perception of us that is totally inaccurate and bears little if any semblance to who we really are. None of us is ready for sainthood, and I would challenge anyone who thinks his or her complete life story is devoid of anything he or she might regret.

OPEC announced this weekend that they are going to hold an emergency meeting in Vienna on the twenty-fourth of October to discuss output in the face of falling oil prices. Chakib Khelil, the group's president, said OPEC oil producers will cut oil supplies at this meeting and the reduction will be significant. I would expect this meeting to thrust our energy policy back onto the front page of the election news and force the candidates to discuss this topic in more detail. McCain and Palin should thank OPEC for this decision, since most voters view the Republican ticket as being stronger on the issue. It was not that long ago that gasoline prices were $4 per gallon, and a gentle reminder that the current drop in price is temporary may be a potent campaign issue once again.

I have not given much thought to the controversy surrounding ACORN, although it is gathering more steam as a potential issue. I know this organization has been actively canvassing to register voters and that the center of the controversy seems to be in Ohio. Coincidentally, this is the state that has seen its share of issues in prior elections, and one where a few thousand votes could determine which column its twenty electoral votes go to. Something sounds fishy about this organization; however, I do not know enough about the specifics yet to render an opinion. I would be offended if voter fraud was uncovered, and if our election was decided by this type of activity. I thought we were beyond "hanging Chad" issues, and, for a country that bills itself as the cradle of democracy, such issues should be non existent.

One other issue that is garnering some discussion is the threat of a terrorist strike during our transition of power. The FBI has some credible information it wants to share with both candidates about the potential threat, to avoid openings to our enemies as a new administration takes over. I am curious to see how much airtime this story receives, since my initial reaction is it would benefit McCain. While on the topic of terrorism, I'm always interested to hear what commentators have to say about profiling. We know that profiling is dangerous, and that there are many dark sides to this practice. I agree its's wrong, but let's be careful not to tip the pendulum so far to the other side that we tie the hands of those who are entrusted to protect us, and prevent our noble law enforcement agencies from doing their jobs. Let common sense enter the equation. Whether we admit it or not, profiling goes on everyday in all walks of life, whether employers screening prospective employees, single individuals looking for a dating partner, or a bank deciding who they'll provide a loan to. I feel fairly confident that regardless your political affiliation (or even if you are a member of the ACLU) your heart would be beating a little faster if someone wearing a turban and was carting a box sat down next to you on the metro or on a bus.

Terrorism, energy, and wealth redistribution have emerged over the last few days as campaign issues. The economy is not going away as a major issue, but it may be joined on the front page by these other developing stories. Will McCain be able to seize these issues to regain momentum?

October 20, 2008

This morning was the first time this season I had frost on my car windows, a sure sign of colder days ahead. We turned on our home heat yesterday, which means our heating costs will be higher next bill. I like the in-between seasons where we don't need air conditioning or heat. My checkbook likes this also. I was hoping to squeeze out a few more weeks until Halloween, but Mother Nature decided otherwise.

OPEC continues to talk of cutting production, which would add to our heating bill this winter. Some of these oil-producing countries got drunk on their oil profits, and now that prices are receding, their cash flow position is weakening. The *USA Today* had an article on the front page about OPEC countries and what oil price they need to keep their budgets in balance. Iran has a breakeven of $90 a barrel, the highest of any of the OPEC countries. Kuwait and the UAE are the lowest at $33 and $23 respectively. Saudi Arabia, the largest producer, has a $50 breakeven point. Venezuela and Russia could also be vulnerable, given their propensity to shower petro dollars to gain influence. As the disparities in breakeven prices indicate, some countries are exposed more than others to drops in oil prices.

It is ironic that our recession is being felt by countries hostile to us, and given their oil-production dependency to fund their governments and their activities, they may actually experience worse side effects than we do? We tend to focus on our oil-importing dependency and overlook the other side of this equation. If we truly want to punish Iran and Venezuela, then why not create an energy policy weaning us off dependency on foreign oil? Their economies are so dependent on Petro dollars that they have no significant substitute with which to balance their budgets. Simple math dictates that, as revenues drop, expenses need to drop as well. We do not practice this discipline in the U.S. because we have foreign investors willing to fund our excess spending. The Petro states do not have this luxury; thus, they need to keep the spigot open. OPEC may unite and say they want to stabilize prices at a certain level, but which countries will reduce output to force the price up? Will Iran or Venezuela cut production, or will they continue to maximize their output? Their influence is built upon spreading dollars to neighboring regimes or terrorist organizations to curry favors. This type of allegiance works both ways, and their fragile relationships can dissipate quickly if they need to rein in their spending. We don't need armies to wreak havoc on these countries; they will bring it on themselves, as their own infrastructure crumbles amid falling oil revenues. Their regimes and leadership are hollow, and are exposed in a climate of lower energy costs. The current situation may only be a temporary reprieve if demand increases, although China's economy seems to be slowing as well and affecting world demand. An effective energy policy by our lawmakers would provide us with a significant weapon to combat these regimes. We do not need to shed American blood on the battlefield and spend hundreds of billions on defense when effective use of these dollars can protect our interests. National security is linked to our energy policy, and let us hope the next administration makes this a top priority.

The polls show some tightening, although they still point toward an Obama victory. Financial markets appear stable this morning, and if this relative calm stays for a couple of weeks, the McCain campaign should benefit. They have been up against it the last few weeks, and they need this calm to resurrect their hopes of winning on November fourth. Some pundits are saying it is too late, and that Obama can rebut any McCain momentum with his sizeable war chest. This strategy is obviously one the Obama camp counted on when they opted out of federal matching funds, and they are positioned to open their wallets and spread the green around to put the finishing touches on this election.

Markets are behaving today, with the Dow and S&P both up over 2 percent at noon. Foreign markets all closed in the green today. There are signs the credit markets are starting to thaw, but companies and investors prefer to see more traction on this before declaring it safe to jump back in. A report today said that the U.S. IPO market has gone ten weeks since a company has held an IPO, a record-setting stretch of inactivity that began back in August.

As the financial crisis continues, some businesses continue to get creative to lure customers. One Texas car dealership has offered fifty shares of GM stock for a new car buyer. Given GM's current stock price, this only equates to about $325, but it is in addition to any incentives offered on the vehicle. I like the strategy to offer something different, since businesses are being forced to be creative to generate sales. More businesses should pursue these types of strategies, versus the common belt-tightening on the expense line. It is easier for me to say this since I am not a small business owner, but sometimes a contrarian strategy might prove beneficial. With a little luck, we could see some small businesses usher in new strategies that jump-start certain segments of consumer spending. Once this crisis passes, these businesses would have an advantage over their competitors, most notably in customer loyalty. If they can attract and retain customers in this environment, they are doing something right.

Bernanke commented today that consideration of a second fiscal stimulus package by congress seems appropriate. This green light should embolden policymakers, and I would expect talk of such to gain momentum. He also hinted at another rate cut at the Fed's meeting next week. I continue to wonder when this stimulus will begin to show positive side effects. We had a $150 billion stimulus package earlier this year, a $700 billion rescue program a month ago, we have a low federal funds rate of 1.5 percent likely to be lowered next week, and now another possible stimulus package. All this medicine has failed to heal the patient, which once again highlights the dire crisis we are in. When things do improve, I would expect all of this built-in stimulus to jolt the system, with some level of tightening needed to stop the runaway inflation train.

Palin's appearance on *Saturday Night Live* drew an audience of 17 million for the first half hour. Only two shows in prime time the prior week had bigger audiences. This free advertising spared the use of precious dollars, and may have been a contributor to a poll movement showing a McCain lift. He is still behind, but his team can draw comfort from the fact that the poll moved in his direction.

Obama drew crowds of 100,000 and 75,000 in Saint Louis and Kansas City this past weekend, unusually high numbers for a campaign in Missouri. This battleground state has moved in Obama's direction, and this appearance may have put the state away for him.

Obama continues to outspend McCain by huge margins in other battleground states, keeping up the pressure he has been relentless in applying. It appears he is going to use every dollar at his disposal to vanquish his opponent. This is legal, and I do not fault his campaign for using this to its advantage. I may not agree with spending this much on a campaign, but a presidential election is the ultimate contest in which one can compete.

Job cuts continue to make the news, with Merrill Lynch's CEO mentioning job cuts to achieve savings targets in their acquisition by Bank of America. Retail stores are talking about cutting back on part-time holiday hiring, which makes sense with the gloomy predictions of holiday season spending.

A recent poll indicated one-third of workers are worried about losing their jobs. This same poll indicated a 25 percent approval rating for Bush, with congress' approval rating at 11 percent. Against this background of an unhappy electorate, an economy that is probably in recession, and a huge money advantage, Obama should be swamping McCain. The Republican is a long shot to win, but he still has life. Maybe the power of Joe the Plumber's appeal, along with Obama's "spreading the wealth" comment have provided a rare opportunity for McCain with fifteen days to go.

The market ended up over four hundred points today on signs of a reviving credit market. Investors are more optimistic as bank-to-bank lending rates continue to ease, and there is also less demand for the safe haven of treasury bills. Throw onto this further fed rate cuts and a second stimulus package, and the market has nowhere to go but up. Recent volatility has taught us that upticks can be fleeting, with a quick reversal to the downside wiping out short-lived gains.

There are ten trading days left until the election, and the Republicans need a continuation of today's upward movement to get people feeling better about their own economic situation. We have short memories, and we tend to allow current situations to dictate our mood. There is no denying the bludgeoning investors took over the last month, with voters' moods mirroring this anger. A rally until Election Day might move the needle some, and as much as McCain took a beating as the market dropped, he could be the recipient of a reverse market movement.

McCain is starting to zero in on Obama's liberal record, and he is trying to capitalize on his opponent's "spread the wealth" philosophy. It may be too late to change the eventual outcome, but an improving market may cause people to revisit their thinking. McCain has been left for dead before, as recently as the early stages of the Republican primary season. This is déjà-vu for him, and he has learned it is not over until the fat lady sings.

Obama is a smart politician, and he seems to have a top-notch team on his side. I would expect him to counter McCain's offensive by continuing to hammer away on his opponent's close relationship with Bush, and attempt to ride this point until Election Day. Momentum can shift suddenly in a campaign, and a candidate's safe lead could evaporate in a short period of time. Commentators and pundits continue to say the election is Obama's, but I think they may be underestimating the possibility of a McCain resurgence in these last days. Obama was called a "transformational" candidate by Colin Powell, which he cited as one of the reasons for endorsing him, and there is certainly a passion and cult-like following displayed by Obama's supporters. Republicans are not as flashy or prone to drooling as their Democratic counterparts, yet they consistently show their passion on Election Day by going out to vote. McCain is counting on this, and the question is whether Obama's army will display this same passion on Election Day.

Given the overwhelming advantage Democrats have in new voter registrations, and the significant campaign contributions received by Obama, it would be hard for McCain to overcome these disadvantages. Obama can spend heavily until Election Day to get his message out, while McCain needs to target just those states he needs to get to the coveted 270 number. His margin for error has narrowed dramatically, and although he faces an uphill battle, it is not impossible. We Americans have a soft spot for the underdog, a position McCain is certainly in now. I find myself rooting for him to come back, although I still have reservations about voting for him. I also have questions about Obama, which is why he has not closed the deal for me yet. Two weeks to go and this election is not over, at least in my mind.

October 21, 2008

Current estimates are that about a third of the electorate is expected to vote early in this election, versus 16 percent in 2000 and 22 percent in 2004. Voters in every state can now cast ballots through early voting or absentee voting programs. Results will not be released until November fourth, but Democrats have been more aggressive than Republicans in this process. Florida started voting yesterday, with reported record crowds heading to the polls and voters waiting hours to cast their ballots. Florida has 4.7 million registered Democrats versus 4.1 million Republicans. There are an additional 2.1 million identifying with neither party. McCain has to repeat Bush's performance in winning the state, since there is no formula for him winning the presidency without its twenty-seven electoral votes. My naive perception of the state is that there are three distinct groups a candidate needs to court: the military, retirees, and Hispanics. McCain should win the military, while, according to the polls, Obama leads in the other two groups. I cannot understand McCain's huge gap with Obama on the Hispanic population, since McCain went against his party in last year's immigration debate. I always assumed McCain would win the retiree vote, but the recent stock market collapse and its effect on retiree savings is influencing this bloc's leaning toward Obama. I am surprised I have not heard or seen more of Governor Crist helping McCain. I also haven't seen much of Jeb Bush, a popular former governor, stumping for McCain. I guess the Bush name is poison to him at this time.

I would tend to think early voting favors Obama, since the McCain momentum is just starting to gain traction. Then again, I would think that those voting early have been decided for awhile, and that those undecided are keeping their options open for another two weeks. McCain needs the independents to come out for him since the Democrats hold the advantage in voter registrations. This will be true in most states, since the Democrats have registered more new voters than the Republicans. Let me draw an analogy to the credit card industry here in that hundreds of millions of direct mail solicitations are sent to prospective customers each year, with most prospects tossing the offer into the trash while a small percentage might actually accept the offer. The real success rate isn't the acceptance rate, but the activation and utilization rate. I wonder how many of these newly registered voters will translate into active voters. We'll find out on November fourth.

As I think of absentee ballots, my mind wanders to my son who is stationed in the Pacific. He wanted to vote in this election, and I hope he mailed his absentee ballot in on time. I am not sure who he is voting for, although some of his emails give me an idea as to his leaning. Another factor I am weighing is which candidate will be a better commander in chief since my son will be directly affected by this election. Our military is involved in various conflicts, and although I understand we live in a dangerous world, I sincerely hope new disturbances requiring our involvement are few and far between. If we unfortunately need to get involved, I would hope our allies would do their fair share to help. This is not meant to belittle all of our allies, but why does it seem we are always shouldering

90% of the military burden. We're helping to protect their interests, yet most times we receive scorn as a thank you from their populace. I wonder how some of our friends will feel when Iran or another rogue nation has nuclear weapons within reach of their borders.

I received my hotel reservation form for the 2009 Penn State fall football season and was disappointed that they are sticking to their policy of a two-night minimum with payment due by the end of this month. Adding insult to injury, they have a 10-percent surcharge for the most desirable game, which next year is Ohio State. Given the state of the economy, I was hoping they would change the advanced payment-in-full policy, but I guess they believe that this year's successful season will only increase the demand for next year. They are probably right, and although I am not happy about it, I will bite the bullet and send in my payment. In their never-ending search for profit enhancements, companies sometimes look at float opportunities. I feel confident that the Days Inn has successfully mastered this concept, as evidenced by their 365-day float on my money. I better exercise some caution here in that I don't want them to pull me off the preferred reservations list for future years.

I would like to see a continuation of yesterday's market gains, and although overseas markets are up this morning, Dow futures are pointing lower. It would be nice to get our first consecutive positive days in what seems like months, and I know the Republican ticket is hoping for this as well. The economy will undoubtedly remain front and center in the remaining days, with the Democrats continuing to pound away on this issue.

The forgotten man of the Democratic ticket, Joe Biden, brought foreign affairs back into the forefront by telling an audience that Obama will be tested by an international crisis shortly after taking office. The McCain campaign quickly pounced on this to highlight Obama's lack of experience on the world stage and emphasize their own candidate's experience in such matters. I would not be surprised if Obama called Biden to scold him for these comments. Why change the focus off the economy and put the spotlight on McCain's perceived area of expertise? Biden has a reputation for shooting his mouth off, and the pundits who said he could not be muzzled are being proven correct. A campaign that has been so devoid of missteps now has two in the last week, each on the ticket responsible for one gaffe. Obama's "spread the wealth" and now Biden's bringing foreign affairs to the forefront were not expected, and I would anticipate the McCain ticket is trying to get as much mileage out of these as possible. A campaign that seemed on its last legs just a week ago is now poised to continue with their recent run of momentum.

Obama announced he will be suspending his campaign for a couple days to visit his ailing grandmother in Hawaii, and this absence should help McCain grab the headlines. I find it noble of Obama to make this visit and would expect the liberal media to emphasize his compassion at such a critical juncture of the campaign. I would be extremely impressed with Obama if he shuns the media while in Hawaii to focus on quiet moments with his grandmother. The media will be relentless in portraying his family values; the question is whether this message will be able to combat a hard-charging McCain. I would expect McCain to offer words of sympathy and encouragement to Obama and his grandmother, and I think most people would believe the genuine nature of this gesture. He could trump Obama's compassion with some of his own, and still hammer away on core issues that people are focusing on. McCain does need to be careful to stay away from any personal attacks while Obama is in Hawaii. I think such an attack at this moment would derail his momentum.

Overseas markets took their cue from the U.S. and finished down, as the Dow and S&P opened lower this morning and stayed there through noon. Investors are cashing in on yesterday's gains and are still cautious of this market. The afternoon session still has to play out, and given the volatility of late afternoon movements, a few hundred points shift in either direction is possible.

Media outlets like to do exit polling, which suggested that John Kerry would be elected president in 2004. I bring up this topic because, in their haste to get the jump on competitors, some media outlets release their exit polling to predict the outcome of an election. Not only do we get inundated with polls every day leading up to Election Day, but as soon as we finish voting, there are pollsters soliciting our decision. Like most Americans, I find this annoying and intrusive and prefer to leave the voting booth and have a few moments to reflect on whom I voted for. If asked, I respectfully decline, but upon persistent questioning I may relent and feed disinformation. My circumstance is not unique, and I would hope that this irritable and annoying exit polling process would go away. In their thirst to "scoop" their competitors, they swoop in like vultures over their prey, hoping to deliver the news to their employer, so they can intelligently tell us what is happening in real-time. I do not want to know; I am content to go home, have dinner, and turn on to the media outlets after the polls close.

The market finished down one hundred, thirty points, wiping out more than one third of yesterday's gain. We will have to wait longer for consecutive up days. Job cuts continue to be announced, with Caterpillar and Yahoo the latest to state their intentions. It seems that earnings season is the time for these announcements, as companies try to offer up expense cuts to offset their dismal results and gloomy outlooks. The holiday season is fast approaching, and the timing of these cuts will make for a less joyful mood in the affected workers' households. Caterpillar is a bellwether stock to many, since a positive economy is usually equated to their business doing well. I view their announced reductions as affirmation that we are in for difficult times.

Obama continues to feast on the sick economy causing these job losses, with each announced reduction improving his standing. He is feeding off the anxiety people are feeling, and offering himself as the candidate most likely to put the economy on the right track and generate job growth. This single important issue has put him within sight of the White House, and his relentless attacks on McCain's policies are the consistent refrain we have heard for the last month. His laser focus on this issue is impressive, and it allows him to remain silent on other issues such as national security.

McCain tried to bring foreign affairs back into the forefront today by talking about his experience during the Cuban Missile Crisis some forty-six years ago, a crisis which Biden alluded to a day earlier. I understand and can relate to McCain's experience, but this crisis was well before a lot of today's voters were born. Is McCain reminding us of his age unintentionally? I have not spoken about this yet, but at seventy-two he would be the oldest president elected to a first term. He seems to be in good shape, and it was encouraging to see his mother healthy in her nineties. There is something to be said for genes, with both my parents alive and well at eighty-seven and ninety-one years of age. I would be lying if I said his age was not a consideration, and Obama looks young compared to him. The presidency is a tough job, and I want someone who will be able to answer that 3 a.m. call in the white house. I must congratulate Hillary's team for that effective advertising pitch during the primary season, which was meant to get voters thinking of the crisis-management experience of her opponent. Although she didn't win her party's nomination, this commercial wins my personal vote as the best thus far, during the 2008 election season.

The market drop today was a gentle reminder to each of us that the economy still has major problems. Each time the market shows signs of life, we get a host of experts who say we have bottomed. Twenty-four hours later, these prognosticators are proven wrong by the market, which continues to exhibit a volatile behavior. McCain cannot shake it, and if he loses, it will be the defining issue of his demise.

The train was extremely crowded on the way home tonight, with a dozen or so fellow commuters having to stand. I feel for them, but I am not giving up my seat.

October 22, 2008

Only thirteen days until the election, but more importantly only about twelve hours until the Phillies open the World Series in Tampa against the Rays. Our last World Series appearance was in 1993, and I still have visions of Joe Carter of the Toronto Blue Jays sending a Mitch Williams pitch over the wall for a walk off title clinching home run. I want them to win a title for our city, which has been starving for a championship in any sport since the 76ers in 1983. Like most Philly fans, I am passionate about our teams, yet cautious in that we have been down this road before, only to be disappointed as another city honors their champions with the traditional victory parade. I want to believe this year will be different, and that this Series will usher in a new era of Philly championships. The Phillies being in the fall classic brings a rush of adrenalin, and allows us to escape the realities of the financial crisis we are experiencing. A few hours of baseball will do more for a lot of Phillies fans than what our politicians have done to try and fix the economy. I am sure there are Philly fans who have lost their jobs during this downturn, and absent securing a new job, a championship will be the best medicine they could receive in these trying times. They need a job to support their families, but they want a title to satisfy a hunger they have felt for far too long.

It looks like another gloomy day in the financial markets. All overseas markets are in the red, most down 4-5 percent.

U.S. futures are pointing toward a lower open as well. Earnings reports have been mixed, but most companies continue to be pessimistic in their future outlooks. This negative forecast is a pretense for more job cuts, which weighs on Middle America's psyche. McDonalds reported stronger earnings than expected this morning, which makes sense given their low-end prices. People prefer their burgers and fries at fast food outlets to more pricey mid-scale establishments when in a cost conscience mood. This retrenchment is consistent with an observable change in habits among consumers, as generic is replacing brand names as the products of choice. Wal-Mart alluded to these changes in comments this morning, which continues to highlight that this economy is still quite some time away from recovering. Companies such as Wal-Mart should thrive in this environment, with their upscale competitors struggling to keep pace. Job losses are sure to come from these shifting habits, and I wonder how many thousands more will be getting their pink slips over the coming weeks and months.

Foreign markets closed down 5 percent today, and U.S. markets are off about 2 percent at midday. They have recovered from steeper losses earlier this morning. The economy seems to be getting worse, and it seems as if we are talking ourselves into a deep recession .The presidential election is feeding into this frenzy with each of the candidates talking about the problems we're facing and how they are going to fix them, although they speak in generalities as opposed to specifics. The devil is in the details, and we are being spared the details.

The current administration continues to caution us on any hopes of a speedy recovery, with Bernanke's comments reinforcing this mood. There is not much to be optimistic about, and I am starting to believe that people need to think that change is on the horizon to improve their psyche and let them start feeling more optimistic about the future. The front page of today's *Wall Street Journal* said Obama has opened up a double-digit lead, taking a commanding lead among independents, suburban voters, and those over sixty-five. These were blocs McCain had to win, and to see Obama enjoying such a margin in these groups is surprising.

Most voters polled said that McCain is better prepared for the White House than Obama, but there are increasing concerns about Palin's readiness to be President. McCain's age is probably influencing this, since it is more likely that a seventy-two-year-old would have health complications than a forty-eight year old. He chose her to appeal to Clinton's followers and to solidify his conservative base, and the analysts are now saying that it was a mistake. I do not buy into this argument, since she is the one generating the enthusiastic crowds to combat Obama's rock-star rallies. My impression is that she has helped McCain, although she has been castigated by the liberal media who went after her with a vengeance. She epitomizes change more than any of the other principals, and I wonder if this is what scares the liberal media. Her conservative values are a polar opposite of liberal ideals, and for whatever reason, they seem to be afraid of her. The problem for the Republican Party is the economy, and nothing McCain or Palin does can shake the blame directed toward Republicans by voters. I do not believe the polls in that I think it is much closer. We will find out in thirteen days.

McCain is stumping more in my home state, although these same polls indicate he trails by ten points or so in Pennsylvania. I thought Obama's infamous "cling to guns and religion" would come back to haunt him, and with Democrat

John Murtha singing the same tune the last couple days, I am surprised voters have not shifted more to McCain. Bush failed to carry Pennsylvania in 2000 and 2004, although he came close in the last election. My discussions with voters indicate a close contest in the Keystone State. We will see if my personal poll is more accurate than the scientific polls.

The Dow closed down more than five hundred points, another rough day for my wallet. This market remains in panic mode, with any negative information triggering severe downward movements. Yesterday and today's losses more than offset Monday's gains. These losses are being felt by everyone, and in all sectors. One group feeling heavy pressure is pension funds, which invest in equities, commodities, real estate, and private equity to diversify their investments. Each of these asset classes is being rocked, and as losses pile up, companies will be forced to increase their pension contributions to offset their liability obligations. The latter is mostly fixed, while the assets are dropping precipitously, causing shortfalls. Companies are already being pressured on earnings, and additional contributions will put additional pressure on the bottom line. The taxpayers may be asked to fund this shortage in certain instances, for example, if state and local municipalities need to raise taxes to offset shortfalls in asset returns. We will be asked to support this funding shortfall, while the affected workers will continue to receive their fixed benefits. Teachers are usually covered under these types of pension plans as well, and it will be hard for us to accept higher taxes while home values continue to plummet. Wealth can be destroyed in many ways, either through existing asset losses or less discretionary income through higher taxes. As I think about it more, I start to appreciate all of the tentacles this crisis has, and how it affects much more than what we might normally think. All facets of our society are affected, and there's no place to hide. This crisis seems to be getting worse, not better.

Another poor day for the markets is another good day for the Democratic ticket. Today's 4-percent drop will give Obama and Biden more ammunition for blaming the Republicans for causing this crisis. They repeat the same lines every day, and voters respond to this by venting anger at McCain. Never before do I remember when a crisis of this magnitude occurred at so pivotal a point in an election. We are not hearing a debate on education, immigration, Iraq, or even Social Security. Every issue is swamped by the economy and its woes.

An AP presidential poll came out this evening and said that the race has tightened to a one-point margin for Obama over McCain with likely voters. This is in direct contrast to the ABC/*Wall Street Journal* survey, and leads one to wonder what is believable with these polls. I felt it was closer than the *Wall Street Journal* survey, although I did not think it was the virtual dead heat that the AP says. The AP poll showed McCain gaining among whites and those making below $50,000. I can understand McCain's pickup with these voters making less than $50,000, because these individuals are working hard to make ends meet, and they are extremely sensitive to people paying no taxes and living under an entitlement safety net, which is what "spreading the wealth" implies. They chose to work and not take a handout, and they expect others to do likewise. Joe the Plumber has provided a lift to McCain.

The weather has gotten cold this week. It feels like someone turned on the cold switch. I am wearing a topcoat to work now, which I will probably be doing for another four or five months. One clothing brand that seems to be the choice of many people is NorthFace, which is easy to ascertain, given its identifiable logo. I'm not sure what this brand has that competitors don't, but it definitely has brand awareness. I would expect this economy to challenge their continued revenue stream, unless of course the need to wear a NorthFace trumps a bad economy. If parents are making the decisions, I would expect to see less of these in the future. Daylight gets shorter now, as we get closer to the holidays. It usually gets festive as the holidays approach, with decorations popping up seemingly overnight. The only remnants I have seen so far were in greeting card stores, but I am sure that will change soon. More than ever this year, people will need that holiday spark to provide an uplifting feeling. We all have neighbors who try to put up their eye-grabbing holiday displays each year, but I'll bet this year we have less Griswalds than in prior years. This has been a difficult year, more so over the past month or so. I started writing this book a little over a month ago, and I could never have imagined that the crisis we are experiencing would have mushroomed to this level. It is not just the evaporation of wealth in the markets that has affected people's lives, but it is also how this crisis has turned people's lives upside down through actual or threatened job losses and a fear about what the future holds. People are afraid, and their habits are changing to confront this deteriorating economy, and I see more frequent usage of the "D" word.

Governments around the world have intervened to help their own economies, and we are seeing unprecedented steps to contain the damage. It continues to spread, and against this backdrop, we have our presidential contest in full swing. People are hurting and angry, and the election presents an opportunity to vent their frustrations. Each candidate is promising the change we want and need, and loyal followers are jumping on their bandwagon to help them win the election prize. I'm not sure voters fully understand what change each of the candidates is offering, but we're being promised such nebulous change nonetheless by both candidates. The winner is going to have a tremendous burden, yet also a tremendous opportunity to make his mark starting on day one.

I need to get my mind away from work and the economy, so I am planning on watching my Phillies tonight. The team that wins game one has gone on to win the World Series ten out of the last eleven years. I hope the Phils win and this trend continues.

I stayed up until midnight to watch the Phillies win game one. I was pumped that they won, although I know they still have to win three more to deliver us our long-overdue title.

October 23, 2008

I thought I would be tired after staying up to watch the game last night, but I feel wide awake and ready to go. I guess the adrenaline from game one is still with me. Foreign markets are down this morning, and Dow futures are pointing toward a negative open. This earnings season still has a couple of weeks left, and all it takes each day is one negative report to send the whole market south. I guess the Phillies' win last night isn't moving the markets the way I was hoping.

A report this morning said that 766,000 homes received at least one foreclosure-related notice during the July to September period, representing a 71 percent increase from the comparable prior year period. Nearly twelve million of the fifty-two million Americans with a mortgage are underwater in that their mortgage amount exceeds the value of their homes. Many experts point to this phenomenon as the center of the crisis we are in. Part of the American Dream is to own a home, and banks and lending authorities were only too happy to accommodate this dream over the last few years. There are a lot of horror stories the media brings to our attention concerning this situation, and most instances end tragically as a family's dream is shattered when the reality sets in that they cannot afford to maintain their home. This must be psychologically devastating to these people, and it only increases their anger at a system they feel has failed them. The government has tried to intervene with various measures, and there are lenders who are proactively trying to work with these families to avoid having to take the keys to their homes. The taxpayers will ultimately pick up the tab for this, either through higher taxes to fund government programs or higher fees to cover the lending institutions' workout costs. It wasn't that long ago when we would see mortgage rates advertised at low teaser rates, with additional enticements, such as only having to make interest payments for the first few years of a mortgage's life. We've often heard the phrase that "if it's too good to be true, it usually is," and many people are in the throes of finding this sums up their predicament. I guess people are blinded by a desire to be homeowners, and they aren't looking more than a year into the future to see what could happen when their payments increase and they're trapped in negative equity.

There is unanimity in experts' conclusions that the financial crisis will be with us until the housing market stabilizes. The timing as to when this occurs is the big question, with some predicting a first-half 2009 easing, while others are forecasting a late 2010 recovery. The disparity in expectations reveals the uncertainty as to how much more pain we will have to endure. Bubbles occur throughout economic cycles, and history shows that when they burst, the heartaches begin. Economists are still debating the root cause of this housing bubble, with some pointing to the previous Fed chairman Alan Greenspan and his low rates and easy money policies. He has vigorously denied the accusations, and he's fighting to ensure his reputation and legacy are not scarred by a kangaroo court looking to place blame at his feet.

McCain is spending some of his time defending his vice presidential pick, which is detracting from his staying on the offensive. He needs to be talking about "Joe the Plumber," "spreading the wealth," and contrasting his leadership skills versus his opponent, especially in the event of an international crisis.

A CNN survey said that Palin's unfavorable rating among independent women has risen dramatically in the last few weeks. The report went on to say that this is a drag on McCain and what momentum he might achieve. I question the reliability of this survey and am suspicious of the motives of the authors. It is fair to question her credentials, but the same scrutiny is not being applied to the lack of experience at the top of the Democratic ticket. One is given a relative free pass while the other gets crucified daily. The media can form their opinion and bludgeon us until we agree with their views.

Many people thought Romney would have been a better VP choice, especially given the financial crisis that is on every voter's mind. McCain did not foresee the severity of the deteriorating economy, and we are left to wonder if Romney would have been his pick if he knew the nasty turn to be thrown at us. Time will tell if this pick costs him the election, and with only twelve days to go we will find out soon enough.

Overseas markets finished mainly on the down side, with Asia off more than their European counterparts. U.S. markets are mixed at midday, with early gains reversed as investors are becoming more nervous about the length and severity of the current recession. Everyone now speaks of not *if* we are in a recession, but *when* it will end. The formal government definition of two consecutive negative growth quarters has not been officially met, but the expectation is that we are in negative growth territory now. Given the state of the economy and the financial crisis we are in, I would hate to think what a recession is like if we are not in one now.

Layoff notices continue to be announced, with Goldman Sachs and Chrysler the latest to announce job cuts. The Goldman cuts highlight that no company is immune from this crisis, with 3,200 unfortunate employees about to join the ranks of the unemployed.

There was an article in the *Wall Street Journal* today about the striking Boeing workers, who have been walking the picket line since September sixth. They are receiving $150 in strike pay from their Union, and most are trying to subsidize the loss of income with part-time jobs. Boeing management seems to be maintaining their tough stance, as are union employees. Both sides have a lot to lose, with Boeing losing a reported $100 million a day in revenue, while employees are losing a reliable earning stream during these difficult times. It will be interesting to see which side blinks first. I was inclined to think the company might, but given the current crisis, I am thinking that management might believe it is better to ride this out even at the risk of paying fees to customers for delayed airplane deliveries. Union employees appear resigned to a long strike, but with the holidays drawing near and the financial crisis intensifying, I would expect some cracks in their armor. As friends and neighbors lose their jobs involuntarily, I find it hard to believe they will voluntarily give theirs up.

I had a business meeting at another AIG location this morning, and on my way to the meeting, I passed a BMW dealership at the corner of Wall and Pearl. I pass this spot a few times a week, and each time, I glance in to see if any customers are in the showroom. Since I started writing this book, I have passed this dealership at least ten times. The next customer I see will be my first sighting in quite some time. This dealership epitomizes the current Wall Street circumstances, with a lack of customer traffic reinforcing the gloomy financial outlook. All indications are that bonuses will be severely curtailed this year, and business establishments like this upscale car dealership will feel the pain.

The Dow ended up one hundred, seventy points or 2 percent on the day. The NASDAQ finished down almost 1 percent. Companies continued job-cutting sprees with Xerox announcing a cut of 3,000 jobs or 5 percent of its work force. The list continues to grow, with Xerox joining Yahoo, Merck, National City, Chrysler, and Goldman Sachs on this week's job-cutting announcements roster. More earnings releases will be coming out tomorrow, which means additional pink slip announcements for the end of the week. I hope the affected employees who have given their blood and sweat to the employers are being given decent severance packages by their employer. It's hard enough for them to have to hit the unemployment line, but it shouldn't compound by giving them a minimal assistance program. A company is usually given a pass on these restructuring costs by investors, so show the employees the respect they deserve with a good faith severance gesture. I think shareholders will understand, and it might actually position such a company as an employer of choice in the future.

OPEC's president said today that the oil cartel will be discussing lowering output at a meeting scheduled for Friday in Vienna. Oil is now selling for $66 per barrel, a level last seen in mid-June 2007. It is now more than 50 percent off its peak, yet the drop at the gas pump has not been nearly as steep. I think OPEC is making a mistake by cutting production, or at least signaling their intention to do such. The worst case for them long term is to have prices go up while we are in the midst of a crisis. They are going to force us to prioritize a strategy around our energy policy to counter this blackmail. A smarter position for them to adopt would be to let the price drop, and allow us to lose sight of the importance of a sound energy policy. We are so near-term focused that we would abandon our urgency and revert to our old habits.

Obama continues to target his campaign rally speeches about McCain's policies being similar to those of George Bush. McCain seems to have found his message of Obama's "welfare" checks to people not paying income taxes. Polls indicate this message may be getting through; however, the issue is whether it is too late. Obama is set to visit his ailing grandmother in Hawaii and lose a day or so on the stump. McCain is not letting up, and he will be going nonstop from now until Election Day. TV Ads continue to run in my area, so both candidates must think there is still some uncertainty over Pennsylvania's outcome. I want my state to be relevant in this historic election, and I have never believed the recent polls that had Obama with a double-digit lead.

I did not get out of work until about 8 p.m. tonight, which means I will miss the first four innings or so of the Phillies' game. I would have originally been happy with a split in Tampa, but now I want two wins to open the series. If ever a city deserved a championship it is Philadelphia. A victory would lift the spirits of the city and its surrounding areas, and provide a needed temporary escape from the real world. I intend to stay up again until midnight to watch the game. I can always catch up on some sleep on the train tomorrow morning. On my ride home from the train station, my car hit a nasty pothole that almost caused me to swerve off the road. Given the tough economic times, I would expect townships will have fewer funds to fix these road sores. Car repair shops should the beneficiary of this, thus I have found my first small business franchise that should do well if the economy continues to deteriorate.

As I think of the events unfolding during this election season, a few stand out as noteworthy. Obama has benefited from a financial crisis that is the only issue people are concerned about. He has been able to effectively lay the blame at Bush's feet and convince a good portion of voters that McCain equals Bush. It is a rather simple strategy in that he does not have to discuss other issues where voters might question his policies.

McCain's campaign has struggled since the financial crisis kicked into high gear around mid September. As the stock market dropped, so did his poll numbers. He seems to have found his footing after Obama's encounter with Job the Plumber and his "spread the wealth" comment. It may have appeared innocent at the time, but it speaks volumes to a philosophy as to how Obama might govern.

When you think about the possible ramifications of this governing philosophy, what strikes me is the long-term strategy of solidifying a base of support that could dwarf any other we have seen in American politics. If he is able to successfully transfer wealth, he will win the hearts and minds of the recipients, creating a very distinct and powerful voting bloc that would passionately pull the Democratic lever to maintain their safety net. Entitlement recipients have leaned Democratic before, but the higher entitlements will increase their level of passion and guarantee their voting preference. If the universe of entitlement recipients increases, so would the number of voters supporting this philosophy in the voting booth. This foundation could be a winnable building block for years to come, especially if they could find a way to draw baby boomers to their side as well.

Boomers are being squeezed in this crisis as they are thinking of retirement, and they blame the current administration for this wealth evaporation. This unusual alliance could set the stage for the Democratic Party to rule Washington for the foreseeable future. Maybe I'm over thinking and analyzing too much, but I can see a scenario unfolding where Obama and the Democratic Party could create their own wealth redistribution revolution. The sudden and severe financial crisis was the catalyst and spark that ignited this movement, and the timing could not have been better scripted by Hollywood.

Is it possible that Obama may just be in the right place at the right time, and has put himself in a position if he wins to make landmark policy decisions that will reverberate throughout America well into the future? People are suffering during this financial meltdown, and their anger demands change. We just have to be cautious in what type of change we want. A convincing Obama victory would energize his party and possibly cause them to overreach their agenda. They might mistake their victory as a call to drastic change; however, far-left influenced change isn't something middle-class America wants. We want jobs and an improving economy before tackling other pressing issues. Change that delivers on this will be greeted with overwhelming support and would provide the new administration with some goodwill, if and when they embark on more sensitive issues. What better symbol of change could we possibly receive than electing the first minority president in the history of our country? This symbolic change would satisfy people's desire, but I am not sure they are looking under the hood to see what they might be getting.

October 24, 2008

The Phillies lost last night, evening their series with Tampa at one game apiece. I went to bed with them trailing 4-0, tired and frustrated at their numerous missed scoring chances. The next three games are in Philly, so there is a chance they could clinch the series at home.

Overseas markets were off sharply this morning, with some indexes down over 10 percent. Quarterly earnings have been disappointing, thus far, with profit warnings coming fast and furious across all industries. This gloom over future-growth expectations is putting some economies and currencies under extreme pressure. Investors are pulling money out of countries in eastern Europe, Latin America, and Asia on fears that vulnerable countries will not only be hit hard by the financial crisis but may also default on debt. Since investors consider the Euro exposed to the vulnerable eastern European markets, it is trading at a two-year low versus the dollar. The British pound has dropped to its lowest level against the dollar since August 2002.

U.S. futures are way off this morning. They dropped so much that they had to be frozen at several points. The U.S. markets are poised to open significantly in the red, following the direction of their overseas brethren. Today is shaping up to be financial Armageddon, and I am sure we will hear phrases such as "panic" and "capitulation" many times over. Everyone now seems to think the world economy is headed for a long and severe downturn, despite the many government rescue efforts that were supposed to help avert this occurrence. Cash is king, and efforts to raise cash and de-lever is only intensifying the selling pressures.

The Federal Reserve is now widely expected to cut rates again next week at their scheduled meeting. There is now talk that the Fed may go where it has never gone before, bringing rates below 1 percent. If banks are not lending, however, it does not matter how low the Fed cuts rates. I almost feel a sense of paranoia setting in, because I find myself looking more closely at the environment surrounding me and being acutely aware of the side effects of this crisis. I was driving to the Trenton train station this morning and it dawned on me that the volume of trucks I see on the road isn't nearly as great as it used to be. I noticed this because I'm used to passing trucks to get into the exit lane for the train station, and then having to wait behind some heavy trucks at the light at the bottom of the off ramp. I would miss many a green light waiting for the trucks in front of me to turn. These types of trucks are one of the primary modes of moving goods throughout the economy, and fewer trucks means fewer goods being produced, due to lower demand. I'll chalk this up as one of my visual leading indicators that foreshadows tough times ahead. As much as I hate the truck traffic, I will greet a slower commute as a sign that things are improving.

Against the global recession, OPEC followed through at its emergency meeting and said it will slash oil production by 1.5 million barrels a day. An official OPEC statement read, "oil prices have witnessed a dramatic collapse—unprecedented in speed and magnitude." How hypocritical. I don't remember the same type of comment when prices witnessed a dramatic increase that was unprecedented in speed and magnitude. Something tells me that some of the OPEC countries do not want to be the one to make the cuts. Absent Saudi Arabia cutting production, the other countries need the oil revenues to fund their own spending. They want higher prices, but more urgently need the revenues. This is precisely the time that countries like Saudi Arabia and Kuwait can show their friendship toward the west and continue pumping at their current levels to help ease the burden of the recession. This would be a bold step, and realistically speaking, one they would probably be reluctant to take. I guess saving Kuwait from Saddam Hussein less than twenty years ago doesn't carry the reward premium we would've expected.

How will the candidates respond to today's impending bloodbath? Obama is in Hawaii visiting his grandmother, so the stage is set for McCain to show leadership in this crisis. I do not know what he can say to help alleviate the panic, but he has been presented with a unique opportunity to sway voters with only eleven days until the election. Obama and the Democrats have battered him over the ills of the economy, and he now has a stage to trumpet what he would do to combat the current meltdown. He needs to play offense today, and put Obama on the defensive. This is his moment. His opponent is thousands of miles away. Will he squander this opportunity?

Markets fought to erase their losses, and overseas, the drop was "limited" to 5 percent. U.S. markets were off their lows at midday, down about three hundred points. Armageddon did not arrive today, although there is still four hours to go until the closing bell. More job-cut announcements came this morning, with Chrysler saying they are going to cut 25 percent of their salaried workforce. This represents another 5,000 people hitting the unemployment lines.

I felt sorry for Alan Greenspan in his grilling at a congressional hearing today. It just seemed like yesterday that this man was treated with reverence, and considered to be one of the most learned economists on the planet. His words were treated as gospel, and markets felt comfortable with his guiding hand on the wheel. He now admits some errors during his tenure as Fed chief, the most telling was his admission that he was "wrong to think banks' ability to assess risk and their self-interest would protect them from excesses." Media-seeking politicians are having a field day with him, doing their obligatory grandstanding for their constituents. None of these congressmen would ever admit guilt or contributory negligence, yet they love to play the role of Monday-morning quarterback to critique others. Voters know their representatives are not blameless, yet they will continue to reelect their incumbents. If we really want change, we should not limit our focus to the top job in the land, rather we should vent our frustrations at the congressional levels more vehemently. What we need is a nice influx of successful business people to help solve the current mess. Don't leave it to career politicians who have never had to make a payroll.

Today's *Wall Street Journal* was unusually heavy, made so by a Century 21 "Fine Homes & Estates" magazine insert. I found it amusing with the housing market in the condition it is in and the severity of the current financial crisis that Century 21 would bother to spend on this type of expenditure. They must have had a prior contractual arrangement, or else they are in a state of denial as to how the economy is doing. There were beautiful homes listed for sale in the magazine, as long as you had a cool $10 million to spend on one. I am a little short on this type of cash at the moment; therefore, I need to pass on these offers. The very rich have not been immune to our current crisis, and I would like to see Century 21's success rates associated with these offers.

I have not yet heard anything from McCain today, so it appears he will squander any opportunity to capitalize on today's market conditions. Maybe the Democrats have even convinced McCain and his team that Obama will be a better steward of the economy and that he should remain silent on the issue. He still has some time left today to step up and be bold, but as the hours go by, I become less convinced that he will do anything.

Thank goodness today is Friday. This has been another brutal week for the markets. Job-cut announcements accelerated this week, and economic news gets gloomier by the day. Unless a drastic turnaround occurs next week, the month of October will go down as one of the worst performing months ever for stocks. This is not limited to the U.S. Every market across the globe is suffering. You could multiply the trillions lost in the U.S. by some factor to get a ballpark loss for investors around the world. Everyone is affected, some more than others. The safest place someone could have put his or her assets was in cash, stuffed into pillow cases for the last month. Cash is certainly king today, and people are hoarding as much as possible. Pawnshops should be doing a brisk business these days, low balling their offers to take advantage of the current environment. People in dire circumstances may be pawning items of special significance to get cash to help them survive. It doesn't seem right for someone to have to trade a memory for a short-term need.

The Dow ended Friday's session down three hundred points. While I was on the metro that takes me to Penn Station, I noticed a couple with a tour book of New York City. I could hear them speaking in what sounded like a German accent. I thought back to how it was normal to see foreigners frequently on the metro, but this sighting reminded me that I had not seen or heard foreign tourists in quite awhile. As recently as six months ago, foreigners were kings over here since the dollar had weakened significantly versus most major currencies. I remembered some establishments in the city were pricing items in Euros to highlight the dollar weakness. I wonder if the rise in the dollar has caused them to change their advertising pitch. Dollar strengthening, coupled with foreign market weakness, means we will be seeing fewer tourists in the months ahead. It also means we will be seeing fewer foreign purchases of real estate, putting further pressure on housing prices. Prior to the dollar strengthening there was a trend of foreigners gobbling up our real estate, benefitting from both their strong foreign currency and our weak housing market. I occasionally see advertisements for investors seeking to benefit in the foreign currency markets. This is another one of those investment spaces primarily geared toward the wealthier investors, although it has been spreading its reach to other income levels. I wonder how many have dipped into this arena, and are now regretting this move. I wonder if I qualify as a novice investor since my only dabbling in foreign currencies is through international stock funds.

Biden was campaigning in West Virginia today, trying to wrestle away a state that went to Bush in 2000 and 2004. McCain spent time in Colorado, while Palin was in both Pennsylvania and Missouri. These states and the other handful of battleground states are where the election will be decided. Some commentators speak as if Obama could win this election in a landslide and have long coattails. Obama is trespassing in Republican states, hoping to grab their electoral votes and obtain a mandate from the voters. There are not many 2004 blue states that McCain is campaigning in, but he and Palin are spending a lot of time in Pennsylvania. Polls have Obama ahead comfortably in the state, but I am close to the ground here, and I see a tighter race. If McCain could somehow win Pennsylvania and its rich twenty-one electoral votes, he could have some protection in the event some 2004 red states defect to Obama. He cannot afford to lose Florida or Ohio, however, because his victory strategy needs him to carry these states as well. The polls indicate tight contests in these states, which guarantees the candidates will be spending a lot of time making their pitch to these voters over the last ten days of the campaign. I would expect to see a lot of TV advertisements in my viewing area as well. More advertising dollars are being spent on this campaign than any previous election. Obama is projected to spend $250 million on ads over the last four months of the campaign to McCain's $110 million. To put into perspective the money machine of Obama, an article today highlighted that there are only two companies that will have spent more than he did on ads—AT&T and Verizon. Presidential politics is big business, and I shudder to think what the 2012 campaign will look like.

I have some work to catch up on tomorrow, but Saturday night is sports heaven. Penn State versus Ohio State and game three of the World Series. It does not get any better than that.

October 25th-26th, 2008

I spent a good portion of Saturday morning and afternoon in my local library doing AIG related work. I prefer to work in the library whenever possible because it's always been a place where I can focus on work or other projects without interruption, and because I save four hours of commute time, which I can devote to doing some real work. The municipal library is usually crowded, and I start to wonder if its operating hours will be affected by the weakening economy. I've always felt education is the key to success, and libraries and education have always been joined at the hip. What a pity if this library and others like it become unfortunate victims of this crisis. As companies think more about saving on expenses, telecommuting should become a more acceptable option. Some companies are active proponents of this, while others choose to stick to the old-fashioned philosophy of having their employees physically present at work. There are obviously times an employee needs to be at meetings; however, with the virtual workplace capabilities that exist today, many companies are missing out on expense-saving opportunities. Rent costs are particularly high in New York City, and employees have the added transportation burden to contend with. Many companies think of themselves as 21st century workplaces, yet they fail to offer the telecommuting benefit. Some are so embedded in their old-fashioned ways that it would be heresy for them to consider such a change. Each company has its own culture, with some willing to change the existing culture, while others remain stuck in their ways. Fear of the unknown drives some companies' thinking, with the perception that physical presence guarantees productivity. I have witnessed throughout my career many instances where employees spend ungodly hours in work, doing numerous non-value-added tasks. These non-value-added tasks usually require the assistance of others, meaning the sphere of influence on non-productivity is increased geometrically. Some companies reward their staff for working all those unnecessary hours, in effect encouraging this type of behavior. These instances give rise to unfavorable work/life balances, with many employees being miserable in their jobs. I do expect telecommuting to become increasingly more prevalent in the future, although it is harder to push for a telecommuting strategy when unemployment is on the rise, since employees want to show the valuable contributions they make to their organizations to bulletproof their employment. Change brings with it a fear of the unknown, with some people more willing to take the chance than others. So it is with this year's election that we are confronted with the idea of change, with both campaigns trying to convince voters why their candidate will be the true change agent. Just what type of change do voters want? Is it as simple as a change in the current economic climate, or is it a desire for fundamental change in the way society operates? As we get ready to cast our ballots in ten days, we need to decide what we want from this election. Voters' frustrations and anger are driving their preference for change, and I share this feeling as well. I want change, both in our current economic situation and fundamental change in the way Washington works; however, I do not want radical change that infringes on my core beliefs and values.

This election presents a unique opportunity to usher in an era of change, brought on and supported by voters' anger and frustration with the current economic climate. Obama is a gifted speaker and has a cult-like spell over his followers. He has been able to capitalize on people's thirst for change by convincing them that he is more apt to be a proponent of change than his opponent. Voters look at the age discrepancy of the candidates and draw a conclusion that the younger one is more likely to implement change. They look at the Washington experience level and could conclude that the longer politicians are in elected office the less likely they are to change. Voters also look at the color of the two candidates and conclude that real change would be electing the first minority to the highest position in our country. This last comment is a sensitive one, and people are hesitant to vocally discuss it. I think it is great that we have come to a point in our history that an African American is on the verge of winning the presidency, and I wonder if this is driving voters to his side. We speak of racism in our country, and the majority of people are beyond this prejudicial view. There are those who may feel that electing an African American would be the final exclamation point to ending the racial divide that was part of this country's history. A reverse discrimination may actually be at play in this election, and Obama is the beneficiary of this shift. In addition to the race factor, people have the perception of Obama's relative newness to the political scene as being more identifiable with change, and he certainly has been playing this up as he links McCain to Bush's policies. Back in 2000, a Washington outsider, who has now occupied the White House for eight years, promised us change. Did we get the change that was promised in his campaign?

This leads me to a rather contradictory conclusion in that I believe change at the presidential level is more likely to come from within the beltway, as opposed to an outsider thinking they can turn Washington upside down. An outsider needs time to see how things work and would be less likely to implement change because of the unknown ramifications of his/her decisions and his or her dependency on Washington insiders to show them how the system works. My profile of a presidential change agent is an insider who understands the good and bad of the current environment, and would be in a better position to more quickly implement change. The key is that the individual needs to be committed to change, and not fearful of ruffling the establishments feathers. In my view, McCain's age and reputation make him the more likely candidate to attempt to implement real change in Washington. The problem he would be confronted with would be a democratically controlled congress that could stymie his efforts to enact change. His own party would have its stalwarts who would challenge him on change as well. These barriers will exist regardless of who wins the election, but I believe McCain has the desire and understanding to have a better chance at making Washington work better. I've also concluded that Congress is where we are in dire need of an infiltration of new blood, and if we want real change we need to have a massive turnover in their numbers. These senators and representatives seem to be in tenured positions, and we need new thinking and ideas at these levels to truly confront the issues that need to be addressed. I think a CEO like McCain with a hungry, energetic, and motivated stable of new blood could really change the way Washington works. I know it's far fetched to think this will happen overnight in one election, but it needs to start at some point. I worry an Obama presidency would be more of the same and that we would see a congress whose approval ratings are barely above 10 percent become even more powerful and reckless in their spending. It's true that giving one party complete power with the House, Senate, and Presidency could get legislation enacted, however are we ready to turn the keys over to Pelosi and Reid and the type of change they might want to place upon us? They might actually reach for the type of change most Americans don't want, and that is a particularly worrisome path we voters need to consider. Bush has been a disaster for allowing spending to grow out of control, but he had a willing accomplice in congress. We keep throwing money at the crisis we are confronted with today, and we will have to pay it back at some time. The spending sprees have to end to get our fiscal house in order, and I believe McCain is better equipped to succeed at this. In addition I believe McCain is more likely to limit the amount of government intrusion into the private sector, thus allowing a system that has served us well to show us the way out of the current economic downturn we're experiencing. McCain also recognizes the spending problem and says he would implement freezes, except for a handful of programs, while Obama says he would take a scalpel to carefully cut expenses. Obama's approach sounds great in theory, but sounds like the old penny wise and pound foolish approach which would render it meaningless as a tool in saving the hundreds of billions that needs to be accomplished. I hear Obama's words, and I foresee a spending blitz that can only result in higher taxes to fund an expanding federal government. We need a greater focus on expense cuts, and I do not feel confident he will accomplish anything on this end.

I have thought a lot about this election and have come to McCain's side, as I more fully weigh what the future would hold under the different administrations. The words I have written have helped lead me to this resting place. Skeptics may say that

I was always leaning toward McCain and that my decision was made much earlier. I would beg to differ because my feelings of anger and frustration back on September eighteenth were real, and if the election had been held then, I very well may have voted for Obama out of this frustration that it couldn't get any worse. Over the next thirty-five days or so, I stayed committed to my promise of making the candidates earn my vote. The more I reflected on what each had to offer and what the future would be under each, I began to fear Obama's "spread the wealth" comment because of its implication that government knows best. Quite frankly, this philosophy scares me, and the innocent manner in which it was delivered two weeks ago has caused me to think through the ramifications of how such a change would not only affect me personally, but what it might mean to America's future. I'm sure there will be pundits who will immediately target my motives as being selfish, and rile on about another greedy American who doesn't care for those less fortunate. Let me remind these attackers that I have said repeatedly that I'm okay with paying higher taxes and accepting structural changes to programs such as social security that would negatively affect me. I have also previously said I will not accept higher taxes to fund an increasing and enhanced entitlement society. If you incent and promote a philosophy of dependency on others then you effectively kill the motivation and hunger that has driven this country to the top of the list. I think back to the modest start of my career, and the hard work and effort put in to get to where I am today. Nothing was handed to me; rather I pursued the American dream through my own sweat and blood. I'm not alone in living this story; rather I'm joined by many millions of middle-class citizens who share this same American journey. There is no common demographic that ties us together, but rather a common psychological thread that bounds us together. It had its roots over 240 years ago when a band of colonists decided to seek their dream of independence, and it carries forward to this day. Our duty is to pass this on, not to reverse course and succumb to a dependency state of mind. The country needs a psychological lift, and it is possible Obama would provide this. My fear is that it would be a temporary lift and that his idea of change would be driven by his fellow elected party members and their desire to grow government beyond its already bloated size. It has taken me awhile to come to my conclusion, but I feel comfortable with my decision. I have seen some polls that say there has been some narrowing in Obama's lead, and I cannot help but feel that maybe others are coming to this realization, as well. As I reflect on this, I realize that my emotions were driving my prior indecision. A worrying thought is that many others will be making a purely emotional decision, with Obama as the beneficiary of this rush to judgment. A "spreading the wealth" philosophy could be much closer than we think, and if Obama is elected, I can see this starting to take hold soon after his inauguration. Let's not be duped by its proponents lauding it as a fair and equitable philosophy, but rather let's expose it for the "government knows best" world they'd want us to enter. They will espouse the morality in going down this path; however, I will respectfully disagree and say that they should check their own moral compass, because this country's founding fathers did not envision this type of government.

Pennsylvania is one of the battleground states that McCain would love to have, and I still believe he has a chance in my home state. I saw Ed Rendell on a news program this weekend, where he sounded a little less certain of Pennsylvania being a sure Obama win, although he said he was still confident it would be Democratic on November fourth.

McCain and Palin continue to campaign hard in the Keystone State, and they realize the importance of its twenty-one electoral votes in deciding the election. This importance was reinforced as political advertisements swamped the airwaves on Saturday night, as I watched the Penn State and Phillies' games with some friends. This was a great sports night for Philly and Penn State fans, since both won nail biters. Their magical seasons continue, and I must confess that staying up until 2 a.m. had me tired on Sunday. I would gladly sacrifice lack of sleep for victories, especially since the Phillies' late night contests will come to an end this week.

McCain campaigned in New Mexico and Colorado, while Obama spent time in Colorado. The campaigns are focused on about ten states, now, and those states are where the candidates will be spending their remaining days. McCain will be in my neighborhood on Tuesday of this week, continuing his push to lure undecideds his way. He has not given up, and I sense his opponent is feeling a little heat. Obama is certainly ahead at the moment, but McCain's message is starting to chip away at the lead. The only thing Obama talks about is McCain and Bush and the economy. He has gotten a lot of mileage out of this, and I suspect he will continue to ride it until Election Day. Never has a candidate faced the challenges McCain has during this election, yet he is hanging in. Obama has not closed the deal yet, leaving McCain with a pulse.

The Eagles won today and the Phillies have a chance to make this an undefeated weekend. I am going to watch the Phillies tonight and keep my fingers crossed. I was twenty-six years old when my city won our last title, and it has been a long quarter of a century wait. My mother called me today and talked about last night's game. Her cable went out and she stayed up to the end listening to the game on the radio. Her passion epitomizes the diehard nature of Philly fans.

This coming week is the last full week of the presidential campaign. Both candidates will be making their final pitches, and they will be criss-crossing the country visiting the battleground states. Polls will be all over the place this week, leaving us confused as to what we should believe. It makes for good reading, but the only poll that counts is the final one on November 4th.

October 27, 2008

I went to bed early last night with the Phillies comfortably ahead and woke up this morning, getting confirmation about their easy victory. They're one game away, and I think tonight will be the clincher. That stadium will be rocking, and the poor Rays will be up against it.

Foreign markets were off significantly this morning, and U.S. markets are poised to follow their lead. McCain and the Republicans aren't getting any relief from the economy, and Obama will continue his relentless attack against the Bush/McCain policies of the last eight years. October has been a month worth forgetting from an economic standpoint, and it's only fitting it'll end this Friday on Halloween. One state that has a particularly interesting senate contest going on is Minnesota, where the Republican incumbent Norm Coleman is in a tight race with the Democratic challenger Al Franken. Obama has a comfortable lead in the state, and his coattails may pull Franken into Washington for the next six years. I wonder about the electorate in a state that could elect Al Franken, although I do remember they elected Jesse Ventura as their governor. This illustrates how frustrated people are with the direction we're headed and causes me to cringe when someone like Franken could possibly be making decisions that affect this country's future. Can you imagine if he is the deciding vote on a major piece of legislation? Worse yet, wouldn't that be something if a Franken victory gave the Democrats their magic "60" in the Senate.

Investors are bracing for a tough day this Monday morning. When I arrived at my office, I got up the courage to check in on foreign markets and on U.S. futures and found that the numbers had deteriorated from just two hours earlier. The Nikkei closed at its lowest level in twenty-six years (about the same time Philly last won a championship), while European markets were down over 4 percent at their mid day trading levels. Against this worsening financial crisis, Obama is set to deliver his closing argument in Canton, Ohio, today, hoping to contrast his policies from McCain, continue his message of change, and link McCain to Bush. McCain continues to attempt to distance himself from Bush, and appears optimistic that the race is tightening and that he has a real chance. Polls continue to point toward an Obama victory, and with nine days to go, there are still undecided voters to be won. The Democrats appear giddy over the prospects of getting their magic number of sixty seats in the Senate and also adding to their sizeable lead in the House. The Republicans are trying to hold on, but each day the Markets fall their hopes fade a little more. Obama could be sworn in on January twentieth with an overwhelming majority of support in both the House and the Senate. I am now shuddering at the thought of an Obama presidency, accommodating a Reid led Senate and Pelosi House. I don't believe they represent mainstream America, and the thought of them dictating a legislative agenda causes me to lose sleep. The damage they could inflict in just two years until the mid-term elections is frightening.

It might take decades to undo their carnage. Unfortunately, this possible scenario is being hidden by the economic problems we're confronted with, allowing the dangers of a Reid/Pelosi agenda to fly under the radar screen.

U.S. markets recovered by noon, with the Dow even for the day. Each economic indicator draws increased scrutiny, and this Thursday's release of third-quarter GDP will take center stage. The expectation is it will show a contraction in the quarter, further supporting consensus views that we're in a recession. The FRB will be meeting prior to the GDP release, and the majority of economists expect a rate cut as high as fifty basis points, which will bring the fed funds rate down to 1 percent. The Treasury is set to start injecting cash into banks today, solidifying their capital positions and hopefully spurring additional bank lending activities. The Treasury is now considering using pieces of the $700 Billion rescue package for insurance companies and the auto industry. It was only a matter of time before its reach was expanded beyond banks. The question then would become how many different industries and companies will be beneficiaries, as well as what the government's level of managing these companies will be. The number of banks getting a piece of the package has increased as well, with SunTrust and Capital One mentioned as potential recipients. Although receipt of some government funds should help strengthen a company's balance sheet, these recipients should pause to consider whether they'll regret this decision later.

The *Wall Street Journal* reported today that there were 2,269 mass layoffs in September. A mass layoff is defined as at least fifty people being let go at once. This was the highest monthly figure since September 2001. While the unemployment rate is at a five year high of 6.1 percent, a broader measure of weakness that includes people who have stopped looking for work or whose hours have been cut to part time is 11 percent—the highest in fifteen years. As these numbers worsen, which they're expected to, people's ability to pay mortgage and credit card bills will weaken. This will put additional pressure on banks as they try to shore up their balance sheets. Those who are unemployed or who have had their hours reduced are an important part of the electorate in this year's election. I would guess a sizeable majority of this bloc would be voting out of anger and frustration for Obama this election.

There are two distinct voter perceptions in this election. The first is that Obama and the Democrats will be better for the economy, while the second is that the Democrats want bigger government and higher taxes to fund growth in the public sector. Up till now, the first perception has cemented Obama's lead in the polls since voters overwhelmingly say that the economy is issue number one. With job losses mounting and the markets in free fall, it's not surprising that this bad news has lifted Obama's poll numbers. The perception of higher taxes and bigger government has flown under the radar screen in most voters eyes, but it appears that voters may be giving it some attention now. People are still very angry about the economy and their personal financial situations, but this rush to judgment may now be getting equal billing with the reality of what an Obama administration might mean one or two years out. McCain and Palin have been delivering this message nonstop for the last few weeks, and voters appear to be finally taking notice. The specter of Reid and Pelosi dictating the legislative agenda with an Obama administration creates fear in the minds of most Republicans. The question is how much fear it causes Independents, because they alone have the power to tip the election in McCain's direction.

The Dow finished down two hundred points today, with almost the entire decline coming in the last ten minutes. Analysts continue to say that one of the contributing forces in the repetitive downward march is mutual funds and hedge funds being forced to sell assets, so they can meet investors' demands for their money. Each day brings more investors throwing in the towel and wanting to liquefy their assets. I can remember having this same question myself at various times over the course of the last 2,000 or so point drop in the Dow. I look back and calculate that I would've saved significant dollars if I had pulled out earlier when my instincts told me to do so. My rationale was that I always thought we were approaching a bottom and didn't want to miss out on the uptick. At some point, this logic has to be correct, doesn't it? I hope it's not after another 20 percent drop. I feel for those who were looking to retire in the next few years and what this downturn has done to extend their working careers. If nothing else, I have learned to be more cautious in my investment strategy, as I draw closer to my retirement. In addition, I discovered a thrifty side of me that I didn't know existed. It's easy to say I'll abandon this new-found savings mentality when the economy improves, but I'm pretty certain some of my lessons will continue for years to come. I wonder how many other *born-again* savers will be resurrected as a result of this crisis.

The *New Mexico Sun News*, a liberal leaning alternative newspaper, printed its bi-monthly issue for the October 26 – November 8th period with the headline, "Obama Wins." This conjures up memories of "Dewey beats Truman" sixty years earlier. A story related to this said that Obama's team is already drafting their inauguration speech. If the latter's true, it once again speaks to the confidence or overconfidence the Democrats have that their ticket is headed for a convincing victory. This fait accompli was echoed today by Karl Rove in one of his commentaries, when he said that barring a major surprise Obama will be the next President and that it may be a landslide with long coattails for the Democratic ticket.

The Phillies play tonight in what will hopefully be their World Series, title-clinching victory. They have an opportunity to win the title at home in front of their passionate fans, who have suffered through twenty-five years of Philadelphia sports misery. Throughout the campaign, each candidate has talked of the suffering people are going through during this financial crisis. My fellow Philly sports fans and I have either been in a long and severe recession or a depression that's lasted for far too many years. McCain has spoken of Joe the Plumber in his campaign speeches, and I'm telling you that a Phillies Championship will heal some of the economic pains being felt by the plumbers, carpenters, and unemployed in Philadelphia. It may only be a brief respite, but it will be welcomed with open arms. It's ironic that the major city that has suffered the most in recent sports futility is on the cusp of winning a title in the midst of what some economists are calling the worst financial crisis in eighty years. In the same way that Philly fans will start a new winning tradition, I hope the economy reverses course and starts to show improvement. I spoke with a friend of mine who was going down to the game tonight. Even though we're in the midst of a gloomy economic climate, he paid five hundred dollars for a bleacher ticket. I guess some things are priceless. I hope his wife doesn't find out.

October 28, 2008

The sports gods are playing with our minds. The Phillies were tied 2-2 in the sixth inning when rain forced the game to be suspended. It'll now be completed tonight, weather permitting. We've waited twenty-five years, so one more day can't be that bad.

Overseas markets are up this morning, as are U.S. futures. We're due for a positive day. Whirlpool was the latest company to announce job cuts this morning in light of the slowing economy. Boeing and their union settled their strike, fifty-two days after it started. I was surprised it lasted this long, especially for the union workers who had to survive on a lot less than they were accustomed to.

This morning on my drive to the Trenton train station, I noticed my township police had set up a speed trap on a road I navigate on my commute. Some poor unsuspecting motorist had been pulled over, evidenced by the blinding police lights highlighting their catch. This road has had speed traps on it before, but I hadn't noticed in awhile. I started connecting the dots and concluded two things: first, local governments will be stepping up their speed traps to help balance their budget in this economy; second, we're nearing the end of the month and the local police are probably trying to hit or exceed their ticket quota for the month. In the same way businesses try to hit production quotas each month, municipalities reach to hit their quotas as well. My rule of thumb has usually been to not go more than ten miles above the speed limit; however I think I need to revisit this in light of the economic conditions, and the belief that municipal quotas will be going up as they try to improve their revenue stream. I surmise that states and cities will follow this strategy and attempt to find additional revenue. Anyone driving on I-95 beware.

The FRB meets today and the expectation is they'll lower rates. The ECB is hinting at rate cuts as well. More central banks are getting the courage to lower rates, given the downward pressure on inflation by lower commodity prices, most notably oil. Oil is currently trading at $65, well off its high of $150 reached just a few months ago.

Overseas markets finished up on the day, some by healthy margins. The U.S. market continued its upward momentum at noon, with the averages up 3 percent. Some experts are saying it feels like we're close to a bottom, yet most investors seem willing to miss a 5-percent uptick when weighed against a continued freefall. This is one time they prefer to be late to the party. GM and Chrysler are pursuing merger talks, and they're asking Washington for $10 billion in aid to move this along. If this happens, the big three automakers will now be the big two, and expectations are that sizeable plant closings and job losses would result from this merger. Given the Treasury funding of banks this week, most people believe they'll fund this merger, obtaining their obligatory equity interest. Fidelity investments, the world's biggest mutual fund company, is reviewing its costs and is rumored to be considering job cuts as large as 4,000 or 9 percent of its workforce. These companies make their money on fee income, which is tied to assets under management. They're getting hit with the double whammy of a down market and investor withdrawal requests. Investors pulled out a record $104 billion from all U.S. mutual funds in September. Other mutual funds, such as Janus Capital Group and Alliance Bernstein, have previously announced job cuts.

McCain and Obama continued to hit the battleground states, with both spending time in Pennsylvania. Palin was also in the state today, making a campaign stop at State College, which happens to be the home to Penn State University and its thousands of student voters. It's generally conceded that Obama will win the youth vote; however, Palin's visit is an attempt to limit the margin the Democrats are counting on. The weather across Pennsylvania today was cold, rainy, and windy, a gentle reminder that a repeat performance one week from today could keep some voters home or, in the case of Penn State University, in their dorm rooms. It's been assumed that the youth vote is a passionate group and that they'll show this on November 4th. I've been reluctant to agree with this hypothesis, and I think the elements may influence the turnout more than some believe. Obama and the Democrats have run an excellent campaign so far, but they can't control the weather, although they certainly have enough campaign funds to make their own stormy weather for McCain. The largest percentage of voters in Pennsylvania is concentrated in the Southeast corner of the state, around Philadelphia. My wife told me there were snowflakes in the area today, which is much too early for this winter type weather.

The nasty weather caused major league baseball to cancel the Phillies World Series game until tomorrow night. We're so close to tasting victory, and now we have Mother Nature throwing us a curve. I'm starting to worry just a little, now, since a seventh game, if the series were to go that far, would be on Halloween. A seventh game series loss would be cruel, yet so fitting to occur on Halloween.

Market volatility returned in the afternoon session; however, it surprisingly moved the market to the up side. The Dow leaped forward almost nine hundred points or 11 percent to record its second largest point gain ever. The S&P 500 and NASDAQ joined the Dow with percentage gains in the 10-percent range. Nothing fundamental happened today to cause this movement, except maybe a realization that the market has been oversold. There's a lot of money on the sidelines, and maybe bargain hunters reached their irresistibility level. It's ironic that this dramatic uptick occurred on the day that consumer confidence plunged to its lowest level on record. Layoffs, plunging home prices, and tumbling investments were the catalyst for this record reading, and economists expect the first two to continue for at least a few more quarters. I should be happy the market jumped like it did, but I realize it could move just as easily in the opposite direction tomorrow. I'd prefer positive movements based on improving fundamentals, which would provide a foundation for continued optimism. I don't see this necessary ingredient in today's positive result, thus my caution.

I continue to be amazed by the different margins in the various polls. Some have McCain must-win states of Florida and Ohio basically even, while others show Obama with a comfortable lead. The one consistency is that Obama hasn't trailed since the financial crisis hit in mid September. Joe the Plumber is basking in his new found fame, and came out to formally endorse McCain. He offered to campaign for him in his home state of Ohio. Poor Joe Biden isn't doing much to help Obama. He showed a level of arrogance during a Florida journalist's interview yesterday about Obama and socialism and, today, he defined the middle class as anyone making less than $150,000. McCain was quick to jump on this showing the progression of the Democratic ticket at first saying that anyone making less than $250,000 would benefit from their tax plan, then saying a family making less than $200,000 would benefit, and now Biden saying less than $150,000. This trend is upsetting, and does make one wonder where the cutoff line will fall. It seems to be creeping lower and lower, probably from a realization that their spending programs would need to be fed by higher taxes.

I realized I may not get a chance to vote in person next week because of work considerations. My wife is picking me up an absentee ballot, and the last day to get it in the mail is Friday. I prefer to vote in person, because I like the way the process works in my community. The line will be long, but it's nice to catch up with some neighbors who I don't get a chance to see much. Some will proudly wear their candidate's button, while others, including me, disdain any form of being a walking billboard for any candidate. On my way into the school where the polling booths are set up, I usually get a last-minute advertising pitch from one of the Candidate's associates and sometimes from one of the local candidates themselves. I can state with certainty that I have never had my opinion changed or my decision altered through one of these encounters. I would hope everyone has his or her mind made up before he or she gets in the waiting line, although there are probably some who are still undecided, until they actually cast their vote. I've already made up my mind that, if I get polled after exiting the voting facility, I intend to spread some disinformation to my interviewer.

I don't think I've ever had to wait more than an hour to vote. I saw a story on the news ticker that said some Georgia residents had to wait up to eight hours to vote. The polls there have been open since September 22nd, and about 200,000 voters cast their ballots on Monday alone. Another 1.2 million people, more than 20 percent of the state's 5.6 million registered voters, have voted early so far. This script seems to be playing out in other states as well, with Florida experiencing long lines of people intent on voting early. This election is truly historic in nature, and the increased early voting trend is probably due to the excitement surrounding the contest. A week from today, I'll be sitting down to watch the returns coming in and hoping that the rout some are predicting doesn't come to bear. I want the election to be close and hope that McCain is able to once again surprise the pundits. There's no senate or gubernatorial race in my state this year, although I will be voting for a representative in the House contest, as well as some state and local candidates and referendums. People will be paying much closer attention to referendums this year, since most involve taxpayer funding. Given the economic climate, I would expect most of these to be defeated, some by considerable margins.

Overseas markets will be opening soon, and most times they seem to follow the previous day's U.S. market trend. People around the world are intently watching our presidential contest, and polls and surveys indicate overwhelming foreign support for Obama. Thankfully, these foreigners don't get to vote in our election, although they're welcome to witness our true democracy at work. The Putins of the world will be watching closely, as well, ready to start their chess game with whoever wins the election. Biden's warning that an international crisis will test the new president shortly after taking office may prove to be true, and I hope our new leader is up to the task.

My wife works as an RN at a senior assisted-living community, and tonight she mentioned to me about some of the units being available. I started thinking that the economic downturn is probably causing some of the residents to search for new living arrangements, either because their investment portfolio has taken significant losses, their portfolio of dividend paying companies has seen a dramatic reduction, or their relatives who are supporting their stay have now decided this expenditure is too rich given their own deteriorating financial condition. This is an unenviable situation for all affected parties, and I would expect, if conditions continue to worsen, we will see many extended families under one roof. This will not be limited to parents moving in with their children, since it will also give rise to extended stays for those in their twenties as well. I'm not criticizing this occurrence; rather, I'm highlighting another development from the crisis we're in.

October 29, 2008

It felt like winter this morning, with a blustery wind accompanying temperatures in the thirties. Overseas markets are following the U.S. lead from yesterday and trending higher this morning. The Nikkei is up almost 8 percent, recapturing some of its huge losses of the last few weeks. U.S. futures are pointing slightly higher this morning with eyes toward a fed cut when the Federal Reserve meeting concludes today. More job cuts were announced this morning, with Time, Gannet, and Motorola delivering the news. The unemployment lines continue to grow, and I fear this trend will be with us for some time.

It would be refreshing to see the market have a relatively quiet day, allowing yesterday's gains to build a foundation. The big move up yesterday occurred in the last hour of trading, consistent with the trends we've experienced over the last few weeks. This volatility is unnerving and makes everyone a little cautious about deciding when to jump back into the market. It's encouraging that some of the investment gurus are starting to comment that there are golden opportunities out there, with Schwarzman of Blackstone offering some optimistic words. Warren Buffet has already weighed in with his bullish comments, so maybe we'll continue to see other influential business leaders do so as well and provide a much-needed boost to the market's confidence.

The media continues to flood us with polling data, which has consistently given the edge to Obama. The election will be won in the battleground states, and polls indicate a split decision in capturing these prizes. The bad news for McCain is that most of these states were red in 2004, and a split decision would give the presidency to Obama. Pennsylvania is the exception in that its twenty-one electoral votes went to Kerry and the Democrats in the prior election. The Keystone State has become pivotal to McCain's strategy of winning the election, because it affords him some margin of error if he loses a Bush state like Virginia. I'm happy to see my state being relevant in this election, and I continue to disbelieve the polls that show Obama with a comfortable lead. Obama will be in Florida today with both Clintons and hoping to use their popularity to gain additional votes. If Obama wins Florida, it doesn't matter what happens in Pennsylvania. That would be game over and a Democratic administration in January 2009. Obama has purchased thirty minutes of airtime on the major networks for tonight, serving as a lead in to the World Series. Money talks and allows Obama to make his case to the American people in prime time. I don't remember any candidate doing this before, but then again no one ever raised $700 million to spend on his or her campaign.

Overseas markets finished up on the day. The Dow is flat at midday, with investors staying on the sideline until the Federal Reserve's announcement on rates this afternoon. The markets are holding their breaths, waiting to see if the Fed delivers on the rate cut already priced into the market. I fear a failure on the Fed's part to cut rates will have a decidedly negative effect to this afternoon's trading activities, which would set us up for a wild end to today's trading session.

Another side effect of this financial crisis is the amount companies will opt to contribute to employee 401 (k) plans. Not only are workers taking a pounding on their vested 401 (k) savings, but the expected employer matching will be less generous than usual. This is to be expected with lower corporate profits and is the risk behind a 401 (k) plan. Other defined contribution plans will suffer, as well, when companies cut back on their voluntary funding to these types of plans. These plans have been supplanting the traditional defined benefit plan as the choice of employers to more appropriately align benefits with company earnings. This is a logical transition for corporations, and the current market declines will only hasten their movement to defined contribution plans. Defined benefit plans have a formula-driven benefit calculation, and future benefits are usually funded by the employers. They invest in a variety of investment options, with equity markets one of their choices. As markets fall, so too does the value of the assets supporting the liabilities, creating a negative mismatch for corporations to cover. In up markets the opposite occurs; however, given that many companies were underfunded in their pension plans before the financial crisis hit, the gap will only get larger. Most companies don't have the earnings or cash to fund their pension obligations; thus, employees hoping for their promised benefits may be in for a surprise. The Pension Benefit Guaranty Corporation is a Federal agency, which provides a backstop to protect retirees; however, there are maximum benefits this organization guarantees. I would expect their commitments to increase due to this financial crisis, with their current surplus position moving into a deficit position in the coming year. They can increase fees they charge to companies with these types of benefit plans, but at some point, the corporations that are fully funded with their pension plans may balk and accelerate their own change to a defined contribution plan. The taxpayers will be left holding the bag, with another bailout the likely outcome.

GM announced that they'll be reviewing their 401 (k) matching, preparing their employees for more bad news. Given GM's financial condition, I can understand their rationale for this move. GM and Chrysler have been involved in merger talks, and a report today said such a combination could cost 25,000 to 35,000 automaker jobs. Hard hit Michigan would bear the brunt of these losses. Additional jobs would be lost at companies that supply parts to GM and Chrysler, swelling the total affected to some multiple above the 35,000 mark. My brother-in-law works for a company that supplies parts to the auto industry, and I would expect his employment to be in jeopardy if this combination were to occur.

The market sighed when the announcement came out that the Fed decided to cut rates fifty basis point to 1 percent. This move was widely expected and didn't initially drive the market higher. In the last hour of trading, volatility returned, with the market jumping up two hundred, eighty points but, by the close, it retreated to a loss of seventy points. The sharp move downward came in the last minutes of the trading day, reminding us that volatility still rules this market.

Obama and McCain continue to campaign in key battleground states, with the Democrat repeating his McCain-Bush linkage theme. McCain maintained his focus on Obama as a liberal high-taxer and big government spender. He also tried to capitalize on a story that the *Los Angeles Times* is refusing to release a tape it has of Obama and Rashid Khalidi socializing together at a meeting. Khalidi was reportedly a former spokesperson for the Palestinian Liberation Organization, a group opposed to Israel. The tape reportedly has footage of Obama toasting Khalidi, which could create some unease in the minds of undecided voters. This could be another defining moment in the campaign, one that could dispel the myths of Obama's friendship with questionable associates or create doubts about his relationship with Khalidi. McCain correctly stated that if it were a tape of him in such a situation, it would've already been released and played on every major media outlet in the U.S. This is an example of the double standard at play in this election. If the tape is released, and it turns out to be harmless, then McCain will suffer the consequences. Voters have a right to see the tape, if it exists, and be allowed to form their own conclusions after viewing it. This could reinforce one of McCain's arguments about Obama and his judgment. Democrats refer to this as part of a right-wing conspiracy to discredit Obama. Given what's at stake on November fourth, we should get the truth about this story now. If McCain's accusations are proven correct, one could make a reasonable argument that, coupled with his twenty-year relationship with Reverend Jeremiah Wright and his friendship with William Ayres, Obama has made some reckless decisions about whom he chooses to confide in. There should be no skeletons left in the closet for someone wanting to be elected to the most powerful position in the world.

It just dawned on me that the right may be brainwashing me. Am I falling victim to the same bias that I accuse the extreme left of inflicting on their puppets? We all like to think we're independent in our thinking, yet the more media we expose ourselves to, the more prone we become to believe their side of the story. It's impossible not to be influenced in some respect, with the key being how successful or willing we are to filter the information and form our own sound opinions. During this election, it's painfully obvious that Fox is heavily for McCain while NBC, MSNBC, and in my opinion even CNN are biased in Obama's favor. A click onto their websites or a five-minute viewing of their programs is all you need to feel the prejudices these outlets have for the candidates. The same holds for local media outlets, which often times take the lead from their national brethren and feel empowered to state their preferences in unabashed fashion. We're free to listen if we want, and we always have the power to turn them off at any time we so desire. I sense from some of the anchors and commentators that they're absorbed in themselves, that they actually believe some of the garbage spewed from their mouths. They view themselves as more important than the story and eliminate any sense of independence from their thinking. They feel their platform gives them a sense of power to speak and have their viewers blindly follow where they're being led. Unfortunately, there are some people who will be swayed by a certain anchor's words, and dismiss any chance that their preacher could be wrong. Fortunately, there are many people who see this scam for what it is and watch respectfully but allow themselves to make their own judgments.

My Phillies play tonight in a continuation of the game suspended from Monday because of inclement weather. It'll pick up in the bottom of the sixth inning, with the game tied at two. I hope this is the night we can let out a collective sigh of relief and finally get the monkey off our backs. I'm sure my mother and father will be watching, as will my one brother who lives and dies with Philly sports teams. I've never seen a temper like his when the home team loses a key game or makes a bonehead play. He's been banned from watching games at my house for safety reasons, and he epitomizes the Philly sports fan that will be living and dying with every pitch tonight.

Obama is giving a thirty-minute infomercial tonight on most of the major networks. Fox is carrying this advertisement before World series game coverage begins at 8:30 p.m. My initial reaction was that this media time would be extremely beneficial for Obama, since he has thirty minutes of commercial-free time to convince voters why he should be our next president. As I think about this more, I start to weigh the benefits and risks associated with this strategy. The obvious benefit is prime time access to voters' living rooms. The risk is that the nation will be getting Obama overkill, with some voters potentially turned off by this show, which will reinforce the money advantage he's enjoyed in this campaign. Voters might perceive this as trying to buy the election, and don't want someone assuming something is already theirs before the American people vote. Poor John McCain is on Larry King Live at 9 p.m., which will be telecast while the World Series game is in progress. He'll try to rebut the Obama arguments presented an hour earlier and contrast the differences between them. One piece of bad luck for McCain is that a lot of the voters in the battleground states of Pennsylvania and Florida will be watching their respective teams in the World Series and miss his interview. I must admit I will be guilty of this offense as well.

October 30, 2008

Overseas markets are way up this morning. Asian shares have surged, with the South Korean market up a record 12 percent and the Nikkei up a healthy 10 percent. U.S. futures are pointing toward a sharply higher opening after yesterday's slight decline. The big economic news today is the preliminary release of third-quarter GDP. Wall Street is expecting GDP to have contracted in the quarter, as concerns about employment drove consumers to be more cautious in their spending.

The Big News for Philadelphia sports fans is that the Phillies won the World Series last night. I remember that, when they won their prior championship in 1980, I was in Denver on a business trip. I spent last night in New York City, so I guess the moral is that I should be away from home if they play in the World Series again. News accounts showed partying in the city to celebrate the victory, but thankfully it didn't look like it got out of control. Philly fans have waited a long time with bottled up emotions, and I would expect the parade down Broad Street to be attended by a million die-hard fans. I've spent the last half of my life without a Philly sports title. In the same respect, my oldest son who is twenty-four years old has never witnessed a Philly title. He did experience a Penn State National Championship back in 1986, but since he was only two years old, I doubt he fully appreciated it. He's a passionate Philly fan, and I'm sure he's gloating to his fellow midshipmen out in the Pacific somewhere. His suffering has ended, as has the rest of Philly nation. Not working in the Philadelphia area has its drawbacks in that I can't share the excitement with fellow Philly fans this morning. There are some of us scattered around the Big Apple, and there's actually a few who work at AIG. Today is our day, and I'm not letting this pass with a whimper. I picked up a few dozen treats at Dunkin Donuts this morning for my New York co workers, and I proudly wore my Phillies hat as well. I hope I don't have to wait another quarter of a century to do this again. Maybe this title will jump start the economy, and now I start dreaming of getting greedy and expecting a double championship in football with the Eagles and Penn State. These types of things run in cycles, and once the dam breaks the momentum pours out. One title has made me delirious. I need to take a deep breath and settle down.

The U.S. economy shrank at a 0.3 annual rate in the third quarter, its sharpest contraction in seven years, as consumers cut spending and businesses reduced investment in the face of rising fears that a recession was settling in. The decline was slightly less than Wall Street had expected. Consumer spending, which fuels two-thirds of U.S. economic growth, fell at a 3.1 percent rate in the third quarter. This represented the first cut in quarterly spending, since the closing quarter of 1991, and the biggest since the second quarter of 1980. Spending on nondurable goods, items like food and paper products, dropped at the sharpest rate since 1950. Futures jumped after the GDP report, since fears of a much worse contraction weren't realized. Other news providing a lift are reports of a $600 billion plan being hammered out by the FDIC and Treasury that could provide guarantees for at-risk mortgages, offering much needed relief to homeowners.

Obama had his infomercial last night, and unfortunately, I missed it. I did see clips of it, with the background setting attempting to portray the oval office. His team has run a great campaign so far, and their motives for this infomercial were well grounded. I'm not sure how the American people responded to this ad or how this will affect the race in the remaining days. McCain was on Larry King Live last night, and due to work commitments, I wasn't able to see his interview, either. Polls continue to show Obama leading, and depending on which one you read, the race could be tight or a comfortable Obama lead. There's only five days to go, and the candidates will maintain their frenetic pace of visiting the battleground states. By all accounts, the electoral map is shrinking for McCain, and his success in defending red states will determine the outcome. The consensus is he'll lose some, and the only blue pickup he has a chance to offset these losses in is Pennsylvania. My home state has become pivotal in McCain's strategy to win the white house. Gettysburg was a defining battle in the civil war, and McCain needs to duplicate the North's success in this epic battle to have any chance of being our forty fourth president. Obama said that he would include Republicans in his cabinet if he wins the election. This outreach to undecided Republicans and Independents is an attempt to steal some votes from McCain and show a bipartisan approach to governing. I don't think those comments will sway any hesitant conservative to his side.

U.S. markets were mixed at midday, with investors trying to determine what the third-quarter GDP reading implies for the future. Markets have historically bottomed in the middle of a recession, with the subsequent uptick based upon an expected improving economy. Investors aren't sure if a long and surefire recession just started, or if the economy will be in a short period of contraction. Money will be won and lost on being able to predict the future, but for now, caution seems to be the prudent approach. Today, Exxon, the world's largest publicly traded oil company, reported earnings of $14.9 billion for the quarter, shattering its own record for the biggest quarterly profit from operations by a U.S. corporation. Obama and the Democrats have used excessive oil company profits as an example of the rich getting richer under Bush and playing to voters' emotions to imply they won't allow this to happen under their watch. I'm trying to interpret what this means, and can only conclude that corporations that are successful will be targeted for being such. I guess "spreading the wealth" relates to corporations as well as individuals. It's easy for each of us to initially sign on to this populist position of taxing the impersonal corporation, but let's not forget that there are millions of us employed by these companies. In addition millions of us own mutual funds which have stakes in these companies. Each additional tax dollar is one less to be spent on hiring, salary increases for each of us, dividends, and even charitable contributions to deserving organizations.

The roll call of companies announcing job cuts continued today, with American Express indicating they'll be slashing 7,000 jobs. This could've been expected, given the migration of deteriorating credit quality from mortgages to credit cards. Companies such as American Express have been tightening underwriting standards, further limiting consumer and business access to credit. Stories about reduced credit lines for customers are normal today, as are initiatives by lending institutions to maximize fee income. This income stream flies under the radar screen in many instances and gets introduced to customers in tossed-aside terms and conditions notifications.

Such fees include over-limit and late fees, and in some cases are the major drivers of a lending institution's bottom line. These fees generally go up in this type of economy because of both customer habits and the lenders' thirst to offset higher credit losses. When markets recover, these fees will stick for a period of time, thus continuing to enhance bottom-line results.

The Dow finished up almost two hundred points today. The more telling news was that it traded in a range of less than three hundred points, well below the four-hundred-point and five-hundred-point swings that have become commonplace. I'd like to think this implies we're entering a period of stability; however, we'll need at least a week of mild swings before I'll seriously entertain any such thoughts. We've been through a lot over the last forty-five days or so, and it's going to take a lot to remove fear, as our initial line of expectation. This crisis has hardened a lot of investors and reminded us that there is a downside risk to investing. The housing industry is a prime example of the risks associated with certain asset classes. Many households are underwater in their home, and are now left pondering how to get out of this predicament. In some cases, the American dream has turned into a nightmare, with families suffering as a result. The government and the private sector are trying to help with various programs, hoping to prevent a bad situation from deteriorating into a calamity. Some people think we're already at this final step and that additional bailouts will only prolong the day of reckoning.

Al Gore traveled to Florida today to campaign for Obama. He and his wife made stops in Pam Beach and Broward counties, the areas at the center of the infamous recount. Most Americans remember the 2000 election and the "hanging chads." This story consumed numerous weeks of our attention after that election. It was eventually decided in Bush's favor, with many people angry it ended the way it did. There have been stories this election season about potential voting machine glitches with touch screen machines and optical scan systems. An article I read today said that for this election, 55 percent of American voters will be casting ballots via optical scan systems, up from 49 percent two years ago. One-third of Americans will be voting by electronic touch screen. The state of New York still votes mostly with the mechanical lever, curtained relics from the 1960s, while several small counties in Maine and Vermont still use old-fashioned paper ballots, counted by hand. It's hard to believe that a country like ours doesn't have more consistency in our voting methods. We should've learned from the 2000 election that the system needed improvement. Regardless of the outcome next week, American voters don't want a disputed election. This year would be especially sensitive, given the historical significance of the race. As I stared out my office window, I noticed a regal looking yacht on the river. The time was about 4 p.m., and what struck me was that this boat was all by itself on the river, with no other traffic to contend with. It had the stage all to itself for what seemed like hours, when, in reality, it was no more than a couple of minutes. I thought of John McCain, as I gazed at the boat, because it was alone on the water, with no companion ships in sight. He seems to be on his own in this election, with few Republicans wanting to risk being seen as his ally. One Republican from Connecticut even went so far as to publicly disclaim McCain at a campaign stop in his tight congressional race. Congressman Shay seems to be saying what he thinks the voters in his district want to hear by compromising his values to win the election. The power and prestige of serving in congress should have its limits, and anyone who throws away their integrity to win an election is someone worth voting against. I'll be checking the results of this race closely, and I hope this incumbent loses his seat. There was an article on the Internet about the presidential election and buyers' remorse. It alluded to the fact that some voters may be having buyers' remorse about their decision to vote for Obama. These voters may be having second thoughts about him and are taking a second look at McCain. Polls indicate some tightening over the last week, which the experts say is normal in an election. The only candidate over the last thirty years to come back from a polling deficit as large as McCain's with a week to go was Ronald Reagan in 1980. McCain quotes Reagan as his idol, and nothing would be sweeter for him than to duplicate the Gipper's come-from-behind win.

October 31, 2008

Somehow it seems fitting that the Phillies' World Series parade is being held on Halloween. All those nightmarish setbacks by Philly teams from the past are now being overshadowed by the Phillies' championship. Estimates of over a million people are forecast for the parade route, and my youngest daughter will be part of this celebration. Her school decided to close today rather than have teachers face empty classrooms. The city of Philadelphia considered having the parade on Saturday but decided on Friday to limit overtime costs for the increased police force needed to control the crowds.

The parking garage at Trenton was empty this morning. The combination of Halloween and interest in taking in the parade was a powerful motivator for people to take the day off. The train ride into New York City was pleasant, with plenty of legroom, since the number of commuters at each stop along the route was significantly less than normal. The weather is forecast to be in the mid sixties with sunshine, perfect weather for both the parade and tonight's trick or treaters. We have had fewer costumed visitors in recent years, but with Halloween on a Friday, I would expect a larger turnout tonight.

Although the economy is slumping, this is another one of those days where we can get our minds off the daily grind of work and the consistent gloomy news about the continuing financial crisis. Obama and McCain costumes should be favorites tonight. My wife always goes overboard in the amount of candy she buys to hand out, but my sweet tooth is okay with this, as long as there are plenty of chocolate bars left over for me to munch on. As is my custom, I will choose one of the masks I have accumulated over the years and make my usual rounds to a few neighbors and pick up some treats for myself. One of my neighbors always gives me a pack of frozen chocolate Tastycakes, and I hope this year is no exception. I'm not sure exactly how many years ago or why this tradition started, but I do look forward to it each year.

My wife and I enjoy seeing the different costumes and the little trick or treaters who parade around as they go to the different houses. I used to take my kids around when they were younger, with my wife staying home to hand out the candy. This was always a fun task, and I have to admit I miss this part of Halloween.

Overseas markets were down this morning, and U.S. futures were pointing in this direction as well. The Dow is off 17 percent so far this month, which puts it on track to be the worst month since October 1987. September was awful as well, and these two months will be remembered as a period of significant wealth destruction the world over. There were minimal bright spots for investors, although shareholders of Wal-Mart can smile, since their stock has led the Dow with a year-to-date gain of 15 percent. Wal-Mart is the only Dow stock in positive territory for the year. McDonalds is second among performers, but they are in the red with a 2-percent drop. GM is the laggard in the group, down 76 percent year-to-date. AIG, which was removed from the list on September 21st, is down 93 percent. I know that quite a few of my fellow employees have realized tremendous wealth destruction, as a result of AIG's problems. Some were counting on their AIG stock to fund their childrens college tuitions. This strategy is now in need of serious overhaul, and the lack of alternate funding sources may necessitate taking out more in loans, or quite possibly considering less costly schools. I am sensitive to their plight and try to remove myself from conversations about this topic.

U.S. markets were up slightly at noon, with European markets closing up about 3 percent for the day. Shares in Asia and Europe had their worst month ever, with investors hoping for a better return in November. Most analysts believe the market has priced in an Obama victory next Tuesday. Common wisdom is that a democratic victory will translate to higher taxes, including an increase in the capital gains and dividend rates. Bush let spending get out of control, and the consensus is that a Democratic victory on Tuesday would bring an acceleration of this spending trend for the next few years. I have said before that I would be okay with higher taxes, as long as spending cuts were being enacted as well. I do not want any tax increase going to increase the size of entitlement programs. One of my biggest fears in an Obama administration is that these programs could grow to a much larger percentage of GDP, moving us closer to a European model of more government dependence in our daily lives. The unfortunate thing is that Bush has opened the door for this transition with programs such as the $700 billion rescue plan. Democratic control of the white house and both houses of congress would only accelerate a movement in this direction. History may show it was begun under a Republican administration and expanded significantly under Democratic leadership.

Pandora's Box has been opened, and we may be entering a period of government intervention unlike any in our history.

We were so concerned with fixing the current financial crisis that there wasn't adequate thought put into the longer-term ramifications of the changes implemented. Legislators adopted Wall Street's mentality of a short-term focus, and in the process, allowed a normal business downturn (although severe in nature) to be the impetus for rushing to solutions. This was the perfect storm in that the financial crisis collided with a historical election season to force our legislators to make decisions to limit the damage. They could not sit idly by during an election season and leave the decision to the next session of congress and the new administration. Their hands were tied, and they opted to have the federal government clean up the mess. We will survive this crisis, but at what long-term costs? The next president will not have an easy job, but the phobia of government intervention has been removed from the equation. The level of intervention becomes the real issue and how amenable our elected officials will be to allow for an unwinding of government ownership in the private sector, once the crisis passes. I fear an Obama victory will move us toward massive government expansion. Once this process takes hold, I worry that government won't know where to stop. I believe the majority of Americans don't want the government telling them how to run their lives.

Obama and McCain continued their campaigning in a number of battleground states. McCain was in Ohio with Arnold Schwarzenegger, while Obama was in Iowa and Indiana. Obama's rallies set attendance records, while McCain's are in smaller settings that attract a few thousand. Obama rallies are like rock concerts, while McCain's can be likened to a family gathering.

On the surface, it would be fair to say that Obama has the more passionate followers, yet time and again, on Election Day,

Republicans have proven to be the more passionate voters. This difference is a major reason I consider most polls to be irrelevant. The Democrats can be likened to a team that talks a good game, while the Republicans usually play a good game. Something does feel different this time, however, and if the vociferous Democratic voters actually follow through and vote, then McCain and the Republicans are in for a long election night. One of the battlegrounds is the "show me" state of Missouri, and until the Democrats show me on Election Day, I will be a skeptic of their passion. Obama is still feeling confident and even a little cocky as evidenced by him spending on ads in McCain's home state of Arizona. A sizeable war chest allows this kind of spending, and if he is elected, I hope his spending habits with taxpayer dollars prove to be more frugal.

McCain has been preaching about Obama's tax philosophy and warning voters that the definition of middle class is a moving target for his opponent. Biden inadvertently reinforced this warning by saying $150,000 of income defines the middle class and, today, New Mexico governor Bill Richardson said, "Obama is looking at $120,000 and under among those that are in the middle class, and there's a tax cut for them." Even if Richardson is not speaking for Obama, it's the philosophy of democratic thinking that should cause us to question what the true income level for tax cuts are. I am not a mathematician, but I do know that the number of people making between $120,000 and $250,000 is a significant amount, especially when both spouses' income is taken into consideration. I'm starting to hold onto my wallet on the train as I write this down.

October is in the books, and the market closed out a horrendous October with a one hundred, forty point gain on the Dow, improving the month's dismal performance to a negative 14 percent (the S&P lost 17 percent in the month). This represented the worst month in twenty-one years. One piece of good news is that the positive gains of yesterday and today was the market's first consecutive plus days in more than a month. October was a wild month, with the average daily trading range from low to high of six hundred points. It also had sixteen down days, the most since August 1973. I like to use benchmarks wherever possible to provide insight into various noteworthy trends or items. I find these are very helpful when put in laymen's terms. Here's one for you to chew on—each one-hundred-point movement in the DOW equates to approximately one hundred billion dollars in paper wealth change. This means that the average trading day range of six hundred points in October meant six hundred billion dollars of wealth changes. How's that for volatility?

I was hoping to get home early tonight, but I left work later than planned and did not get home until after 7 p.m. The train was deserted on the ride to Trenton tonight, and the few people I did see were napping on the way home. As I stared out the window of the train as it headed south through New Jersey, I could see residential streets lit up to help the little ones navigate their way from house to house for their treats. I also saw a high school football field lit up for a game, with pregame drills going on. I started thinking of these American traditions of Halloween and football, and how these core ideals will continue, regardless of who wins next Tuesday's election. We might disagree over who will make a better president, but we cherish our American traditions. We have a lot more in common than we think, and this bond will bring us together to support the next president. The beauty of our political system is that we elect people to work for us, and if they invalidate our trust, we can send them to the unemployment line. Nowhere is this more prevalent than every four years in our presidential contest. It energizes most of us and causes us to rethink where we want our country to go and who is best equipped to lead us. This four-year checkup is vital to our democracy, and our participation in the process is a necessary ingredient to ensure its longevity.

November 1ˢᵗ-2ⁿᵈ, 2008

November 1ˢᵗ-2ⁿᵈ, 2008

This is the last weekend before we go to the polls. The last forty-three days have witnessed events that some have characterized as unprecedented in our history. We have experienced a financial crisis that has led to the evaporation of wealth in both corporate and Main Street America. What started on our shores quickly spread overseas and spawned a global economic tidal wave. Economists had been theorizing that one of the results of globalization was that the rest of the world's economies had decoupled from the U.S., and that American influence had lessened. This current crisis has proven that hypothesis to be false, and may actually prove that the rest of the world is more dependent on the U.S. economy than ever. It is a shame we needed the worst financial crisis in eighty years to dispel the decoupling myth, but at least the question seems to have been put to rest. Unprecedented government intervention in the U.S. and across the globe was a result of this meltdown and leaves one to wonder if the baton has been passed to the public sector as the primary driver in determining future economic health. This may be a stretch; however, it will take years to see if this intervention is temporary or a permanent realignment. I fear that a Democratic Party triumph in a few days will usher in even greater governmental intrusion into the private sector. The irony is that the current economic crisis has provided the impetus to gain support among the electorate. We may be witnessing an unusual alliance among baby boomers, who are frustrated with their wealth evaporation as they approach retirement, and entitlement recipients, who are being promised an open-ended continuation of their current lifestyle. I think both are too focused on the short term in that hefty tax increases will be in store for all of us down the road. Income tax increases will hit the middle and upper-income classes, while the lower income class is in store for stealth increases, which will be just as lethal. Let's see their surprise when taxes on utility bills and cell phone services start going higher. Speaking of cell phones, have you ever tried to understand your cell phone bill? I pay it every month, but must admit I don't know what a "regulatory cost recovery charge", a "Federal universal service charge", or a "mobile purchases and downloads communication charge" are for. I wouldn't be surprised if some Democrats start whispering for a value-added tax (VAT) to help cure our ills. A lot of learned and respected people the world over have helped cobble together the band-aid approaches to contain the damage and bring stability to the economic universe. We have witnessed coordinated efforts among governments and central banks to fix the problems, and other global issues have been relegated to the back page as economic issues dominate both governmental and individual attention. Terrorism, genocide, climate control, and world hunger are as prevalent now as before, but the pressing need to resolve them has lessened, as we attempt to get our finances in order. These other issues are not going away; however, if a globally coordinated effort succeeds in stabilizing the world's economies, why can't the same collective strategy be followed to cleanse these other scars? Why can't the global cooperation achieved in this financial crisis be used as a blueprint for solving other world problems? Political motives will be raised, as a barrier to this idea, since other strategic interests may be in play, but logic would imply such a course of action is urgent and necessary. Individual citizens can see the problems and resolutions, yet our leaders can't or won't act in a unified way to seek global solutions.

Against the backdrop of this financial crisis, our country is in the midst of a historic presidential election. We have a lame-duck president who has not instilled confidence with his actions during the crisis, and we have candidates who are more interested in placing blame and distancing themselves from the current downturn than solving the problem. Business leaders in the private sector seemed to be as perplexed about the crisis as anyone, and they have further influenced a panic mood among investors with their own gloomy and pessimistic outlooks on the economy. This was a prime example of a leadership vacuum in one of the most perilous financial times in our history. Perception often becomes reality, and as investors see distress and panic among their leaders, it is only natural they too would feel this way.

Until mid September, McCain was leading in the polls. As the crisis unfolded and worsened, people's anger intensified and was directed at our country's CEO, President Bush. This shareholder wrath needed someone to punish, but Bush is immune from punishment since he will be leaving office voluntarily. Obama and his campaign were quick to pounce on this opportunity by marrying McCain to Bush, thereby redirecting people's anger toward Bush's surrogate. Once Obama got the high ground on this issue, it became his single biggest weapon, and as the markets deteriorated, his standing with the voters improved. Never has a candidate been handed such a Christmas gift during a campaign, and to his credit, he maximized all the benefits he could from this situation. His areas of weakness such as foreign policy became non-issues, and he was afforded the opportunity to play offense and keep McCain on his heels. Even the price of oil has played to his favor, as its drop has lessened the cries of consumers and relegated any discussion of an energy policy to the backburner.

Against this onslaught, McCain's campaign was treading water. Obama was able to deliver rousing populist speeches that did nothing more than pound his opponent and his alliance with Bush. Obama is a great speaker and orator, and to give him this issue was like putting a kid in a candy store. If the election were two weeks ago, he would have won handily and would have been able to claim a mandate from the people. Then Joe the plumber entered the campaign, and an unusual slip of the tongue by Obama about spreading the wealth gave McCain his long-awaited opening, and he has been attempting to maximize its effectiveness ever since. It has caused people to rethink Obama and take another look at McCain, just as the pundits and commentators were anointing the presidency to Obama. The frontrunner has seen his lead narrow; however, he still leads in most of the battleground states if you believe the polls.

Obama has been urging people to vote early to gain an advantage and eliminate these voters as potential defectors as we move closer to Election Day. They say that early voting has seen record participation, which should benefit Obama. The question is how many of these voters were undecided at one time and pulled the trigger before this recent McCain surge? I would suspect the early voters were diehard supporters of a particular candidate, and that nothing could have swayed their decision. If I am wrong, then Obama probably wins the election, although I wonder how many of these early birds wish they had waited until Tuesday to vote.

McCain's task is certainly daunting but not impossible. The fact that Obama has not closed the deal yet is a tribute to McCain's tenacity and people's caution about Obama. We really do not know what we would get with Obama, except a dominance of the Democratic regime in Washington. They could be given an opportunity to enact game-changing legislation that would be felt for years to come, and government expansion programs could be accelerated with the recent interventionist steps taken to stem the current financial crisis. Any of us hoping for a quick unwinding of the recent steps would be disappointed, and government intrusion into the private sector would be the norm as opposed to the exception. We have had economic setbacks before, and most times reckless investors were punished for their missteps. There has certainly been pain felt by all during this crisis, but government has tried to mitigate the level of damage. Experts say this was necessary to prevent a reenactment of the 1930s, and if so, we should all be thankful we will not have to live through that type of suffering.

Now that October is officially in the record books, a quick recap of the carnage is in order. U.S. equity markets had their worst performance in twenty-one years, with foreign markets feeling the pain by as much or more than the U.S. Japan's Nikkei slumped to its lowest levels in twenty-six years, and October proved to be a bloodbath for commodities as well. Crude oil posted its worst one-month loss in history, while gold had its worst monthly drop since 1980. Copper and aluminum had their largest drop in twenty years, and sugar its biggest monthly fall in a decade. We are witnessing a massive revaluation of assets, and commodities were hit just as hard as other asset classes.

Investment experts talk of diversification to minimize risk, but in this tsunami, cash was the only safe asset to be in. My foreign and domestic investments got pummeled, and the severity and acceleration of this caught everyone by surprise. November has to be an improvement, or else this holiday season will slump well below the already bleak forecasts of most economists.

The Phillies provided me and other Philly fans with a needed diversion from the real world, and we still get a positive jolt from their recent World Series victory. Life goes on, however, and each passing day draws us back closer to facing the crisis we are confronted with. The victor in this election will have great challenges and a phenomenal opportunity. As voters have felt the pain over the last month and a half we take solace in the fact that history shows us things will get better. The question is how the foundation will be laid for future years, because a short-term gain at the expense of long-term pain is not a tradeoff I covet.

While driving my youngest son to bowling this weekend, he mentioned to me that Christmas music was now playing non-stop on a certain radio station until December 25th. I didn't believe him until he turned the dial to 97.5 FM and, sure enough, I was listening to Christmas songs. That means fifty-five days of holiday sounds to improve our mood. I actually think this station is on to something because, after I dropped my son off, I found myself singing along with the tunes I love. It put me into a relaxed mood and had me thinking of all the positive things that come with the holidays. If ever we needed this mood change it is now, and with the holidays on the horizon, I am looking forward to better days ahead.

Penn State had off this weekend, and the Eagles have a late Sunday afternoon game on the West coast against the Seahawks.

This weekend is extremely calm after last weekend's multitude of sporting activities. I am focused on the election and anxious to see how it turns out. The polls are predicting an Obama victory, but I sense it's gonna be closer than people think. I keep thinking my state is in play and that there may be a surprise on Election Day. As I sat in the barber's chair on Saturday, the proprietor and I struck up a conversation. I asked him if business had slowed down, and he replied in the affirmative and alluded to return visits by customers being extended out a few extra weeks. We then talked about the election, and he said that in his conversations with customers, he thought McCain had a seven- or eight-to-one dominance over Obama. We are an upper middle-class suburb of Philadelphia, and the polls keep saying we are solidly behind Obama. Jim's poll tells a different story, the same one I have been feeling for a while. I mentioned this to my wife later in the day, and she said a visit to a hair salon with predominately women customers would provide a completely opposite polling result.

We turned the clocks back an hour this weekend, and although I will see daylight on the way to work, darkness will descend upon us before 5 p.m. McCain would probably like the clocks turned back about forty-five days to when the contest was close and before the financial crisis kicked into overdrive. When I go to vote on Tuesday morning, I will be greeted with sunshine and temperatures in the fifties. No excuses for people due to the weather.

A few stories of note came out this weekend, one concerning Obama's aunt from Kenya living in the U.S. illegally. Obama's campaign did not dispute the authenticity of the story, but questioned the suspicious nature of its timing. I do not think this story will have a significant affect on the election, but you never know how many undecideds will take this into consideration when casting their vote. A second story was Obama saying in Iowa that his faith in the American people had been vindicated on the day of the Iowa caucus during the Democratic primary. McCain seized on this by saying, "my country has never had to prove anything to me. I've always had faith in it, and I've been humbled and honored to serve it."

McCain appeared on *Saturday Night Live* and was rather funny. Free advertising at this time of the campaign can only help.

Commentators and pundits continue to predict an Obama victory, some by overwhelming margins. I sense a much closer election, and believe Pennsylvania could be 2008's November surprise. McCain visited my area on Saturday, with his campaign probably sensing the same momentum shift I feel.

Obama's campaign kicked a few reporters off his plane due to space considerations. The affected reporters happened to be members of newspapers that officially endorsed McCain. What a childish move, especially from a campaign that talks of change and starting a new era of governing. If he does win, I hope he shows more bipartisanship in his dealings with Republicans.

November 3, 2008

After a busy weekend, the candidates are rushing to key states for one final campaign push before tomorrow's Election Day.

McCain started his quest for the presidency back in 2000 when he challenged George Bush during the Republican primary season. He had no choice but to support the incumbent in 2004, and after a slow start in this year's primary, New Hampshire saved his candidacy and propelled him to his party's nomination. Coincidentally, he scheduled a last-minute stop in the granite state to hopefully succeed in prying it loose from the Democrats. At seventy-two years of age, this is certainly his last presidential campaign, unless of course he is fortunate enough to be running for reelection in 2012.

Obama started his quest for the presidency back in 2004 when he gave the keynote address at the Democratic convention. His charisma has been his biggest asset, and although he is only a first-term U.S. senator, he was able to wrestle the nomination from the heavily favored Hillary Clinton. His slogan of change caught on and catapulted him to the top of his party's ticket. His lack of experience has been virtually a nonissue in both the primary and general elections, overshadowed by his theme of change. He was able to strike a nerve with the populace, and the deteriorating economy has positioned him as the favorite to become the forty-fourth president of the United States. His substantial war chest of contributions has enabled him to boldly go where no one has gone before, and his campaign has successfully expanded the electoral map to the point where the word "landslide" has been used by various commentators. His party and followers are so optimistic about his chances that they appear giddy over the potential mandate he will receive tomorrow. Who would have thought when he first stepped onto the national spotlight four years ago that he would enjoy such a meteoric rise to the top of the U.S. political scene? This rapid rise to stardom has negated his opponents and detractors from fully vetting his shortcomings, and I am left wondering who he really is and what he stands for. I worry that his "share the wealth" slip was a prelude to his governing philosophy. Most middle-class voters might initially sign onto this philosophy, but when their government starts taking bigger bites out of their paychecks to fund larger entitlement programs, the realization of a socialist shift will hit home. Middle-class America will have no one to blame but itself for electing someone who will create or expand programs that reward those who are content to do nothing but take a government handout. He has promised hope and change, but so do most candidates. What strikes me about him is that he has a cult-like following that gives him a pass on crucial issues. The race card seems to be working in his favor, with critics hesitant and reluctant to critique him on the chance they will be labeled racist. We have become so sensitive to this topic that we tiptoe around it and go out of our way to avoid any semblance of being an accomplice to it. He has used this to his advantage, and I credit him for seizing this opportunity.

The Republicans play rough, and I thought this young and inexperienced novice would be exposed in the general election. They did not count on the worst financial crisis in eighty years to neutralize their argument, and the anger of voters feeling the effects of wealth destruction to turn toward the Democrat promising hope and change. The stars have aligned perfectly for him, and he has taken full advantage of the situation. The polls continue to show it is only thirty-six hours or so to his victory, and the *USA Today*/Gallup Poll has him with a 53 percent to 42 percent lead among likely voters. This is the poll's largest margin thus far, and would indicate momentum is on his side. I continue to be in a state of disbelief about the accuracy of polls showing a double-digit Obama advantage. The *Business Investor's Daily* reported a 2-percent Obama advantage, which is much more in line with the close race I am sensing. This poll was the closest to predicting 2004's actual margin, thus I am hoping it continues its reliability streak.

McCain will be making a last minute stop in Pennsylvania today, which stresses the importance of the Keystone State for him to achieve the necessary 270 electoral votes. My home state could very well decide the election, and I would expect a huge turnout tomorrow. The weather is forecast to be perfect, and the pundits have said a large turnout favors Obama. The young voters are in his corner, but I am still not sold on their reliability to actually vote. We will find out tomorrow. During the primary season, Clinton trounced Obama in Pennsylvania, a result much different than the polls suggested.

Seventeen-term Democratic Congressman John Murtha made his infamous slight at his constituents recently, and some may feel he deserves to be put out of work. His constituents may be quick to forgive him, however, since he consistently delivers generous earmarks to his district, which helps prevent high unemployment to his electorate. This is one of the benefits of incumbency and seniority in Congress. If voters decide against returning him to Washington, McCain could be the beneficiary of these defections. It is interesting that Bill Clinton is scheduled to make a campaign stop with Murtha today to attempt to limit the damage. Obama has been conspicuously absent from any Murtha gatherings, and would prefer people in the rural sections of Pennsylvania to forget his ill-fated comments on "clinging to guns and religion." He probably wishes he had not made those remarks, and now the voters toward whom those words were directed have a chance to have the final say. Pennsylvania polls close at 8 p.m., and the result will determine whether we are in for a long or short election night.

Markets were mixed overseas this morning, and U.S. futures are pointing toward a slightly positive open. I would not expect volatile movements today, since everyone is fixated on the election. The hope for change is in the air, and investors are hoping for a psychological lift, once this election comes to an end. October was a month to forget, and coupled with September, gave us a one-two punch that won't soon be forgotten. We need a positive week or month, and I hope, November will deliver a much-needed boost of optimism.

The markets are relatively calm today, with the Dow up marginally at mid-day. Circuit city announced today they will be closing 15-20 percent of their U.S. stores. The number two consumer electronics retailer will be cutting thousands of jobs with this move. A measure of U.S. manufacturing activity plummeted to its lowest level in twenty-six years in October, as the credit crisis and hurricane Ike disrupted business from plastics companies to lumberyards. It seems that bad news just continues to roll in.

Obama and McCain are making their mad dash to battleground states to attempt one last persuasive argument for their candidacy. Obama's itinerary on this last day includes Florida, Virginia, and Indiana, while McCain's more ambitious agenda takes him to Florida, Pennsylvania, Indiana, New Mexico, Colorado, and Nevada, before ending with a rally in his home state of Arizona. Biden was set to campaign in Missouri, Ohio, and Pennsylvania, while Palin was scheduled to appear in Ohio, Missouri, Iowa, Colorado, and Nevada. Each of the candidates is keeping to a hectic schedule, and I would expect a few slices of pizza to be on the menu to keep them refreshed as much as possible. They realize this is it, that decision day is only twenty-four hours away. They can rest tomorrow while the returns come in.

A new administration makes its own appointments to thousands of positions in Washington. Filling these patronage jobs is part of the victor's spoils, and if Obama wins, you can expect a much greater turnover than if a repeat Republican victory were to occur. People's lives will be turned upside down, with jobs being lost and gained when the new administration takes office. Starting on Wednesday, the job seekers will be lined up if Obama wins, and his transition team will move quickly to fill key positions. Those leaving Washington will be facing a tough job climate, although the more senior level people should not have a problem, given their stable of old boy networks. The moving trucks will be busy in January, both moving people in and out. Eight years is a long time to live in one place in our transient society, and each of the people hired when the Bush administration took over knew that it would have to end at some point. The home rental market should be bustling, especially in a larger government under Democratic rule. Civil servants with children will be transferring schools in mid-year, further disrupting their families' lives. The newcomers will be jockeying to get Redskins tickets so they can be seen at the big sporting events. These movements into Washington can be equated to move-in day on college campuses. A larger government role, which would require more hirings, should help insulate the DC metro area from the housing slump being experienced in many areas around the country. The new administration could affect AIG also, since they could opt to accelerate strategies that will temper people's outrage at the lifeline we were given. This is a wild card, something employees can't be oblivious to.

The Dow finished the day's trading at about the same level as it started. The session was the calmest in recent memory, with the Dow moving in a range of just over one hundred, thirty points, far from the wild swings common in October. Major auto companies reported weak sales for the month of October. GM said its sales plunged 45 percent in October because of weak consumer confidence and tight credit markets. Ford said its sales fell 30 percent, while Toyota dropped 33 percent, as the gloomy economic climate scared customers away from showrooms. Sales for the industry as a whole may be the worst in twenty-five years. With many people having concerns over job security it's understandable that new car sales would be hurting. That 125,000 mile driven Ford or Chevy may be asked to live another 25,000 miles or so. I would think this will help the auto repair shops. This delayed new car purchasing will create a huge demand at some point in the future, and the auto manufacturers, car dealers, and materials producers will be the beneficiaries of this, assuming they survive to enjoy the rebound. Ford is scheduled to release its financial results this Friday, and the down sales raise the possibility of further plant closures or shift cuts. Ford said it will continue to reduce production to match consumer demand. In another development, GM's financing arm, GMAC financial services, said it was tightening its lending standards to require a credit score of at least seven hundred, potentially shutting out some buyers. The auto industry is struggling mightily, and it employs hundreds of thousands of workers. The state of Michigan is feeling the brunt of this slowdown more than any other state, and their hope is that a Democratic win tomorrow will bring with it a sympathetic ear to their cries for help. I'll go out on a limb here and predict that an Obama victory will lead to bailouts for the auto industry and a return to prominence of unions. Without a fundamental change in their business models, this will be nothing more than a giveaway.

A Democratic victory tomorrow will bring with it supporters and donors getting in line for their special-interest projects. This happens with Republican administrations also, so I am not pointing a menacing finger only at the Democrats. One group that has been waiting for a change in power has been the legal profession, in particular the attorneys I will refer to as the ambulance chasers. They would like nothing more than to see legislation that would roll back limitations on personal injury and class-action lawsuits. If successful, tort reform would be a thing of the past, especially if the Democrats achieve the magic "60" in the senate.

As I ride the train home tonight, I feel at peace with my decision to vote for McCain. I want change as much as any other voter in this election, and although Obama is the picture of change, I believe McCain has a better chance of delivering the right kind of change. I believe he seeks the presidency because he loves his country, not because he seeks the power and prestige associated with it. He has served this country with honor and dignity, sacrificing five years of his life in captivity. This is not itself a reason to vote for him, rather it complements the other attributes he possesses to make him the right leader at this important time in our history. He knows what needs to be changed in Washington, and I believe he will fight to make it happen. Candidates usually tell us what is wrong with our country during the course of a campaign. Rarely do they focus on the good things this country has going for it. We all agree that times are difficult now, but we know that things will turn around and that our best days are still ahead of us. I sense McCain believes this regardless of who wins this election, while I am not sure Obama does. Obama views himself as a savior, while McCain views himself as a humble leader who will continue the great tradition of the prior forty-three men who shared the office before him. I will enthusiastically vote for John McCain and give him one more mission.

November 4, 2008

Election Day is finally here. This campaign has been exciting, and a part of me is sad to see it come to an end. One of the candidates will be our next president, while the runner up will return to his duties in the Senate. The experts continue to say this will be a knockout for Obama, but I'm not sold on this yet.

I got to the polls early this morning, anxious to cast my ballot for McCain. I have meetings at work this morning, so I arrived at the polling location forty minutes prior to the 7 a.m. opening to ensure I wouldn't have a long wait in line. I value this opportunity to vote and feel that my vote can make a difference. Millions of voters throughout this great country will be voting today, and I hope they cherish this responsibility as much as I do. We will be electing someone to the most powerful position in the world. People throughout the world will watch our election intently, amazed at the system we have for selecting our leaders. World events will be shaped by our decisions, and we will have an orderly transition of power unlike any in the rest of the world.

As I drove up to the polling location, I was greeted with a parade of signs along the way. There was what seemed like hundreds of candidate posters for my viewing pleasure. After parking my car, I walked inside to wait and found myself to be the seventh person in line. Lucky seven, is that an omen for McCain's chances of pulling an upset? As I waited in line, this annoying person came up to me and was peddling a sample ballot of his candidates. I politely declined, but he was persistent in trying me again. I was getting more irritated, and the peddler sensed my anger and went to the next voter in line. Two things dawned on me from this encounter. The first was that this person was hawking his slate of candidates aggressively. This campaign has evoked passion in many people, and this level of intensity has been maintained until Election Day. Supporters are not giving up, and each campaign is fighting until the end. They have driven the length of the field and now they are trying to punch it in for a touchdown. The second observation I had was about the undecided voters, and how many were still uncertain as to how to cast their votes. Estimates are that this undecided block could still constitute up to 10 percent of likely voters at this late stage. Could any of these fence sitters be persuaded by annoying supporters like the one I had just encountered? I would hope not, but the candidates and their supporters are leaving nothing to chance as they hope to garner a few extra votes from their last-minute canvassing.

The polls opened at 7 a.m., right on time. It didn't take me more than a few minutes to sign in, and before I knew it, one of the attendants directed me to machine number two of the four that were available. He whispered instructions to me as I entered, and then the curtain closed behind me and I was left to the business of casting my vote. There were a couple referendums regarding debt issuances that I immediately pushed the "NO" button on. The recent federal government rescue program has hardened me on the need for fiscal conservatism, and unfortunately, my township will be feeling the wrath of my dissatisfaction with my rejection of the referendums. Any other year I would have probably voted for it, but not this year. I then moved on to the candidate selections below the referendums. The Democratic Party had the pole position, with the Republican slate next in line. I smiled as I saw the third party's list of candidates, knowing full well that Nader would be hoping for a spoiler role. It is safe to say I will not be voting for Ralph.

I made my selections and pressed the vote button to put closure to my selection. The attendant told me it had been recorded, and the curtain flung open, and I departed the voting booth. I felt a sense of contentment as I walked away, knowing that I had made my mark on this election. I could have opted to leave by the exit immediately behind the polling booth but decided to walk back the way I had entered to get a glimpse of the size of the line and the composition of those in line. As I walked proudly out and down the school corridor where the line had formed, I saw a few familiar faces and engaged in some small talk. None of the conversations touched on voting preferences, which is a tradition I have noticed throughout my recurring voting excursions. The line had grown to over a few hundred people by the time I reached the exit. Those at the end of the line were in for over an hour wait, plenty of time for them to be approached by the candidates' vultures hoping to secure the votes of their unsuspecting prey. The line included a mixture of blue-collar and white-collar workers, with my sole criteria for categorizing someone into either bucket based on their dress. This stereotyping is not scientific, but it is the best I could do (some reading this might actually accuse me of profiling). Most of the people waiting in line were over thirty years of age, with the preponderance being those in my age category. Male and females were about even, and conspicuously absent were any of the young voters, which I have heard so much about during this election season. I reasoned they were probably late risers after a late night out yesterday.

As I drove away from the polling location, I saw a crowd of cars looking for places to park. Some had chosen to park a block or so away, which I deduced from the steady stream of walkers passing by. I am encouraged with what I saw this morning. I can feel a heavy turnout coming, which implies people are concerned with where this country is headed. They want change and recognize that it is within their control to choose the future path we embark on. The election will bring with it a psychological lift to the country, regardless of who wins. This is a final exclamation point to the Bush presidency, and although the inauguration is over two months away, people will know change is coming.

As I drove toward the train station, I turned on 97.5 fm to listen to Christmas songs. The combination of voting for change and listening to holiday songs put me in an upbeat mood for the day. The weather was accommodating, as well, removing this as a crutch for people to lean on as a defense for not voting.

As I rode the train to New York, I looked out to my left and right and wondered how many people in the surrounding areas would actually vote. Statistics indicate there are approximately 150 million registered voters, and I would hope at least 65 percent or almost two thirds actually participate in this election. The historical nature of this campaign has juiced people up with a passion I have not seen before.

As the train pulled into Penn Station, I realized that no one collected my train ticket. Wow, I just saved $12.50. Given the constant delays we NJT riders experience, I doubt any of my fellow passengers will regret this oversight. On my way to the metro, I passed my troubadour flutist who was playing a song that was familiar, but I could not remember from where. A few minutes later, it dawned on me that the flutist was playing the theme from "Popeye the sailor man." I remember Popeye loved his spinach, but I must confess I stay away from this vegetable at all costs.

As I exited the metro at south ferry and ascended to street level, I was greeted by heavily armed officers who were noticeably present in the Staten Island ferry terminal. Machine guns were visible, and I immediately thought of 9/11 and the world trade center site, which is only a few blocks away. I thought of Biden's warning that an international incident would happen soon after our election, although I did not think it would happen today. A terrorist attack on Election Day would be a stunning event to our country, negating this administration's claim of no attack on our soil since 9/11. I was not aware of any incident by noon today, which made me think the extra security was meant to be a deterrent to possible perpetrators. This extra security underscores that we live in a dangerous world, and that our next president will not only have economic issues to contend with but the threat of terrorism as well.

Last night's polls continued to show a likely Obama victory today, although they showed tightening in some key battleground states. McCain is actually breaking tradition today, campaigning at rallies in Colorado and New Mexico before returning to Phoenix to watch election night returns. I arrived in the office later than normal, since I needed to vote. I asked a few of my coworkers if they had voted and most had not, although they were planning to do so in the evening. Those residing in New York and New Jersey have some interesting local and state elections to be decided, but their presidential vote is irrelevant to the final outcome since their states are a gimme for the Dems. My state is relevant, and my vote will help decide who will be the next president.

The Dow finished up three hundred points today to reach its highest close in four weeks. This was the biggest Election Day rally for the Dow, topping the gain seen in 1984 when Reagan defeated Mondale. Prior to 1980, the market was closed on Election Day. Some analysts said the markets rose on relief the election was about to be over, while others did not want to miss out on the start of a year-end recovery. This sentiment was echoed by the noted Vanguard guru John Bogle who said stocks were oversold.

Election results will start rolling in shortly after 7 p.m. when Indiana and Virginia's polls close. These two battleground states will be joined at 7:30 p.m. by North Carolina and Ohio, and at 8 p.m. by Florida, Missouri, and Pennsylvania. These battleground states comprise 116 electoral votes, and McCain needs to win 80 percent of them to make it an interesting night. If Obama carries just a few of these, the commentators will be proclaiming him our next president, since the pressure is squarely on McCain, since he has little if any margin of error to get to 270 electoral votes.

Every news channel will have some type of election coverage tonight. The major stations will have their night set up for election coverage only, and each will try to add their own individual touches to grab and keep viewers. My remote will get a workout tonight similar to when I try and watch a smorgasbord of sports events that run simultaneously. The usual cast of characters will be on tonight with each trying to outdo the other with their analysis of the election. For once, I would like to hear one of these supposed geniuses admit they were wrong about something. That is wishful thinking on my part, because I know their egos would not allow such an admission to be breathed from their mouths. I am not sure what channel I will start at, but if McCain gets momentum early, and people start talking about a possible upset, I will switch to Obama's surrogate stations of NBC and MSNBC to see how the commentators discuss their chosen one in this unforeseen close race. In the event McCain makes it a tight race some of these "independent" commentators will visibly and verbally show their disgust at the proceedings and blabber on about this unfortunate turn of events. If form holds true and Obama wins comfortably, these same people will speak with reverence of our newly elected president and the intelligence of the American people in selecting him. It will be an interesting night either way.

Not to be outdone by McCain, Obama made a final campaign stop in Indiana, hoping to win the electoral votes in a state that has not been kind to the Democratic party in recent presidential contests. Before travelling to Indiana, he cast his own ballot at an elementary school in Chicago. Obama voted a few minutes after his neighbor William Ayres.

As the train headed south through New Jersey, we passed New Brunswick, Metro Park, Jersey Avenue, and Edison. I noticed a lot of car lights to each side of the train as we sped toward Trenton, causing me to wonder how many people were rushing to vote before the polls closed. Some might opt to sit this one out if they believe the election is already decided as the polls indicated, but given the voter passion displayed throughout this campaign, I would expect the nonvoters to be a distinct minority.

As we approached Princeton, I thought of the youth vote in the form of Princeton University students and whether they would come out in the large numbers the Obama camp was predicting. My oldest daughter who graduated from college last year voted today, while my daughter who is at Boston University was not allowed to vote because they said she was not registered. She swears she was properly registered to vote, and I find it ironic that she recently received a jury duty summons, yet they say she is not registered. Massachusetts does not have to worry about the Democrats losing an election, since Republicans win there about as often as a Philly sports team wins a world championship. I am not sure if my son in the navy got his ballot in, since I have not heard from him in a couple weeks. My youngest two (Kyle and Kerry) are not yet eligible to vote, but this has not dampened their interest in the election. Kyle will be able to vote in the 2010 mid term election, and I can ascertain from his comments where his leanings are. Kerry's first official vote will be in the 2012 presidential election, and I can foresee her being politically active based on her preference to watch political programs as opposed to more normal teenage programming. Women such as Hillary Clinton and Condoleezza Rice have successfully blazed a path for women in the political arena, and I would be surprised if Kerry doesn't follow in their footsteps. President Kerry Krouchick has a nice ring to it. I hope she allows my wife and I, as well as her siblings, to attend some of her formal state dinners.

Election Night

The polls had already closed in a number of states by the time I got home around 7:45 p.m. Key battleground states such as Indiana, Virginia, North Carolina, and Ohio were considered too close to call at this early stage. These states comprise the swing states, where the election will be won or lost, and each campaign will be monitoring the results closely to see if their strategies have paid off. With sophisticated analytics, it is not surprising that some states are called a minute after the polls close.

The polls in Pennsylvania closed at 8 p.m., and ABC news declared Obama the victor soon thereafter. I was shocked that my home state was a quick call and switched to another channel to see if it was unanimous among the networks. I was relieved that other networks had it still in play, but worried that the die had been cast.

I remembered a recent presidential election, when Ohio had been inadvertently called and the networks were forced to eat crow on their premature declaration. When Fox called Pennsylvania for Obama around 9 p.m., I knew my state had remained in Democratic control for the fifth straight time. I was surprised at what the final margin was projected to be, and did not understand how it could turn into such a lopsided victory for Obama. I would later find out that the suburban Philadelphia areas did not give McCain the lift he needed and, combined with lopsided Obama support in Philadelphia, eliminated any chance McCain had of pulling off the upset. Any hopes of a November surprise evaporated completely when New Mexico was called for Obama immediately after the polls closed at 9 p.m. and Ohio was declared for Obama around 9:15 p.m. New Mexico does not have many electoral votes, but it was a swing state McCain invested a lot of time in. The dagger was Ohio and its twenty electoral votes going to Obama. Bush received 286 electoral votes in 2004, and if you subtract Ohio he would have been at 266 and John Kerry would have won the election.

McCain needed to protect Bush states as he was counting on Pennsylvania to offset some possible defections. Once the neighboring states of Ohio and Pennsylvania went blue, the race to the white house was effectively over. This verdict was reinforced at about 9:30 p.m. when Nicole Wallace, a senior advisor to the McCain campaign, gave a semi-concession speech to Fox news. She spoke of the difficulties the Republicans faced this year and how it was a tribute to McCain that he made it a race. It was now clear there would not be a November surprise, and that an African American had ascended to the most powerful position in the world. He came out of nowhere four years ago and is now headed to the White House. This rags-to-riches story could only happen in America, and although I am disappointed McCain did not win, I am proud that a candidate's race was not a factor in this election. African Americans voted almost unanimously for Obama. But let's not lose sight of the fact that so did many Hispanics and whites. He could not have won without their support.

Although the final tally will not be available for a few days, preliminary estimates are that this election achieved a 65 percent turnout, which would beat the prior record set when

JFK won in 1960. Analysts will be dissecting this election for years, and both parties will hope to learn from the results to refine their strategies for 2012.

The 2008 presidential election is in the books, and I am certain that plans are already being discussed for 2012. This election showed us that a bad economy trumps every other issue and that a sitting president and his party are held responsible as the primary patriarch of economic conditions. Pundits will say this was a game -changing political event, and that its effects will be felt for years to come. I do not discount the historical significance of Obama winning, but I believe if economic conditions do not improve, the American people will elect a new president in 2012. By giving Obama the presidency, the electorate took a huge step forward in showing the world what we are about. Thoughts of a minority president would have been scoffed at in our recent history, and I hope that this election has graduated us into a new phase in our history.

It should be noted that Democrats expanded their majority in both the senate and the house, thus achieving their triumvirate. Obama has the opportunity to push through major legislation during this next session, and I hope he tries to stay to the middle where he shifted during the election season. Although he has been ranked as one of the most liberal members of the senate, we need to remember that four years as a senator does not constitute a long enough term to develop a consistent voting pattern. We really do not know much about Obama and what his agenda will be. He may want to do certain things that he discussed during the campaign, but the reality is that he is inheriting a mess of an economy. His hands will be tied until the situation improves, limiting the amount and timing of initiatives he would like to move on.

Biden spoke of Obama being tested early on with an international incident. I worry more about him being tested by his own party to push through an agenda of expanding government beyond its already bloated and intrusive scope. I fear that veteran politicians such as Pelosi and Reid will try to bully our new president into policies that the majority of Americans would not take too kindly. Groups such as the teachers union and the trial layers that have supported the Democrats will want to cash in their chips as soon as possible. They understand that their window may be short, since an angry electorate could reverse this year's Democratic gains in the 2010 mid term election cycle. Obama will be pressured by the left to deliver, and this will be his first true test as President. I think he is a smart person and will moderate his agenda. The Democrats' dossier on him is as thin as the Republicans', leaving both parties to wonder how he will govern as President. He built his campaign on change, which the electorate embraced. Change can mean a lot of things to different people. It does not have to mean drastic government regulation or universal health care; rather, it could be as simple as reaching across the aisle to find common ground. We need bipartisanship more than ever to move this country forward. Politicians can get drunk with power and, in the process, forget that they work for the people. It would be easy for Obama and the Democrats to rush their agenda through, but it would be more prudent to govern in the middle. We are still a centrist country, with some claiming we tilt to the right and others saying we are left leaning. If the pendulum swings too far, we get uncomfortable and react in a negative manner. Obama is positioned to be a two-term president if he stays close to the center. The economy will probably be better two years or four years from now, given the normal cycles we experience, thus absent some major policy blunders, this issue should not hurt him in his re-election bid.

There are many challenges he will confront during the next four years. This is a pivotal moment in our history, and we need a leader to move this country forward. There is no "how-to guide" for this job and there is no formal job description. Each of his forty-three predecessors carved their own niche in presidential history. We can debate the levels of success each of the prior forty-three presidents achieved, but we collectively understand that we need number forty-four to be successful.

Epilogue

The 2008 election was a historic moment for our country. Electing an African American to the presidency will be cited by historians years from now as a turning point in American history. I would like to think the race issue has been officially laid to rest with this epic victory and that gender bias will soon follow suit. Any concern or apprehension of whether American voters could elect a minority president were wiped out by the worst financial crisis since the Great Depression. We learned that anxiety over job security and how to pay the bills are still the primary drivers of our election moods.

We are taught in this country that everyone has the same prospects for success, regardless of background. This guiding principle had a hollow sound to some people, but this year's election reinforced and solidified its true meaning to Americans. Not only did we witness this changing of the guard, but we voted to make it happen. Some of us voted for McCain in this election because we believed in his ideals and values. When I compared the candidates, I saw black and white differences in their proposals and not in the color of their skin. John McCain lost this election, but he is still an American hero who places country above all else. An overwhelming majority of Americans were frustrated with where the country was headed, and early on, Obama's battle cry of change struck a nerve with the voters who decided in his favor.

When a true Republican remains undecided for as long as I did, it speaks volumes about the issues confronting this country and the challenges the Republican Party was up against. I came home to my party for Election Day, but my hesitancy was a preview of the uphill climb facing the Republican Party this year. Anger and frustration surfaced throughout the election, but so did passion and hope. The American people wanted to be heard in this election and turned out in record numbers to make a statement. This enthusiasm and acceptance of the political process was refreshing to see, and I would hope that first-time participants continue to embrace their responsibility in the future. This sends a strong message to our citizens and the rest of the world that we take our voting privilege seriously, and that "we the people" have the power to decide our future direction.

I have always been proud to be an American, because I believe we are the greatest country in the history of civilization. It has a touch of conceit to it but reveals why we are the envy of the world. We want the gold medal, not the silver. We have our setbacks as everyone does, but we move forward and believe our best days are ahead of us. I have come full circle during this election. I was undecided for a period of time, and wanted change as much, or more, than my fellow citizens. I came back to my core beliefs for Election Day, but only after an extended and deliberative soul-searching process. I have accepted the outcome of the election and respect the will of my fellow citizens. I hope our new President tackles some of the many issues confronting us in the bipartisan manner he spoke of during the campaign. His limited experience was a positive for him during the campaign, but now comes the difficult task of actually governing. We will soon find out what path he chooses to pursue, and whether his "spreading the wealth" comment was political hyperbole or a defining philosophy, which will guide his agenda. The electorate voted for change, although I'm still not sure anyone knows the specifics of the change we voted for. Our new President is inheriting an economy that continues to worsen. He is also being handed a public sector that has extended its reach into our economy, affording him the convenient fallback position that his predecessor initiated this shift. He will need to decide if this is a temporary fix until the economy improves, or if it should be a more lasting, fundamental change to our future. He will have willing accomplices to the path he chooses with a democratically controlled senate and house. Given this trifecta of power, they are positioned to dictate change that could be game changing, with voters not getting their say until the mid-term elections in 2010. Two years may not seem like a long time, but given the difficulties in governing without a dominant majority, the changes they enact may in fact become as close to permanent as one can get. This forty-seven-day period may well prove to be the catalyst that ushers in dramatic change to America. Let's hope they make change we are comfortable with, and not the type that will bring regret and buyer's remorse to many who enthusiastically voted for our forty-fourth president.

January, 2010

Obama's victory on Election Day was truly historic in nature. The election is now fourteen months in our rear view mirror, and the change we voted for has begun. Cap and Trade and Universal healthcare, referred to by the current administration as healthcare reform, is being passionately debated. Everyone understands that costs can't continue to increase as they historically have; however, the political parties have differences on how to contain these cost increases. The Government is focused on increased regulations regarding the financial system, and is on its way to enacting some form of greater oversight and regulations. The Administration has attempted to open a dialogue with Iran, and is showing an increased preference to accommodate Russian concerns over issues, such as U.S. missile deployments in Poland and the Czech Republic. The Obama administration confidently predicted the unemployment rate wouldn't go above 8 percent if their stimulus plan was passed, and we now know that they badly misjudged as unemployment currently hovers around 10 percent, representing about fifteen million Americans out of work. The stock market hit its low in March of 2009, some 60 percent below the peak it achieved in 2007. It has recovered somewhat, but is still 30 percent below its peak.

I personally feel better about the economy than I did back on Election day when it seemed we would never escape the grips of the financial meltdown, but five million more Americans are unemployed now than on election day. Many of these are middle-class Americans, and the hopes of the ranks of the unemployed aren't being helped by continued warnings that unemployment will not peak until sometime in mid to late 2010. This isn't entirely the current Administration's fault, but at some point, the Obama team will have to take ownership and stop blaming their predecessor for every negative occurrence in our country. Middle class America prefers results to whining.

There is a lot of talk about the dawning of socialism in America, assuming of course that the Administration's agenda is able to successfully work its way through Congress. The dissidents to this agenda are saying that it is a dramatic shift in our way of life, and that we should recognize this for what it is. Its proponents use the cover of the financial collapse as a justification for increased government intervention, arguing that, without this course of action, we are bound to repeat the actions that caused the recent meltdown. Populist rhetoric reigns in Washington, and the President is using his bully pulpit to not only defend his policies, but also to position any critique as a willing return to the economic brink. He and his fellow Democrats are full speed ahead with their agenda, recognizing that the power they have attained is something they shouldn't waste. There are no signs of bipartisanship in the nation's capital, with each side pointing to the other as the reason for the lack of cooperation. One fact that both parties should never lose sight of is that we are a country that likes to be governed in the middle, and if we shift too far to one side, we quickly get a tug that pulls us back to the center. When you cut through it, we are a country that professes to want change, but when change comes knocking, we shudder, hesitate, and express displeasure at the thought of change actually occurring. This seems like a Jekyll and Hyde mentality, but it may be recognition that we like what we have and are afraid of the growing pains associated with change.

We accept a little change, but what we perceive as a major shift isn't part of our culture. The far left and far right would like change skewed toward their way of thinking; however, the middle, middle left, and middle right ensure that we don't stray too far from what the majority actually wants. This is how it should work in a pure democracy, and as long as we maintain this system, we'll always govern from the middle. We'll get the isolated instances where our elected leaders will promote radical changes, but most times this type of agenda will never get enacted. The key question is what we define as radical. A prime example is healthcare reform, for which Obama has said there is agreement on 80 percent of the issues. If that's truly the case, then why not pass legislation that incorporates the mutually agreed 80 percent common ground. Why does either party feel it needs to get the whole loaf of bread? Sometimes, the political parties delude themselves into thinking they have a mandate and go full speed ahead to jam through their agenda for their self-proclaimed mandate. Middle-class America gives no one a mandate and prefers bipartisanship to rule the day. If either party violates this code and acts in a partisan manner, they do so at their own peril. Mid-term elections are on the horizon, and if the majority party doesn't exercise restraint, but rather embarks on a heavily tilted agenda, they will quickly become the minority. Middle-class America wants change, but not radical change that causes unease. We want change, but not change that will dramatically alter the American way of life. What makes us great is that we are different from the rest of the world, and we believe in the American way. I hear comments that we need to be more accommodating to the rest of the world, and that America needs to change. This has been espoused by our elected president, and this tone completely dismisses or ignores that the reverse is more appropriate. We have the greatest nation in the history of the world, and I'm confounded by why we need to change. As much as I worry about my children achieving a standard of living greater than mine, I am comforted that America will get past the current crisis and find a way to keep us at the head of the class. A drop-off is simply not acceptable.

May, 2010 (last entry)

I'm still employed at AIG, and I continue to bring my "A" game each and every day. We recently announced the sales of a couple of our foreign life insurance companies, and the government will be the recipient of some cash pay downs on its investment. I'm even thinking of wearing my AIG golf shirt the next time I hit the links.

What prompted me to start writing this book nineteen months ago was a desire for change. I couldn't really define what change meant back then, except to say that the current situation wasn't acceptable. I put the book on hold after the election, focusing entirely on my AIG responsibilities, but wondering all the time if my words would have any meaning to readers. As events unfolded over the course of this administration's first year in office, I concluded that my observations during the forty-seven days prior to the election warranted telling in that it shows elections truly matter, and that sometimes frustrations and emotions can lead to decision-making that discounts longer-term ramifications. I worried that I might be perceived as overreaching, but I believe I represent a majority of Americans who sense the country's path veering in a direction we do not want. As I now think back on my desire for change, I realize that my thirst for it wasn't being driven by a desire for significant cultural change, but rather an emotional tug that was more general than specific in it's nature. I was certainly affected by the circumstances surrounding AIG and also felt the despair brought on by a weakening economy and a corresponding deteriorating personal wealth situation. Prudent advice is to never let emotions dictate decisions; however, I forgot this golden rule and let emotions get the best of me and influence my thinking. It took me awhile to remove emotions from my decision-making process in the 2008 Presidential election. I've now come to believe that many others did not, and in the process ignored the warning signs of what the future would have in store for us if Obama and his party seized control of Washington. Fortune smiled on Barack Obama, as well as on his fellow Democrats who were swept into power in 2008. They achieved control of the Presidency, House, and Senate and have since embarked on a campaign of change that I believe a majority of Americans did not sign up for. They have passed a bill they refer to as healthcare reform, although the only bipartisanship achieved in the voting tally was that some Democrats sided with Republicans to vote against it. The House vote was 219-212; in effect a four-vote swing is ushering in a massive change to our economy. By itself, this change is significant, but it multiplies when you combine it with other legislative priorities of this administration. The term *socialism* has been used to describe this shift, and although Democrats dispute this characterization of their agenda, they have not riled against it. Obama's words to Joe the Plumber are certainly proving prophetic, and shame on us for not believing he would follow through on a big government redistribution philosophy of "spreading the wealth around." In its simplest terms, he believes government knows better than each of us what to do with our hard-earned wages. I recognize that there are some believers in this philosophy, however I am confident that most of my fellow middle-class Americans do not agree with this position.

The left believes they win the moral argument when they say that all Americans are entitled to healthcare coverage, and that an individual shouldn't be denied coverage for a pre-existing condition. They miss the point, however, in that most people, including Republicans, would agree with them that these are noble goals. The shortsightedness with this thinking is that ensuring our fiscal sanity is a precursor to providing universal healthcare coverage. Sound fiscal policy needs to rule before embarking on a program that will cost trillions of dollars. We all know how this program will be paid for, and that's with tax increases. The Administration claims that only the wealthy will see an increase, yet this logic disregards basic math. Combine this with budgetary problems at the state and local levels, and one could make a cogent argument that we are on the precipice of major tax increases across all bands of Americans. Taxes are necessary to provide each of us some basic items such as safety; however, it becomes blurred as to what constitutes necessities versus luxuries. Taxes in effect represent the value of government services we need, and a higher tax implies an expanded list of needs. Each tax dollar takes the spending decision out of the individual's hands, and allows for government to best decide how to allocate these dollars. I think even the far left would have to admit that each of us is more apt to better control spending than a government bureaucrat who has no skin in the game. This is not a difficult concept to grasp, yet I continue to be amazed that learned people make it more complicated than it is. No sane person will disagree that we need a strong government that will protect us and help provide for various basic necessities. A fair debate, however, would be to determine what government safety net we want and the level of dollars we are willing to allocate for this safety net. For example, do we want to continue to be the world's only superpower and spend the hundreds of billions of dollars necessary to maintain this status? In the same respect, do we feel spending a trillion dollars plus each year on entitlements is appropriate? On the latter question, is it possible that a safety-net mentality is a natural progression and resting place in our country's history? I glance overseas and see some of the problems confronting the European Union (specifically Greece), and wonder if that's our destiny. This is one American who hopes not, and firmly believes there are many more who share my beliefs.

In addition to higher Federal taxes, higher state and local taxes are on the horizon to pay for unfunded promises, and the stealth tax increases that all income levels will feel will follow. This is just the tip of the iceberg. Items such as "sin" taxes will soon be extending to soda drinkers, and then to whatever else they can think of putting into the sin bucket. I use this as an example because I don't believe soda consumption is limited to the wealthy. It will never end, and the bureaucracies that will be created with this funding will only get larger. Most Americans would agree that the focus needs to be on spending cuts, not increased levels of expenditures. Why is it this administration only seems to think of adding to spending and increasing the line at the trough? The administration will stubbornly point out that the CBO says that healthcare reform will reduce the deficit by $150B over ten years, and neglect to point out that ten years of tax increases are needed to cover six years of costs for the program. Did I hear someone once use the term "fuzzy math"? What Kool-Aid are they drinking? We all know how this is going to play out, and that's with higher taxes.

You can put lipstick on a pig, but it's still a pig. Employers will want to stay competitive in the global economy, and in some cases will drop healthcare coverage for their employees. They'll opt to pay the penalty, which will be less than the subsidies they provide employees, forcing more people into the government program. As more are forced into this plan, the government will be forced to either pay the increasing costs or try to hold the line on expenditures by making healthcare choices for us, in effect telling us what treatments are available to us, with historical results dictating what a person might be eligible for. How would you like to be a 60 year old with a chronic condition that needs surgery, but are told that the 40% success rate for someone your age disqualifies you from having the procedure done? Do you think the odds of America succeeding in the Revolutionary war were above 40%? What makes us great is that we constantly beat the odds, whether entrepreneurs starting their own businesses or a brave soldier performing a heroic deed to save his mates from sure defeat. Don't tell middle class America they can't do something. Our history is emblazoned with individuals and teams beating the odds.

We don't want bureaucracy telling us how to live our lives. On the contrary, we want limited interference from government and the right to make our own personal decisions. There are those who will say I'm exaggerating about any impending government dictation of our daily lives, but even the hint of a shift in this direction should be met with loud cries of dismay. The financial Armageddon we avoided in this last recession may very well rear its ugly head, as the recently passed healthcare program mushrooms into the major entitlement program we all know it will become. Why is it so hard for supposed learned individuals to grasp that the only way to really control healthcare spending is for each of us to have skin in the game and make our own decisions on what to spend our healthcare dollars on. Groups such as the tea party have formed, and as long as their motives remain peaceful and respectful, I believe they will grow in size and influence. These types of movements recognize we may be at a crossroads in our democracy, and that it doesn't take long for a tiny leak in a dike to turn into a rush of water producing a flood. This is how our democracy should work, with peaceful yet noteworthy objections to policies we disagree with. Elections matter, and let's see if the electorate embraces the current path this administration and willing accomplices in the senate and house has us on or resoundingly rejects their philosophy in the voting booth.

I recently read that this is the first year that Social Security will be paying out more than it takes in, in essence operating at a cash flow deficit. Can you imagine how we're going to right the Social Security ship when we have another Titanic in healthcare waiting to happen? This is insane, and most taxpayers know it. For the current administration, it all comes down to the solution of taxes. Every American will feel the brunt of this. I mentioned earlier in the book about the VAT (value added tax), which is really a national sales tax. This is what our socialist allies use to help fund their safety programs. We're following their lead in creating a safety net for various constituencies, and the VAT will certainly get more prominence in future discussions of how to solve our funding mismatch problems. Former Federal Reserve chairman Volker is now vocally putting this on the table as an option. The trial balloon has officially been launched. To put it into perspective, Germany has a VAT of 19 percent, France and Italy 20 percent, and most of Scandinavia 25 percent. Do we Americans want this added onto each of our consumption purchases? I think not, especially when it becomes incremental as opposed to a substitute for the current tax code. The poor will feel this more than the wealthy, since it will affect basic necessity purchases, unless of course the government tries to offset this with some kind of credit based upon income levels. This requires more government oversight, which requires a larger bureaucracy, which means an increasing burden on taxes. I'm getting nauseous just thinking of this interventionist attitude, and most people I talk to share my dismay at this proposition.

The current Administration has us headed toward a path of socialism. To claim otherwise is simply being disingenuous. They may outwardly dispute this notion, but secretly they can't deny its drift. This may all be part of a grand design to cater to two strong constituencies, those being the entitlement recipients and the baby boomers. These two groups may seem like an odd couple, but you could make the argument that they are directly linked by their desire for a safety net. The allure of this safety net is enticing, but the temptation can be quickly drowned out when we analyze where costs to cover this will be coming from. The financial meltdown we experienced provided an election opportunity for Obama and the Democrats. They have tried to capitalize on their victory by reaching for change that most Americans do not want. I heard Nancy Pelosi make a comment during the healthcare debate that I'm paraphrasing, but it went somewhat along the lines that "we need to pass the bill so we can tell the American people what's in it." If it was such a good bill, then why the secrecy over the contents of the two thousand, four hundred pages in the legislation? This implies to me that it couldn't stand on its own merits in front of the American people. Isn't it ironic that lending institutions have been told to simplify their terms and conditions by our elected officials so that borrowers can more easily understand what they're getting, yet the people authoring the healthcare legislation do the exact opposite in what they have just passed into law? Do as I say, not as I do. Lawyers will be having a field day with this bill, and its many opportunities for interpretation. I wouldn't be surprised if some law firms are already forming healthcare divisions in their law practices. Many corporations are probably hiring attorneys to help them understand how the bill will impact their business. I guess this should help lower the unemployment rate among lawyers. The arrogance and disdain shown by Washington surrounding this bill is hard to fathom. Wouldn't you think that a bill that affects such a large piece of our economy would be understandable to each of us? I learned a while ago that the more pages you present in a business meeting, the less effective your presentation becomes. I'm sure this bill has been carefully wordsmithed to provide the necessary ambiguity to allow for flexibility in its application; however, I'm equally certain that danger lurks in the depths of the bill's seemingly endless pages that will tie our hands for years to come. I was fortunate to have had a chance to visit Hawaii recently, and during our trip we visited the USS Missouri, which is docked at Pearl Harbor. The Japanese terms of surrender was signed on this battleship in Tokyo harbor, effectively ending World War II. You know how many pages in length this document was – one page. How's that for simplicity? Isn't it ironic that the young people who overwhelmingly voted for Obama may be the ones servicing the huge debt he will be running up? This should serve as a cautious reminder to them that elections matter, that their actions do have consequences, and in their haste to vote for change, they completely dismissed the future repercussions that will fall on their shoulders.

The one lasting impression I had from the one-day healthcare summit that Obama chaired was his comment that "elections matter, and the presidential election is over." I agree wholeheartedly with his comment, and would respectfully remind him that the more recent governor's elections in New Jersey and Virginia matter, as does the senate election of Scott Brown in Massachusetts. If I remember correctly, Brown campaigned vociferously against Obamacare, and his win in possibly the most liberal state in the country should have served notice that the majority of Americans are not in favor of his plan. Rather than heed their warning, and respect the will of the people and their disdain for this legislation, the President and his party went in the opposite direction and signed the bill into law. The arrogance amazes me and a majority of Americans, as the bill's passage implies they know what's better for us than we do. This is a recurring theme in their way of governing. As I write this, I'm now starting to get it that they do understand that elections matter, and that the recent Brown victory told them they had no choice but to pass the bill, because if they waited until November, there would be a mandate against it. They are more concerned with passing something they consider to be their holy grail and attaching their names to what they are calling a historic piece of legislation. Yes, in the eloquent words of our vice president it is a big f-----g deal, but in the real world we recognize that a truly bad plan is worse than doing nothing, and that this plan is a fiscal time bomb. Their hope is that the economy will improve, which it should given the depth and severity of the recent recession, and that this improvement will allow the American people to be duped and give them a mulligan for legislation we are united against. They have badly miscalculated in their analysis, and over reached for change we did not want. You may have passed your bill, but in the process you made clear to the American people what your true intentions are. The current Democratic regime is truly attempting to change the American way of life, and shame on them for thinking they could get away with it. How dare you go against our wishes and implement the kind of change we don't want. You may have interpreted your victory in last year's election as a mandate, but didn't those recent elections caution you in pursuing your agenda? Whether we like it or not, we are probably stuck with this healthcare albatross since a dominant majority like the Democrats currently have is a necessary ingredient to pass this type of legislation. I sincerely doubt the Republicans will attain this type of majority in the mid term elections, and I'm not optimistic the various state attempts to rule it unconstitutional will be successful. Let's hope however, that the legislation can be altered to lessen its price tag. Inadvertently, you have awoken a middle class sleeping giant, and now have more people energized than ever to ensure that we the people win out over a select few who feel it's their destiny to change America to their liking. Thomas Jefferson and other founding fathers needn't turn over in their graves worrying about your attempt to change America into something they wouldn't recognize. We the people get it, and will ensure this democracy endures under the guiding principles it was founded on.

Don't automatically assume from my comments that this is a glowing endorsement of the Republican party and its stable of politicians. There is no free pass or get out of jail free card they can use. I'm certainly more aligned with their general philosophy, but if they want my enthusiastic support going forward they need to put forth specific proposals that will address the many serious issues confronting us. Simply criticizing the other party isn't the answer. Give me and other middle class Americans a reason to support you by laying out ideas that provide a roadmap of what you intend to do and how it will help us overcome the challenges presented to us. Make your case and don't be afraid to state specifics. I know it's risky to do this, but a clear vision will allow us to make clear choices. We can critique all we want over the current administration and congress' actions, but at least they put a marker to contrast their policies and vision with. The ball is in play, and it's up to the Republican Party to respond. Middle class America wants to embrace somebody or something. The current party in power assumed we embraced and endorsed their radical agenda when in fact we endorsed creating jobs and improving the economy. They have squandered their honeymoon period and failed to get middle class America to embrace their doctrine. We'll survive the current economic crisis, but the longer term path we're on is being shaped as I write these words.

I'm not going to threaten to live in another country like some of our celebrities have indicated they would during the Bush years over policies they disagreed with. If I did convey such a threat, I would have the guts to carry it out, however, which would differentiate me from these entertainers. My plan is to respectfully and peacefully help the many millions of Americans who share my desire to avoid getting stuck in the socialism drift. We need to maintain our entrepreneurial and innovative spirit and not succumb to a contentment phase. We are currently being teased with this security carrot, and the current economic climate is helping to reinforce its attractiveness to various members of the voting population. The Robert Frost poem seems appropriate as a guidepost for us now when he said, "Two roads diverged into a wood and I took the one less traveled by, and that has made all the difference." I hope we follow his advice and do not follow the path of least resistance, but rather continue blazing America's path to greatness on our own terms. This makes us different from the rest of the world, and it's what makes us the envy of the rest of the world.

Biography

Bob has over twenty-five years experience in the financial services industry. He has been employed at both large and mid sized companies in various financial roles. He received an undergraduate BS degree in accounting and an MBA in finance from LaSalle University in Philadelphia. He is a certified public accountant.

Mr. Krouchick has been married to his wife Helene since 1981, and they have five children. They live in Pennsylvania, in the same house they have lived in since 1982. Bob and his family enjoy traveling and spending time together. His favorite hobby is coaching basketball, which he has done for over twenty years. His commute to New York City precludes him from coaching currently, but his fantasy is to some day coach a high school basketball team. He was born in Philadelphia and is an avid Philly sports fan, and he also has a passion for the Penn State Nittany Lions.

Bob has always enjoyed writing but has never authored a book. The historic nature of this election piqued his interest, and his frustration over his company being effectively taken over by the government and his concerns over where the country was headed drove him to put pen to paper. The financial crisis intensified after September eighteenth, and Bob felt a need to discuss how this economic meltdown affected middle-class Americans like himself. Bob enjoyed writing this book and hopes you find it interesting, entertaining, and real.